CONTENTS

BPP
LEARNING MEDIA

A NOTE ABOUT COPYRIGHT

Dear Customer

What does the little © mean and why does it matter?

Your market-leading BPP books, course materials and e-learning materials do not write and update themselves. People write them: on their own behalf or as employees of an organisation that invests in this activity. Copyright law protects their livelihoods. It does so by creating rights over the use of the content.

Breach of copyright is a form of theft – as well as being a criminal offence in some jurisdictions, it is potentially a serious breach of professional ethics.

With current technology, things might seem a bit hazy but, basically, without the express permission of BPP Learning Media:

- Photocopying our materials is a breach of copyright

- Scanning, ripcasting or conversion of our digital materials into different file formats, uploading them to facebook or emailing them to your friends is a breach of copyright

You can, of course, sell your books, in the form in which you have bought them – once you have finished with them. (Is this fair to your fellow students? We update for a reason.)

And what about outside the UK? BPP Learning Media strives to make our materials available at prices students can afford by local printing arrangements, pricing policies and partnerships which are clearly listed on our website. A tiny minority ignore this and indulge in criminal activity by illegally photocopying our material or supporting organisations that do. If they act illegally and unethically in one area, can you really trust them?

INTRODUCTION

This is BPP Learning Media's AAT Question Bank for Financial Statements. It is part of a suite of ground breaking resources produced by BPP Learning Media for the AAT's assessments under the qualification and credit framework.

The Financial Statements assessment will be **computer assessed**. As well as being available in the traditional paper format, this **Question Bank is available in an online environment** containing tasks similar to those you will encounter in the AAT's testing environment. BPP Learning Media believe that the best way to practise for an online assessment is in an online environment. However, if you are unable to practise in the online environment you will find that all tasks in the paper Question Bank have been written in a style that is as close as possible to the style that you will be presented with in your online assessment.

This Question Bank has been written in conjunction with the BPP Text, and has been carefully designed to enable students to practise all of the learning outcomes and assessment criteria for the units that make up Financial Statements. It is fully up to date as at June 2012 and reflects both the AAT's unit guide and the practice assessment(s) provided by the AAT.

This Question Bank contains these key features:

- tasks corresponding to each broad topic area. Some tasks are designed for learning purposes, but most of them are of assessment standard

- the AAT's practice assessment(s) and answers for Financial Statements and further BPP practice assessments

The emphasis in all tasks and assessments is on the practical application of the skills acquired.

Approaching the assessment

When you sit the assessment it is very important that you follow the on screen instructions. This means you need to carefully read the instructions, both on the introduction screens and during specific tasks.

When you access the assessment you should be presented with an introductory screen with information similar to that shown below (taken from the introductory screen from one of the AAT's Practice Assessments for Financial Statements).

This assessment is in TWO sections.
You must show competence in BOTH sections.
You should therefore attempt and aim to complete EVERY task in EACH section.
Each task is independent. You will not need to refer to your answers to previous tasks.
Read every task carefully to make sure you understand what is required.

Please note that in this practice assessment only your responses to tasks 1.1, 1.2, 1.4, 1.5 and 2.1 will be marked.
The equivalents of tasks 1.3, 2.2 and 2.3 in the live assessment will be human marked.

In tasks 1.1, 1.2 and 1.5 you will see there are tables that can be used as workings for your proformas. You don't need to use the workings to achieve full marks on the task, but data in the workings will be considered if you make errors in the proforma.

Where the date is relevant, it is given in the task data.

Both minus signs and brackets can be used to indicate negative numbers UNLESS task instructions say otherwise.

You must use a full stop to indicate a decimal point.
For example, write 100.57 NOT 100,57 or 100 57

You may use a comma to indicate a number in the thousands, but you don't have to.
For example, 10000 and 10,000 are both OK.

Other indicators are not compatible with the computer-marked system.

Section 1   Complete all 5 tasks

Section 2   Complete all 3 tasks

The actual instructions will vary depending on the subject you are studying for. It is very important you read the instructions on the introductory screen and apply them in the assessment. You don't want to lose marks when you know the correct answer just because you have not entered it in the right format.

In general, the rules set out in the AAT Practice Assessments for the subject you are studying for will apply in the real assessment, but you should again read the information on this screen in the real assessment carefully just to make sure. This screen may also confirm the VAT rate used if applicable.

A full stop is needed to indicate a decimal point. We would recommend using minus signs to indicate negative numbers and leaving out the comma signs to indicate thousands, as this results in a lower number of key strokes and less margin for error when working under time pressure. Having said that, you can use whatever is easiest for you as long as you operate within the rules set out for your particular assessment.

You have to show competence in both sections of assessments and you should therefore complete all of the tasks. Don't leave questions unanswered.

In some assessments written or complex tasks may be human marked. In this case you are given a blank space or table to enter your answer into. You are told in the practice assessments which tasks these are (note: there may be none if all answers are marked by the computer).

If these involve calculations, it is a good idea to decide in advance how you are going to lay out your answers to such tasks by practising answering them on a word document, and certainly you should try all such tasks in this question bank and in the AAT's environment using the practice assessments.

When asked to fill in tables, or gaps, never leave any blank even if you are unsure of the answer. Fill in your best estimate or enter zero.

Note that for some assessments where there is a lot of scenario information or tables of data provided, you may need to access these via 'pop-ups'. Instructions will be provided on how you can bring up the necessary data during the assessment. For example, the following is taken from the introductory screen from one of the AAT practice assessments for Financial Statements.

Note:

Data is provided in tasks 1.1, 1.2, 1.5 and 2.1 in the form of pop-ups. You can open, close and re-open the pop-ups as often as you want and you can position them anywhere on the screen.

To launch the pop-ups and see the data, just click on the buttons you'll find find in these tasks. The buttons appear at the top of each task, and look like these examples:

| Click here for trial balance | Click here for further information |

Finally, take note of any task specific instructions once you are in the assessment. For example you may be asked to enter a date in a certain format or to enter a number to a certain number of decimal places.

Remember you can practise the BPP questions in this question bank in an online environment on our dedicated AAT Online page. On the same page is a link to the current AAT Practice Assessments as well.

If you have any comments about this book, please e-mail paulsutcliffe@bpp.com or write to Paul Sutcliffe, Senior Publishing Manager, BPP Learning Media Ltd, BPP House, Aldine Place, London W12 8AA.

Question bank

Drafting financial statements

Task 1.1

Given below is the trial balance for Paparazzi Ltd as at 30 June 20X2.

	£'000	£'000
Land and buildings: Cost	2,100	
Plant and machinery: Cost	1,050	
Motor vehicles: Cost	1,000	
Retained earnings		1,131
Share capital		2,500
Share premium		300
Trade receivables	2,500	
Trade payables		1,400
Inventories at 1 July 20X1	690	
Accruals		50
Prepayments	40	
Sales		14,700
Purchases	10,780	
Land and buildings: Accumulated depreciation		280
Plant and machinery: Accumulated depreciation		194
Motor vehicles: Accumulated depreciation		404
Bank	567	
7% bank loan (repayable 20X9)		1,200
Allowance for doubtful debts		92
Dividend paid	120	
Interest paid	84	
Distribution costs	1,200	
Administrative expenses	2,120	
	22,251	22,251

Further information:

- The inventories at 30 June 20X2 cost £710,000

- The corporation tax charge for the year is estimated at £130,000

(a) **Draft the statement of comprehensive income for Paparazzi Ltd for the year ended 30 June 20X2.**

Paparazzi Ltd

Statement of comprehensive income for the year ended 30 June 20X2

	£'000
Continuing operations	
Revenue	
Cost of sales	
Gross profit	
Distribution costs	
Administrative expenses	
Profit/(loss) from operations	
Finance costs	
Profit/(loss) before tax	
Tax	
Profit/(loss) for the period from continuing operations	

Working

Cost of sales	£'000
Opening inventories	
Purchases	
Closing inventories	

(b) **Draft the statement of financial position for Paparazzi Ltd as at 30 June 20X2**

(Complete the left hand column by writing in the correct line item from the list provided)

Paparazzi Ltd

Statement of financial position as at 30 June 20X2

	£'000
Assets	
Non-current assets:	
▼	
Current assets:	
▼	
▼	
▼	
Total assets	
Equity and liabilities	
Equity:	
▼	
▼	
▼	
Total equity	
Non-current liabilities:	
▼	
Current liabilities:	
▼	
▼	
Total liabilities	
Total equity and liabilities	

Picklist for line items:

Bank loan
Cash and cash equivalents
Inventories
Property, plant and equipment
Retained earnings
Share capital
Share premium
Tax liabilities
Trade and other payables
Trade and other receivables

Workings

Property, plant and equipment	£'000
Land and buildings – Cost	
Plant and equipment – Cost	
Motor vehicles: – Cost	
Accumulated depreciation – land and buildings	
Accumulated depreciation – plant and equipment	
Accumulated depreciation – motor vehicles	

Trade and other receivables	£'000
Trade and other receivables	
Allowance for doubtful debts	
Prepayments	

Retained earnings	£'000
Retained earnings at 1 July 20X1	
Total profit for the year	
Dividends paid	

Trade and other payables	£'000
Trade payables	
Accruals	

....

Task 1.2

You have been asked to help with the preparation of the financial statements of Bathlea Ltd for the year ended 30 September 20X8. The extended trial balance for the year ended 30 September 20X8, is set out below.

The following further information has been supplied.

- The tax charge for the year has been calculated as £11,000.

- Depreciation has been charged on all assets for the year and included in the trial balance figures for distribution costs and administrative expenses.

- The interest on the long-term loan is charged at 12% per annum and is paid monthly in arrears. The charge for the first eleven months of the year is included in the trial balance.

- A customer owing Bathlea Ltd £10,000 went into liquidation on 2 October 20X8. This has not been accounted for.

BATHLEA LIMITED: EXTENDED TRIAL BALANCE 30 SEPTEMBER 20X8

Description	Trial balance		Adjustments		Statement of comprehensive income		Statement of financial position	
	Debit £'000	Credit £'000	Debit £'000	Credit £'000	Debit £'000	Credit £'000	Debit £'000	Credit £'000
Land and buildings – cost	300						300	
Fixtures and fittings – cost	220						220	
Motor vehicles – cost	70						70	
Office equipment – cost	80						80	
Land and buildings – accumulated depreciation		65						65
Fixtures and fittings – accumulated depreciation		43						43
Motor vehicles – accumulated depreciation		27						27
Office equipment – accumulated depreciation		35						35
Sales		3,509				3,509		
Purchases	1,691				1,691			
Inventories	200		250	250	200	250	250	
Receivables	370						370	
Allowance for irrecoverable debts		5						5
Prepayments			10				10	
Bank overdraft		3						3
Payables		350						350
Accruals				9				9
Distribution costs	860		7	10	857			
Administrative expenses	890		2		892			
Interest charges	11				11			
Interim dividend	15						15	
Share capital		500						500
Retained earnings		70						70
Long-term loan		100						100
Profit (loss)					108			108
Total	4,707	4,707	269	269	3,759	3,759	1,315	1,315

8

(a) **Draft the statement of comprehensive income for Bathlea Ltd for the year ended 30 September 20X8.**

Bathlea Limited

Statement of comprehensive income for the year ended 30 September 20X8

	£'000
Continuing operations	
Revenue	
Cost of sales	
Gross profit	
Distribution costs	
Administrative expenses	
Profit/(loss) from operations	
Finance cost	
Profit/(loss) before tax	
Tax	
Profit/(loss) for the period from continuing operations	

Workings

Cost of sales	£'000
Opening inventories	
Purchases	
Closing inventories	

Administrative expenses	£'000
Administrative expenses	
Bad debts	

(b) **Draft the statement of financial position for Bathlea Ltd as at 30 September 20X8**

(Complete the left hand column by writing in the correct line item from the list provided)

Bathlea Limited

Statement of financial position as at 30 September 20X8

	£'000
Assets	
Non-current assets	
▼	
Current assets	
▼	
▼	
Total assets	
Equity and liabilities	
Equity	
▼	
▼	
Total equity	
Non-current liabilities	
▼	
Current liabilities	
▼	
▼	
▼	
Total liabilities	
Total equity and liabilities	

Picklist for line items:

Bank overdraft
Cash and cash equivalents
Inventories
Long-term loan
Property, plant and equipment
Retained earnings
Share capital
Tax liabilities
Trade and other payables
Trade and other receivables

Workings

Property, plant and equipment	£'000
Land and buildings – Cost	
Fixtures and fittings – Cost	
Motor vehicles – Cost	
Office equipment – Cost	
Land and buildings – Accumulated depreciation	
Fixtures and fittings – Accumulated depreciation	
Motor vehicles – Accumulated depreciation	
Office equipment – Accumulated depreciation	

Trade and other receivables	£'000
Trade and other receivables	
Allowance for irrecoverable debts	
Bad debt	
Prepayments	

Retained earnings	£'000
Retained earnings at 1 October 20X7	
Total profit for the year	
Dividends paid	

Trade and other payables	£'000
Trade and other payables	
Accruals: trial balance	
Additional interest accrual	

Task 1.3

The directors of Howardsend Ltd have asked you to prepare the financial statements of the company for the year ended 30 September 20X6. An extended trial balance (ETB) as at 30 September 20X6 has been taken from the computerised accounting system. Some of the balances need to be adjusted. The ETB is on the next page.

Additional data

- Credit purchases relating to September 20X6 amounting to £2,403,000 had not been entered into the accounts at the year end.

- An allowance for doubtful debts is to be maintained at 2% of trade receivables. The doubtful debts expense is included in administrative expenses.

- The inventories at the close of business on 30 September 20X6 cost £8,134,000.

- The company employed an advertising agency during the year to promote a new product. The cost of the advertising campaign was agreed at £57,000, but no invoices have yet been received for this expense and no adjustment has been made for it in the ETB. This is to be included in distribution costs.

- Interest on the long-term loan for the last six months of the year has not been included in the accounts in the trial balance. Interest is charged at 7% per annum.

- The corporation tax charge for the year has been calculated as £1,382,000.

- Land that had cost £9,600,000 has been revalued by professional valuers at £11,600,000. No adjustment has yet been made in the balances in the ETB. The revaluation is to be included in the financial statements for the year ended 30 September 20X6.

- All the operations are continuing operations.

HOWARDSEND LTD
EXTENDED TRIAL BALANCE AS AT 30 SEPTEMBER 20X6

Description	Trial balance		Adjustments		Statement of comprehensive income		Statement of financial position	
	Debit £'000	Credit £'000	Debit £'000	Credit £'000	Debit £'000	Credit £'000	Debit £'000	Credit £'000
Inventories at 1 October 20X5	7,158				7,158			
Administration expenses	9,086		90		9,176			
Interest	350				350			
Sales		53,821				53,821		
Accruals				214				214
Purchases	24,407				24,407			
Allowance for doubtful receivables		53						53
Distribution costs	12,092		124		12,216			
Long-term loan		10,000						10,000
Ordinary share capital		8,000						8,000
Share premium		1,000						1,000
Cash at bank	579						579	
Property, plant and equipment – cost	57,149						57,149	
Property, plant and equipment – accum depn		14,523						14,523
Trade receivables	6,600						6,600	
Trade payables		2,577						2,577
Final dividend paid for 20X5	960						960	
Interim dividend paid for 20X6	480						480	
Retained earnings		28,887						28,887
Profit for the year					514			514
TOTAL	118,861	118,861	214	214	53,821	53,821	65,768	65,768

(a) **Draft the statement of comprehensive income for Howardsend Ltd for the year ended 30 September 20X6.**

Howardsend Ltd

Statement of comprehensive income for the year ended 30 September 20X6

	£'000
Continuing operations	
Revenue	
Cost of sales	_____
Gross profit	
Distribution costs	
Administrative expenses	_____
Profit/(loss) from operations	
Finance costs	_____
Profit/(loss) before tax	
Tax	_____
Profit/(loss) for the period from continuing operations	
Other comprehensive income	
Gain on revaluation	_____
Total comprehensive income for the year	_____

Workings

(Complete the left hand column by writing in the correct narrative from the list provided)

Cost of sales	£'000
▼	
▼	
▼	

Picklist for narratives:

Accruals
Closing inventories
Opening inventories
Prepayments
Purchases

Distribution costs		£'000
	▼	
	▼	

Picklist for narratives:

Accruals
Allowance for doubtful debts
Distribution costs
Prepayments

Administrative expenses		£'000
	▼	
	▼	

Picklist for narratives:

Accruals
Administrative expenses
Allowance for doubtful debts
Prepayments

(b) **Draft the statement of financial position for Howardsend Ltd as at 30 September 20X6.**

(Complete the left hand column by writing in the correct line item from the list provided)

Howardsend Ltd

Statement of financial position as at 30 September 20X6

	£'000
Assets	
Non-current assets	
▼	
Current assets	
▼	
▼	
▼	
Total assets	
Equity and liabilities	
Equity	
▼	
▼	
▼	
▼	
Total equity	
Non-current liabilities	
▼	
Current liabilities	
▼	
▼	
Total liabilities	
Total equity and liabilities	

Picklist for line items:

Cash and cash equivalents
Inventories
Long-term loan
Property, plant and equipment
Retained earnings
Revaluation reserve
Share capital
Share premium
Tax liabilities
Trade and other payables
Trade and other receivables

Workings

(Complete the left hand column by writing in the correct narrative from the list provided.)

Property, plant and equipment		£'000
	▼	
	▼	
	▼	

Picklist for narratives:

Property, plant and equipment – Accumulated depreciation
Property, plant and equipment – Cost
Revaluation

Trade and other receivables		£'000
	▼	
	▼	

Picklist for narratives:

Accruals: trial balance
Additional distribution costs accrual
Additional distribution costs prepaid
Additional interest accrual
Allowance for doubtful debts
Prepayments
Trade payables
Trade receivables

Retained earnings		£'000
	▼	
	▼	
	▼	

Picklist for narratives:

Dividends paid
Other comprehensive income for the year
Retained earnings at 1 October 20X5
Revaluation
Total comprehensive income for the year
Total profit for the year

Trade and other payables		£'000
	▼	
	▼	
	▼	
	▼	

Picklist for narratives:

Accruals: trial balance
Additional distribution costs accrual
Additional distribution costs prepaid
Additional interest accrual
Allowance for doubtful debts
Dividends
Prepayments
Tax liabilities
Trade payables
Trade receivables

Task 1.4

You have been asked to help prepare the financial statements of Benard Ltd for the year ended 31 October 20X7. The company's trial balance as at 31 October 20X7 is shown below.

Benard Ltd

Trial balance as at 31 October 20X7

	Debit	Credit
	£'000	£'000
Share capital		12,000
Trade and other payables		3,348
Property, plant and equipment – cost	58,463	
Property, plant and equipment – accumulated depreciation		27,974
Trade and other receivables	6,690	
Accruals		387
7% bank loan repayable 20Y2		16,000
Cash at bank	1,184	
Retained earnings		12,345
Interest	560	
Sales		50,197
Purchases	34,792	
Distribution costs	6,654	
Administrative expenses	4,152	
Inventories as at 1 November 20X6	8,456	
Dividends paid	1,300	
	122,251	122,251

Further information

- The sales figure in the trial balance does not include the credit sales for October 20X7 of £3,564,000.

- The inventories at the close of business on 31 October 20X7 cost £9,786,000.

- The company paid £48,000 insurance costs in June 20X7, which covered the period from 1 July 20X7 to 30 June 20X8. This was included in administrative expenses in the trial balance.

- Interest on the bank loan for the last six months of the year has not been included in the accounts in the trial balance.

- The corporation tax charge for the year has been calculated as £1,254,000.

- All of the operations are continuing operations.

(a) **Draft the statement of comprehensive income for Benard Ltd for the year ended 31 October 20X7.**

Benard Ltd

Statement of comprehensive income for the year ended 31 October 20X7

	£'000
Continuing operations	
Revenue	
Cost of sales	
Gross profit	
Distribution costs	
Administrative expenses	
Profit/(loss) from operations	
Finance costs	
Profit/(loss) before tax	
Tax	
Profit/(loss) for the period from continuing operations	

Workings

(Complete the left hand column by writing in the correct narrative from the list provided.)

Cost of sales		£'000
	▼	
	▼	
	▼	

Picklist for narratives:

Accruals
Closing inventories
Credit sales for October 20X7
Opening inventories
Prepayments
Purchases

Administrative expenses		£'000
	▼	
	▼	

Picklist for Narratives:

Accruals
Administrative expenses
Prepayments

(b) **Draft the statement of financial position for Benard Ltd as at 31 October 20X7**

(Complete the left hand column by writing in the correct line item from the list provided.)

Benard Ltd

Statement of financial position as at 31 October 20X7

	£'000
Assets	
Non-current assets	
▼	
Current assets	
▼	
▼	
▼	
Total assets	
Equity and liabilities	
Equity	
▼	
▼	
Total equity	
Non-current liabilities	
▼	
Current liabilities	
▼	
▼	
Total liabilities	
Total equity and liabilities	

Picklist for line items:

Bank loan
Cash and cash equivalents
Inventories
Property, plant and equipment
Retained earnings
Share capital
Tax payable
Trade and other payables
Trade and other receivables

Workings

(Complete the left hand column by writing in the correct narrative from the list provided.)

Trade and other receivables		£'000
	▼	
	▼	
	▼	

Picklist for narratives:

Accruals: trial balance
Administrative expenses accrual
Administrative expenses prepaid
Additional interest accrual
Credit sales for October 20X7
Prepayments
Trade and other payables
Trade and other receivables

Retained earnings		£'000
	▼	
	▼	
	▼	

Picklist for narratives:

Dividends paid
Other comprehensive income for the year
Retained earnings at 1 November 20X6
Total comprehensive income for the year
Total profit for the year

Trade and other payables		£'000
	▼	
	▼	
	▼	

Picklist for narratives:

Accruals: trial balance
Administrative expenses accrual
Administrative expenses prepayment
Additional interest accrual
Credit sales for October 20X7
Dividends
Prepayments
Tax payable
Trade and other payables
Trade and other receivables

Task 1.5

You have been asked to help prepare the financial statements of Laxdale Ltd for the year ended 31 October 20X8. The company's trial balance as at 31 October 20X8 is shown below.

Laxdale Ltd

Trial balance as at 31 October 20X8

	Debit	Credit
	£'000	£'000
Share capital		25,000
Trade and other payables		2,798
Land and buildings – cost	35,152	
Land and buildings – accumulated depreciation at 1 November 20X7		7,000
Plant and equipment – cost	12,500	
Plant and equipment – accumulated depreciation at 1 November 20X7		7,400
Trade and other receivables	5,436	
Accruals		436
8% bank loan repayable 20Y2		15,000
Cash at bank	9,774	
Retained earnings		9,801
Interest	600	
Sales		58,411
Purchases	41,620	
Distribution costs	5,443	
Administrative expenses	4,789	
Inventories as at 1 November 20X7	9,032	
Dividends paid	1,500	
	125,846	125846

Further information

- The inventories at the close of business on 31 October 20X8 were valued at £7,878,000.

- Depreciation is to be provided for the year to 31 March 20X1 as follows:

Buildings	2% per annum	Straight line basis
Plant and equipment	20% per annum	Reducing balance basis

Depreciation is apportioned as follows:

	%
Cost of sales	40
Distribution costs	40
Administrative expenses	20

Land, which is non-depreciable, is included in the trial balance at a cost of £15,152,000.

- The company began a series of television adverts for the company's range of products on 1 October 20X8 at a cost of £45,000. The adverts were to run for three months and were to be paid for in full at the end of December 20X8. Advertising expenses are included in distribution costs.

- Interest on the bank loan for the last six months of the year has not been included in the accounts in the trial balance.

- The corporation tax charge for the year has been calculated as £970,000.

- All of the operations are continuing operations.

(a) **Draft the statement of comprehensive income for Laxdale Ltd for the year ended 31 October 20X8.**

Laxdale Ltd

Statement of comprehensive income for the year ended 31 October 20X8

	£'000
Continuing operations	
Revenue	
Cost of sales	
Gross profit	
Distribution costs	
Administrative expenses	
Profit/(loss) from operations	
Finance costs	
Profit/(loss) before tax	
Tax	
Profit/(loss) for the period from continuing operations	

Workings

(Complete the left hand column by writing in the correct narrative from the list provided.)

Cost of sales	£'000
▼	
▼	
▼	
▼	

Picklist for narratives:

Accruals
Closing inventories
Depreciation
Opening inventories
Prepayments
Purchases

Distribution costs	£'000
▼	
▼	
▼	

Picklist for narratives:

Accruals
Depreciation
Distribution costs
Prepayments

Administrative expenses		£'000
	▼	
	▼	

Picklist for narratives:

Accruals
Administrative expenses
Depreciation
Prepayments

(b) **Draft the statement of financial position for Laxdale Ltd as at 31 October 20X8.**

(Complete the left hand column by writing in the correct line item from the list provided.)

Laxdale Ltd

Statement of financial position as at 31 October 20X8

		£'000
Assets		
Non-current assets		
	▼	_____
Current assets		
	▼	
	▼	
	▼	_____
		_____
Total assets		_____
Equity		
	▼	
	▼	_____
Total equity		_____

	£'000
Non-current liabilities	
	————
Current liabilities	
	————
	————
Total liabilities	
Total equity and liabilities	————

Picklist for line items:

Bank loan
Cash and cash equivalents
Inventories
Property, plant and equipment
Retained earnings
Share capital
Tax liabilities
Trade and other payables
Trade and other receivables

Workings

(Complete the left hand column by writing in the correct narrative from the list provided.)

Property, plant and equipment		£'000
	▼	
	▼	
	▼	
	▼	

Picklist for narratives:

Accumulated depreciation – land and buildings
Accumulated depreciation – plant and equipment
Land and buildings – Cost
Plant and equipment – Cost

Retained earnings		£'000
	▼	
	▼	
	▼	

Picklist for narratives:

Dividends paid
Other comprehensive income for the year
Retained earnings at 1 November 20X7
Total comprehensive income for the year
Total profit for the year

Trade and other payables		£'000
	▼	
	▼	
	▼	
	▼	

Picklist for narratives:

Accruals: trial balance
Additional distribution costs accrual
Additional distribution costs prepaid
Additional interest accrual
Dividends
Prepayments
Tax payable
Trade and other payables
Trade and other receivables

Task 1.6

You have been asked to help prepare the financial statements of Cappielow Ltd for the year ended 31 March 20X0. The company's trial balance as at 31 March 20X0 is shown below.

Cappielow Ltd

Trial balance as at 31 March 20X0

	Debit	Credit
	£000	£000
Share capital		10,000
Revaluation reserve at 1 April 20W9		2,000
Trade and other payables		1,347
Property, plant and equipment – cost/value	36,780	
Property, plant and equipment – accumulated depreciation		19,876
Trade and other receivables	2,133	
Accruals		129
6% bank loan repayable 20X6		12,000
Cash at bank	7,578	
Retained earnings		2,595
Interest	720	
Sales		35,547
Purchases	27,481	
Distribution costs	1,857	
Administrative expenses	2,235	
Inventories as at 1 April 20W9	3,790	
Dividends paid	920	
	83,494	83,494

Further information:

- The inventories at the close of business on 31 March 20X0 were valued at £4,067,000.

- Depreciation has already been provided on property, plant and equipment for the year ended 31 March 20X0.

- On 31 March 20X0 items of plant with a cost of £12,750,000 and accumulated depreciation of £3,100,000 were found to have a fair value less costs to sell of £8,500,000 and a value in use of £8,200,000. Any adjustment should be included in cost of sales.

- Land, which is non-depreciable, is included in the trial balance at a value of £5,150,000. It is to be revalued at £7,500,000 and this revaluation is to be included in the financial statements for the year ended 31 March 20X0.

- The company hired some office copiers for the period 1 March to 30 June 20X0. The contract price for the four months was £164,000 and this was paid in full on 3 March.

- The company sourced extra warehousing space, for the storage of goods prior to their sale, for a period of three months from 1 February to 30 April 20X0. The invoice for the full three months of £114,000 was paid on 16 April. No entry has been made in the accounts for this transaction.

- The corporation tax charge for the year has been calculated as £874,000.

- During February 20X0 the directors decided to close one of the company's six operating divisions, probably during June 20X0. They have estimated that this will result in redundancy and other costs of £2,500,000. At 31 March 20X0 the directors had not yet announced the closure to the public or to the workforce and had not yet drawn up a detailed plan or timetable.

- On 15 April 20X0 one of the company's customers went into liquidation. Trade receivables at 31 March 20X0 include a balance of £95,000 owed by this customer. The directors have been advised that they are unlikely to receive any of this amount.

- All of the operations are continuing operations.

  (a) **Draft the statement of comprehensive income for Cappielow Ltd for the year ended 31 March 20X0.**

  (b) **Draft the statement of financial position for Cappielow Ltd as at 31 March 20X0.**

Note:

Additional notes and disclosures are not required.

Cappielow Ltd

Statement of comprehensive income for the year ended 31 March 20X0

	£'000
Continuing operations	
Revenue	
Cost of sales	
Gross profit	
Distribution costs	
Administrative expenses	
Profit/(loss) from operations	
Finance costs	
Profit/(loss) before tax	
Tax	
Profit/(loss) for the period from continuing operations	
Other comprehensive income for the year	
Gain on revaluation of land	
Total comprehensive income for the year	

Workings

(Complete the left hand column by writing in the correct narrative from the list provided.)

Cost of sales	£'000
▼	
▼	
▼	
▼	

Picklist for narratives:

Accruals
Closing inventories
Impairment loss
Opening inventories
Prepayment
Purchases

Distribution costs		£'000
	▼	
	▼	

Picklist for narratives:

Accruals
Bad debt
Distribution costs
Prepayment

Administrative expenses		£'000
	▼	
	▼	
	▼	

Picklist for narratives:

Accruals
Administrative expenses
Bad debt
Impairment loss
Prepayment

Cappielow Ltd

Statement of financial position as at 31 March 20X0

(Complete the left hand column by writing in the correct line item from the list provided)

	£'000
Assets	
Non-current assets:	
▼	
Current assets:	
▼	
▼	
▼	
Total assets	
Equity and liabilities:	
Equity	
▼	
▼	
▼	
Total equity	
Non-current liabilities:	
▼	
Current liabilities:	
▼	
▼	
Total liabilities	
Total equity and liabilities	

Picklist for line items:

Bank loan
Cash and cash equivalents
Inventories
Property, plant and equipment
Retained earnings
Revaluation reserve
Share capital
Tax payable
Trade and other payables
Trade and other receivables

Workings

(Complete the left hand column by writing in the correct narrative from the list provided.)

Property, plant and equipment		£'000
	▼	
	▼	
	▼	

Picklist for narratives:

Impairment loss
Property, plant and equipment: Accumulated depreciation
Property, plant and equipment: Cost/value

Trade and other receivables		£'000
	▼	
	▼	
	▼	

Picklist for narratives:

Accruals: trial balance
Administrative expenses accrued
Administrative expenses prepaid
Bad debt
Distribution costs accrued
Distribution costs prepaid
Trade and other payables
Trade and other receivables

Revaluation reserve		£'000
	▼	
	▼	

Picklist for narratives:

Dividends paid
Other comprehensive income for the year
Retained reserves at 1 April 20W9
Revaluation reserve at 1 April 20W9
Total comprehensive income for the year
Total profit for the year

Retained earnings		£'000
	▼	
	▼	
	▼	

Picklist for narratives:

Dividends paid
Other comprehensive income for the year
Retained earnings at 1 April 20W9
Revaluation reserve at 1 April 20W9
Total comprehensive income for the year
Total profit for the year

Trade and other payables		£'000
	▼	
	▼	
	▼	

Picklist for narratives:

Accruals: trial balance
Administrative expenses accrued
Administrative expenses prepaid
Bad debt
Distribution costs accrued
Distribution costs prepaid
Dividends
Tax payable
Trade and other payables
Trade and other receivables

The statement of cash flows and the statement of changes in equity

Task 2.1

An extract from a company's statement of comprehensive income for the year ended 31 December 20X1 is given:

	£
Revenue	560,000
Cost of sales	300,000
Gross profit	260,000
Other expenses	160,000
Profit from operations	100,000

Other expenses include £20,000 of depreciation. Interest paid was £10,000. The tax paid for the year was £25,000.

Extracts from the statement of financial position are also given below:

	20X1	20X0
	£	£
Inventories	30,000	25,000
Trade receivables	40,000	42,000
Trade payables	28,000	32,000

(a) **Prepare a reconciliation of profit from operations to net cash from operating activities using the indirect method.**

Reconciliation of profit from operations to net cash from operating activities

	£
Profit from operations	
Depreciation	
Increase/decrease in inventories	
Increase/decrease in trade receivables	
Increase/decrease in trade payables	
Cash generated from operations	
Interest paid	
Tax paid	
Net cash from operating activities	

(b) **Complete the table below to show net cash from operating activities using the direct method.**

	£
Operating activities	
Cash receipts from customers	
Cash paid to suppliers and employees	
Cash generated from operations	
Interest paid	
Tax paid	
Net cash from operating activities	

Workings

Cash receipts from customers	£
Opening trade receivables	
Revenue	
Closing trade receivables	

Cash paid to suppliers and employees	£
Opening trade payables	
Total purchases (W)	
Closing trade payables	

Total purchases	£
Cost of sales	
Opening inventories	
Closing inventories	
Other expenses	
Depreciation	

Task 2.2

Given below is an extract from a company's statement of financial position:

	Year ended 31 March	
	20X2	20X1
	£'000	£'000
Trade payables	340	380
Corporation tax	100	94
Accrued interest	8	13

The statement of comprehensive income shows that interest payable for the year was £32,400 and the corporation tax charge was £98,000.

Calculate the figures that would appear in the statement of cash flows for:

(a) **Interest paid**

£

(b) **Tax paid**

£

•••

Task 2.3

An extract from a company's statement of financial position is given below:

	Year ended 30 June	
	20X2	20X1
	£'000	£'000
Property, plant and equipment at cost	1,340	1,250
Less: accumulated depreciation	(560)	(480)
	780	770

During the year items with a cost of £140,000 and net carrying amount of £98,000 were sold at a loss of £23,000.

Calculate the figures for:

(a) **Cash paid to acquire property, plant and equipment during the year**

£

(b) **Proceeds of the sale of property, plant and equipment in the year**

£

(c) **The depreciation charge for the year**

£

•••

Task 2.4

During the year ended 30 April 20X2 a company made a profit of £110,000. On 1 May 20X1 there were already 500,000 £1 ordinary shares in issue. On that date the company issued a further 200,000 ordinary shares at a price of £1.40 per share.

During the year the company revalued some of its non-current assets upwards by £70,000. An ordinary dividend of £35,000 was paid.

Share capital and reserves at 1 May 20X1 (before accounting for the share issue) were as follows:

	£
£1 ordinary shares	500,000
Share premium	100,000
Revaluation reserve	30,000
Retained earnings	180,000
	810,000

Draft a statement of changes in equity for the year ended 30 April 20X2.

Statement of changes in equity for the year ended 30 April 20X2

	Share capital	Share premium	Revaluation reserve	Retained earnings	Total equity
	£	£	£	£	£
Balance at 1 May 20X1					
Changes in equity for 20X2					
Total comprehensive income					
Dividends					
Issue of share capital					
Balance at 30 April 20X2					

Task 2.5

You are presented with the following information for Evans.

Evans

Statement of comprehensive income for the year ended 31 October 20X1

	£'000
Continuing operations	
Revenue	2,000
Cost of sales	(1,350)
Gross profit	650
Gain on disposal of non-current assets	10
Distribution costs	(99)
Administrative expenses	(120)
Profit from operations	441
Finance costs	(23)
Profit before tax	418
Tax	(125)
Profit for the period from continuing operations	293

Evans

Statements of financial position as at 31 October

	20X1		20X0	
	£'000	£'000	£'000	£'000
Assets				
Non-current assets				
Property, plant and equipment		1,180		1,010
Current assets				
Inventories	486		505	
Trade receivables	945		657	
Cash	2		10	
		1,433		1,172
Total assets		2,613		2,182
Equity and liabilities				
Equity				
Share capital	1,200		1,000	
Share premium	315		270	
Retained earnings	363		110	
		1,878		1,380

Non-current liabilities

12% bank loan		50	150

Current liabilities

Trade payables	560		546
Tax payable	125		106
		685	652
Total liabilities		735	802
Total equity and liabilities		2,613	2,182

Additional information for the year ended 31 October 20X1

- Vehicles which had cost £155,000 were sold during the year when their net carrying amount was £65,000.

- The total depreciation charge for the year was £190,000

- There were no prepaid or accrued expenses at the beginning or end of the year.

- Dividends of £40,000 were paid during the year.

(a) **Prepare a reconciliation of profit from operations to net cash from operating activities for Evans Ltd for the year ended 31 October 20X1.**

Reconciliation of profit from operations to net cash from operating activities

	£'000
Profit from operations	
Adjustments for:	
Depreciation	
Gain on disposal of property, plant and equipment	
Adjustment in respect of inventories	
Adjustment in respect of trade receivables	
Adjustment in respect of trade payables	
Cash generated by operations	
Interest paid	
Tax paid	
Net cash from operating activities	

(b) **Prepare the statement of cash flows for Evans Ltd for the year ended 31 October 20X1.**

Evans Ltd

Statement of cash flows for the year ended 31 October 20X1

	£'000	£'000
Net cash from operating activities		
Investing activities		
Purchase of property, plant and equipment		
Proceeds on disposal of property, plant and equipment		
Net cash used in investing activities		
Financing activities		
Proceeds of share issue		
Repayment of bank loan		
Dividends paid		
Net cash from financing activities		
Net increase/(decrease) in cash and cash equivalents		
Cash and cash equivalents at the beginning of the year		
Cash and cash equivalents at the end of the year		

Workings

Proceeds on disposal of property, plant and equipment (PPE)	£'000
Carrying amount of PPE sold	
Gain on disposal	

Purchase of property, plant and equipment (PPE)	£'000
PPE at start of year	
Depreciation charge	
Carrying amount of PPE sold	
PPE at end of year	
Total PPE additions	

(c) **Draft the statement of changes in equity for Evans Ltd for the year ended 31 October 20X1.**

Evans Ltd

Statement of changes in equity for the year ended 31 October 20X1

	Share Capital	Other Reserves	Retained Earnings	Total Equity
	£'000	£'000	£'000	£'000
Balance at 1 November 20X0				
Changes in equity for 20X1				
Profit for the year				
Dividends				
Issue of share capital				
Balance at 31 October 20X1				

Task 2.6

For the year ended 31 October 20X7 you have been asked to prepare:

- A reconciliation between profit from operations and net cash from operating activities
- A statement of cash flows for Lochnagar Ltd.

The statements of financial position of Lochnagar Ltd for the past two years and the most recent statement of comprehensive income are set out as follows:

Lochnagar Ltd

Statement of comprehensive income for the year ended 31 October 20X7

	£'000
Continuing operations	
Revenue	22,400
Cost of sales	(12,320)
Gross profit	10,080
Gain on disposal of property, plant and equipment	224
Distribution costs	(4,704)
Administrative expenses	(2,240)
Profit from operations	3,360
Finance costs – interest on loans	(91)
Profit before tax	3,269
Tax	(1,344)
Profit for the period from continuing operations	1,925

Lochnagar Ltd

Statements of financial position as at 31 October

	20X7	20X6
Assets	£'000	£'000
Non-current assets		
Property, plant and equipment	25,171	24,100
Current assets		
Inventories	3,696	2,464
Trade and other receivables	3,360	2,464
Cash and cash equivalents	0	129
	7,056	5,057
Total assets	32,227	29,157
Equity and liabilities		
Equity		
Share capital	2,200	2,000
Share premium	800	500
Retained earnings	24,990	23,065
Total equity	27,990	25,565
Non-current liabilities		
Bank loans	1,300	800
Current liabilities		
Trade and other payables	1,232	1,848
Tax liability	1,344	944
Bank overdraft	361	0
	2,937	2,792
Total liabilities	4,237	3,592
Total equity and liabilities	32,227	29,157

Further information

- The total depreciation charge for the year was £3,545,000.
- Property, plant and equipment costing £976,000 with accumulated depreciation of £355,000 was sold in the year at a profit of £224,000.
- All sales and purchases were on credit. Other expenses were paid for in cash.

(a) **Prepare a reconciliation of profit from operations to net cash from operating activities for Lochnagar Ltd for the year ended 31 October 20X7.**

(Complete the left hand column by writing in the correct line item from the list provided.)

Lochnagar Ltd

Reconciliation of profit from operations to net cash from operating activities for the year ended 31 October 20X7

		£'000
	▼	
Adjustments for:		
	▼	
	▼	
	▼	
	▼	
	▼	
Cash generated by operations		
	▼	
	▼	
Net cash from operating activities		

Picklist for line items:

Adjustment in respect of inventories
Adjustment in respect of trade payables
Adjustment in respect of trade receivables
Depreciation
Gain on disposal of property, plant and equipment
Interest paid
New bank loans
Proceeds on disposal of property, plant and equipment
Profit after tax
Profit before tax
Profit from operations
Purchases of property, plant and equipment
Tax paid

(b) **Prepare the statement of cash flows for Lochnagar Ltd for the year ended 31 October 20X7.**

(Complete the left hand column by writing in the correct line item from the list provided.)

Lochnagar Ltd

Statement of cash flows for the year ended 31 October 20X7

	£'000	£'000
Net cash from operating activities		
Investing activities		
▼		
▼		
Net cash used in investing activities		
Financing activities		
▼		
▼		
Net cash from financing activities		
Net increase/(decrease) in cash and cash equivalents		
Cash and cash equivalents at the beginning of the year		
Cash and cash equivalents at the end of the year		

Picklist for line items:

Adjustment in respect of inventories
Adjustment in respect of trade payables
Adjustment in respect of trade receivables
New bank loans
Proceeds of share issue
Proceeds on disposal of property, plant and equipment
Purchases of property, plant and equipment

Workings

(Complete the left hand column by writing in the correct narrative from the list provided.)

Proceeds on disposal of property, plant and equipment (PPE)	£'000
▼	
▼	

Picklist for narratives:

Carrying amount of PPE sold
Depreciation charge
Gain on disposal
PPE at end of year
PPE at start of year

Purchases of property, plant and equipment (PPE)	£'000
PPE at start of year	
▼	
▼	
▼	
Total PPE additions	

Picklist for narratives:

Carrying amount of PPE sold
Depreciation charge
Gain on disposal of PPE
PPE at end of year

Task 2.7

You have been asked to prepare the statement of cash flows for Thehoose Ltd, for the year ended 31 March 20X9. The most recent statement of comprehensive income and statements of financial position of Thehoose Ltd for the past two years are set out below.

Thehoose Ltd

Statement of comprehensive income for the year ended 31 March 20X9

	£'000
Continuing operations	
Revenue	37,680
Cost of sales	(22,608)
Gross profit	15,072
Gain on disposal of property, plant and equipment	376
Distribution costs	(6,782)
Administrative expenses	(3,014)
Profit from operations	5,652
Finance costs	(280)
Profit before tax	5,372
Tax	(1,484)
Profit for the period from continuing operations	3,888

Thehoose Ltd
Statements of financial position as at 31 March

	20X9	20X8
	£'000	£'000
Non-current assets		
Property, plant and equipment	27,570	21,340
Current assets		
Inventories	5,426	4,069
Trade and other receivables	3,768	4,145
Cash and cash equivalents	335	0
	9,529	8,214
Total assets	37,099	29,554
Equity and liabilities		
Equity		
Share capital	4,500	3,000
Share premium	3,000	2,000
Retained earnings	21,854	17,966
Total equity	29,354	22,966
Non-current liabilities		
Bank loans	4,000	1,500
Current liabilities		
Trade and other payables	2,261	4,069
Tax liability	1,484	887
Bank overdraft	–	132
	3,745	5,088
Total liabilities	7,745	6,588
Total equity and liabilities	37,099	29,554

Further information:

- The total depreciation charge for the year was £3,469,000.

- Property, plant and equipment costing £764,000, with accumulated depreciation of £347,000, were sold in the year.

- All sales and purchases were on credit. Other expenses were paid for in cash.

(a) **Prepare a reconciliation of profit from operations to net cash from operating activities for Thehoose Ltd for the year ended 31 March 20X9.**

(Complete the left hand column by writing in the correct line item from the list provided.)

Thehoose Ltd

Reconciliation of profit from operations to net cash from operating activities for the year ended 31 March 20X9

		£'000
	▼	
Adjustments for:		
	▼	
	▼	
	▼	
	▼	
	▼	
Cash generated by operations		
	▼	
	▼	
Net cash from operating activities		

Picklist for line items:

Adjustment in respect of inventories
Adjustment in respect of trade payables
Adjustment in respect of trade receivables
Depreciation
Gain on disposal of property, plant and equipment
Interest paid
New bank loans
Proceeds on disposal of property, plant and equipment
Profit after tax
Profit before tax
Profit from operations
Purchases of property, plant and equipment
Tax paid

(b) **Prepare the statement of cash flows for Thehoose Ltd for the year ended 31 March 20X9.**

(Complete the left hand column by writing in the correct line item from the list provided.)

Thehoose Ltd

Statement of cash flows for the year ended 31 March 20X9

	£'000	£'000
Net cash from operating activities		
Investing activities		
▼		
▼		
Net cash used in investing activities		
Financing activities		
▼		
▼		
Net cash from financing activities		
Net increase/(decrease) in cash and cash equivalents		
Cash and cash equivalents at the beginning of the year		
Cash and cash equivalents at the end of the year		

Picklist for line items:

Adjustment in respect of inventories
Adjustment in respect of trade payables
Adjustment in respect of trade receivables
Dividends paid
New bank loans
Proceeds of share issue
Proceeds on disposal of property, plant and equipment
Purchases of property, plant and equipment

Workings

(Complete the left hand column by writing in the correct narrative from the list provided.)

Proceeds on disposal of property, plant and equipment (PPE)	£'000
▼	
▼	

Picklist for narratives:

Carrying amount of PPE sold
Depreciation charge
Gain on disposal
PPE at end of year
PPE at start of year

Purchases of property, plant and equipment (PPE)	£'000
PPE at start of year	
▼	
▼	
▼	
Total PPE additions	

Picklist for narratives:

Carrying amount of PPE sold
Depreciation charge
Gain on disposal of PPE
PPE at end of year

Task 2.8

You have been asked to prepare a statement of cash flows and a statement of changes in equity for Adlington Ltd for the year ended 31 October 20X9. The most recent statement of comprehensive income and statements of financial position of the company for the past two years are set out below.

Adlington Ltd

Statement of comprehensive income for the year ended 31 October 20X9

	£'000
Continuing operations	
Revenue	45,500
Cost of sales	(27,300)
Gross profit	18,200
Gain on disposal of property, plant and equipment	455
Distribution costs	(6,825)
Administrative expenses	(5,005)
Profit from operations	6,825
Finance costs – interest on loan	(595)
Profit before tax	6,230
Tax	(1,757)
Profit for the period from continuing operations	4,473

Adlington Ltd

Statements of financial position as at 31 October

Assets	20X9	20X8
Non-current assets	£'000	£'000
Property, plant and equipment	31,989	22,246
Current assets		
Inventories	6,552	4,914
Trade and other receivables	4,550	4,641
Cash and cash equivalents	450	0
	11,552	9,555
Total assets	43,541	31,801
EQUITY AND LIABILITIES		
Equity		
Share capital	10,000	8,000
Share premium	4,000	3,000
Retained earnings	15,462	11,489
Total equity	29,462	22,489
Non-current liabilities		
Bank loan	8,500	3,000
Current liabilities		
Trade and other payables	3,822	4,368
Tax liabilities	1,757	658
Bank overdraft	–	1,286
	5,579	6,312
Total liabilities	14,079	9,312
Total equity plus liabilities	43,541	31,801

Additional data

- The total depreciation charged for the year was £4,398,000.

- Property, plant and equipment costing £568,000 with accumulated depreciation of £226,000 was sold in the year.

- All sales and purchases were on credit. Other expenses were paid for in cash.

- A dividend of £500,000 was paid during the year.

(a) **Prepare a reconciliation of profit from operations to net cash from operating activities for Adlington Ltd for the year ended 31 October 20X9.**

(Complete the left hand column by writing in the correct line item from the list provided.)

Reconciliation of profit from operations to net cash from operating activities for the year ended 31 October 20X9

		£'000
	▼	
Adjustments for:		
	▼	
	▼	
	▼	
	▼	
	▼	
Cash generated from operations		
	▼	
	▼	
Net cash from operating activities		

Picklist for line items:

Adjustment in respect of inventories
Adjustment in respect of trade payables
Adjustment in respect of trade receivables
Depreciation
Gain on disposal of property, plant and equipment
Interest paid
New bank loans
Proceeds on disposal of property, plant and equipment
Profit after tax
Profit before tax
Profit from operations
Purchases of property, plant and equipment
Tax paid

(b) **Prepare the statement of cash flows for Adlington Ltd for the year ended 31 October 20X9.**

(Complete the left hand column by writing in the correct line item from the list provided.)

Adlington Ltd

Statement of cash flows for the year ended 31 October 20X9

	£'000	£'000
Net cash from operating activities		
Investing activities		
▼		
▼		
Net cash used in investing activities		
Financing activities		
▼		
▼		
▼		
Net cash from financing activities		
Net increase/(decrease) in cash and cash equivalents		
Cash and cash equivalents at the beginning of the year		
Cash and cash equivalents at the end of the year		

Picklist for line items:

Adjustment in respect of inventories
Adjustment in respect of trade payables
Adjustment in respect of trade receivables
Dividends paid
New bank loans
Proceeds of share issue
Proceeds on disposal of property, plant and equipment
Purchases of property, plant and equipment

Workings

(Complete the left hand column by writing in the correct narrative from the list provided.)

Proceeds on disposal of property, plant and equipment (PPE)	£'000
▼	
▼	

Picklist for narratives:

Carrying amount of PPE sold
Depreciation charge
Gain on disposal
PPE at end of year
PPE at start of year

Purchases of property, plant and equipment (PPE)	£'000
PPE at start of year	
▼	
▼	
▼	
Total PPE additions	

Picklist for narratives:

Carrying amount of PPE sold
Depreciation charge
Gain on disposal of PPE
PPE at end of year

(c) **Draft the statement of changes in equity for Adlington Ltd for the year ended 31 October 20X9.**

(Complete the left hand column by writing in the correct line item from the list provided.)

Adlington Ltd

Statement of changes in equity for the year ended 31 October 20X9

	Share capital £'000	Other reserves £'000	Retained earnings £'000	Total equity £'000
Balance at 1 November 20X8				
Changes in equity for 20X9				
Profit for the year				
Dividends				
Issue of share capital				
Balance at 31 October 20X9				

Task 2.9

You have been asked to prepare the statement of cash flows and statement of changes in equity for Forthbank Ltd for the year ended 31 March 20X1.

The most recent statement of comprehensive income and statement of financial position (with comparatives for the previous year) of Forthbank Ltd are set out below.

Forthbank Ltd – Statement of comprehensive income for the year ended 31 March 20X1

Continuing operations	£'000
Revenue	54,000
Cost of sales	(32,400)
Gross profit	21,600
Dividends received	650
Loss on disposal of property, plant and equipment	(110)
Distribution costs	(11,420)
Administrative expenses	(4,860)
Profit from operations	5,860
Finance costs	(301)
Profit before tax	5,559
Tax	(1,113)
Profit for the period from continuing operations	4,446

Forthbank Ltd – Statement of financial position as at 31 March 20X1

	20X1	20X0
	£'000	£'000
ASSETS		
Non-current assets		
Property, plant and equipment	26,660	19,140
Current assets		
Inventories	5,832	4,860
Trade and other receivables	5,400	4,320
Cash and cash equivalents	587	0
	11,819	9,180
Total assets	38,479	28,320
EQUITY AND LIABILITIES		
Equity		
Share capital	8,000	6,000
Share premium	3,000	2,000
Retained earnings	18,826	14,840
Total equity	29,826	22,840
Non-current liabilities		
Bank loans	4,300	800
	4,300	800
Current liabilities		
Trade payables	3,240	3,564
Tax liabilities	1,113	908
Bank overdraft	0	208
	4,353	4,680
Total liabilities	8,653	5,480
Total equity and liabilities	38,479	28,320

Further information:

- The total depreciation charge for the year was £3,366,000.

- Property, plant and equipment costing £812,000 with accumulated depreciation of £475,000 was sold in the year.

- All sales and purchases were on credit. Other expenses were paid for in cash.

- A dividend of £460,000 was paid during the year.

(a) **Prepare a reconciliation of profit from operations to net cash from operating activities for Forthbank Ltd for the year ended 31 March 20X1.**

(Complete the left hand column by writing in the correct line item from the list provided.)

Reconciliation of profit from operations to net cash from operating activities

		£'000
	▽	
Adjustments for:		
	▽	
	▽	
	▽	
	▽	
	▽	
	▽	
Cash generated by operations		
	▽	
	▽	
Net cash from operating activities		

Picklist for line items:

Adjustment in respect of inventories
Adjustment in respect of trade payables
Adjustment in respect of trade receivables
Depreciation
Dividends received
Loss on disposal of property, plant and equipment
Interest paid
New bank loans
Proceeds on disposal of property, plant and equipment
Profit after tax

63

Profit before tax
Profit from operations
Purchases of property, plant and equipment
Tax paid

(b) **Prepare the statement of cash flows for Forthbank Ltd for the year ended 31 March 20X1.**

(Complete the left hand column by writing in the correct line item from the list provided.)

Forthbank Ltd

Statement of cash flows for the year ended 31 March 20X1

	£'000	£'000
Net cash from operating activities		
Investing activities		
▼		
▼		
▼		
Net cash used in investing activities		
Financing activities		
▼		
▼		
▼		
Net cash from financing activities		
Net increase/(decrease) in cash and cash equivalents		
Cash and cash equivalents at the beginning of the year		
Cash and cash equivalents at the end of the year		

Picklist for line items:

Adjustment in respect of inventories
Adjustment in respect of trade payables
Adjustment in respect of trade receivables
Dividends paid
Dividends received
New bank loans
Proceeds of share issue
Proceeds on disposal of property, plant and equipment
Purchases of property, plant and equipment

Workings

(Complete the left hand column by writing in the correct narrative from the list provided.)

Proceeds on disposal of property, plant and equipment (PPE)	£'000
▼	
▼	

Picklist for Narratives:

Carrying amount of PPE sold
Depreciation charge
Loss on disposal
PPE at end of year
PPE at start of year

Purchases of property, plant and equipment (PPE)	£'000
PPE at start of year	
▼	
▼	
▼	
Total PPE additions	

Picklist for narratives:

Carrying amount of PPE sold
Depreciation charge
Loss on disposal of PPE
PPE at end of year

(c) **Draft the statement of changes in equity for Forthbank Ltd for the year ended 31 March 20X1.**

Forthbank Ltd

Statement of changes in equity for the year ended 31 March 20X1

	Share Capital £'000	Other Reserves £'000	Retained Earnings £'000	Total Equity £'000
Balance at 1 April 20X0				
Changes in equity for 20X1				
Profit for the year				
Dividends				
Issue of share capital				
Balance at 31 March 20X1				

Accounting standards and The Conceptual Framework – written tasks

Task 3.1

The accounting equation of a company is as follows:

Assets £1,200 – Liabilities £800 = Equity £400

The company subsequently makes two transactions.

- It purchases inventories costing £120 on credit
- It sells these inventories for £180 cash

(a) **Explain what is meant by 'assets', 'liabilities' and 'equity'.**

(b) **Explain the effect of each transaction on the elements in the statement of financial position.**

(c) **State the accounting equation for the company after the two transactions have taken place.**

(d) **Draft a simple income statement for the two transactions.**

Task 3.2

The purpose (objective) of financial statements is to provide financial information about the reporting entity that is useful in making decisions about providing resources to the entity. Financial statements provide, among other things, information about the equity of the company.

Prepare brief notes to answer the following questions:

(a) **According to the IASB's** *Conceptual Framework for Financial Reporting*, **who are the most important (primary) users of financial statements (general purpose financial reports)?**

(b) **Explain how the financial statements might be used by a user who is interested in finding out how well a company has managed working capital.**

(c) **What is meant by 'equity'? How is it related to other elements in the accounting equation?**

Task 3.3

The accounting equation is:

Assets – Liabilities = Equity

(a) **Define the following elements of financial statements**

　　(i)　**Assets**
　　(ii)　**Liabilities**
　　(iii)　**Equity**

(b) **Explain why inventories are an asset of a company.**

Task 3.4

Leonard Martin plans to invest in shares in a private company. He has identified two companies that might be suitable. He has obtained the latest financial statements of the companies in order to learn more about the risk inherent in, and the return he can expect from, a potential investment in these companies.

(a) **State the objective of general purpose financial reporting according to the IASB's *Conceptual Framework for Financial Reporting.***

(b) **Identify the type of user of financial statements described above and explain how financial statements can be used to meet the objective of financial statements in these circumstances.**

Task 3.5

The IASB's *Conceptual Framework for Financial Reporting* explains that relevance and faithful representation are the two fundamental qualitative characteristics of useful financial information. It also sets out and explains four further qualities which enhance the usefulness of information that is relevant and faithfully represented.

(a) **Briefly explain what is meant by:**

　　(i)　**relevance**

　　(ii)　**faithful representation**

　　according to the *Conceptual Framework for Financial Reporting*

(b) **State the four enhancing qualitative characteristics of useful financial information**

Task 3.6

The directors of Chopin Ltd are interested in the principles to be followed in selecting accounting policies for the company.

They are aware that IAS 1 *Preparation and Presentation of Financial Statements* identifies two important assumptions (or concepts) of going concern and accruals that are fundamentally important to the preparation of financial statements and to the selection of accounting policies.

(a) **Explain these two assumptions (or concepts).**

(b) **According to IAS 8 *Accounting policies, changes in accounting estimates and errors*, how should an entity decide what accounting policies should be adopted?**

Task 3.7

The directors of Aston plc are considering acquiring another subsidiary. They have obtained the latest financial statements of the company they wish to purchase and have had some preliminary discussions with the directors of this company. They are unclear about some of the accounting treatments in the financial statements of the company and have asked you to come to a meeting to explain them.

Prepare notes for a meeting with the directors to explain the accounting treatment of the following issues:

(a) The company owns the freehold of a building which it constructed for investment purposes. The building is currently rented to another company on commercial terms. The property is not recorded at its historical cost and has not been depreciated.

(b) A note to the accounts states that there was a fire in the warehouse of the company that occurred after the year end and resulted in considerable losses of property and inventories. No adjustment for these losses appears to have been made in the year-end financial statements.

(c) There is a liability for something called 'deferred taxation' in the statement of financial position of the company.

Note: You should make reference, where appropriate, to relevant accounting standards.

Task 3.8

IFRS 5 requires separate disclosure of the post-tax profit or loss of discontinued operations.

Prepare notes to explain:

(a) **What is meant, in IFRS 5, by 'discontinued operations'.**

(b) **Why it is useful to distinguish between continuing operations and discontinued operations for the purposes of financial reporting.**

Task 3.9

You have been asked to help prepare the financial statements of Sandringham Ltd for the year ended 30 September 20X4 and to advise the directors on the accounting treatment of certain items.

Prepare brief notes to answer the following questions that have been asked by the directors of Sandringham Ltd. Where appropriate, make reference to relevant accounting standards.

(a) (i) **Why is an adjustment made for closing inventories in the financial statements?**

   (ii) **How should inventories be valued in the financial statements?**

(b) (i) **When would an impairment review of non-current assets be necessary?**

   (ii) **What would you do in an impairment review?**

....

Task 3.10

You have been asked to help prepare the financial statements of Merched Ltd for the year ended 31 March 20X3. Legal proceedings have been started against the company because of faulty products supplied to a customer. The company's lawyers advise that it is probable that the entity will be found liable for damages of £250,000.

Explain how you would treat the probable damages arising from the legal proceedings in the financial statements. Refer, where relevant, to accounting standards.

....

Task 3.11

Houghton Ltd owns and operates a department store. During the year, the directors decided to offer refunds to dissatisfied customers, provided that these were claimed within three months of the date the goods were purchased. There are large notices explaining this policy on every floor of the store. Since the policy was introduced, refunds have been claimed on roughly 2% of all sales.

Prepare brief notes for the directors of Houghton Ltd to answer the following questions:

(a) **When should a provision be recognised, according to IAS 37 *Provisions, contingent liabilities and contingent assets*?**

(b) **How should the policy of refunding customers be treated in the financial statements for the year?**

(c) **How should the policy of refunding customers be disclosed in the notes to the financial statements?**

....

Task 3.12

The directors of Lavendar plc are considering acquiring a subsidiary. They are unclear about the criteria for an entity to be a parent of a subsidiary, and would like you to clarify this for them. They would like to write off any goodwill that arises on the acquisition of the subsidiary immediately, and have asked for your opinion on the correct accounting treatment.

Prepare brief notes to answer the following questions that have been asked by the directors of Lavendar plc:

(a) **What are the criteria for an entity being the parent of a subsidiary?**

(b) **Explain the accounting treatment that has to be adopted for the goodwill in the consolidated statement of financial position of Lavendar plc**

Note: Your answer should make reference to relevant accounting standards.

....

Accounting standards and regulation – objective test questions

Task 4.1

Which one of the following is responsible for governance and fundraising in relation to the development of International Accounting Standards?

International Financial Reporting Standards Foundation	
International Accounting Standards Board	
International Financial Reporting Standards Interpretations Committee	
International Financial Reporting Standards Advisory Council	

Task 4.2

The role of the International Accounting Standards Board (IASB) is to oversee the standard setting and regulatory process.

Is this statement true or false?

True	
False	

Task 4.3

IAS 1 *Presentation of financial statements* requires some items to be disclosed as separate line items in the financial statements and others to be disclosed in the notes.

1   Depreciation
2   Revenue
3   Closing inventories
4   Finance cost
5   Dividends

Which two of the above have to be shown as line items in the statement of comprehensive income, rather than in the notes to the financial statements?

1 and 4	
3 and 5	
2 and 3	
2 and 4	

Task 4.4

If a company changes the depreciation method for its motor vehicles from the straight line method to the reducing balance method, this is not a change in accounting policy.

Is this statement true or false?

True	
False	

Task 4.5

After the financial statements for the year ended 31 December 20X3 had been published, it was discovered that one of the accounts staff had committed a fraud. As a result, the purchases figure in the 20X3 financial statements is overstated. The amount involved is material.

When preparing the financial statements for the year ended 31 December 20X4, the correct course of action is to:

Adjust opening retained earnings and comparative figures	
Adjust the financial statements for the current period	

Task 4.6

A decrease in trade receivables is deducted from operating profit in the reconciliation of profit from operations to net cash from operating activities.

Is this statement true or false?

True	
False	

Task 4.7

Which of these transactions would be reported in a statement of cash flows?

1   A bonus issue of shares
2   Dividends paid

1 only	
2 only	
Both 1 and 2	
Neither 1 nor 2	

Task 4.8

The components of the cost of a major item of equipment are given below.

	£
Purchase price	780,000
Import duties	117,000
Site preparation	30,000
Installation	28,000
General overheads	50,000
	1,005,000

What amount should be recognised as the cost of the asset, according to IAS 16 *Property, plant and equipment*?

£888,000	
£897,000	
£955,000	
£1,005,000	

Task 4.9

A property was purchased on 1 April 20X0 for £160,000. Depreciation policy is to depreciate properties over a period of 40 years. On 1 April 20X2 the property was revalued to £200,000.

What is the depreciation charge for the year ended 31 March 20X3?

£4,000	
£4,211	
£5,000	
£5,263	

Task 4.10

A machine was purchased on 1 January 20X0 for £80,000 and was depreciated over a period of 10 years using the straight-line method. On 1 January 20X2 it was decided that the machine had a total useful life of just 7 years.

What is the depreciation charge for the year ending 31 December 20X2?

£9,143	
£11,429	
£12,800	
£18,286	

Task 4.11

On 1 January 20X0 a building was purchased for £240,000. At that date its useful life was 50 years. On 1 January 20X4 it was revalued to £460,000 with no change in estimated useful life. On 31 December 20X5 the building was sold for £500,000.

What is the profit on disposal?

£40,000	
£58,400	
£60,000	
£288,800	

Task 4.12

Swale Ltd took out a bank loan to finance the purchase of a new machine for immediate use in the business.

According to IAS 23 *Borrowing costs*, Swale Ltd should recognise the interest on the loan as an expense.

Is this statement true or false?

True	
False	

Task 4.13

Undine Ltd purchased a piece of land on 31 October 20X0 for £500,000. On 31 October 20X4 the fair value of the land was £700,000. The latest valuation report, dated 31 October 20X8, values the land at £450,000.

The land is investment property and Undine Ltd has adopted the fair value model in accordance with IAS 40 *Investment property*.

Which ONE of the following shows the correct accounting treatment in Undine Ltd's financial statements for the year ended 31 October 20X8?

Loss of £250,000 in other comprehensive income	
Loss of £200,000 in profit or loss	
Loss of £250,000 in profit or loss	
Loss of £50,000 in profit or loss; loss of £200,000 in other comprehensive income	

Task 4.14

Totterdown Ltd has a non-current asset that is held for sale.

According to IFRS 5 *Non-current assets held for sale and discontinued operations*, where should the carrying amount of the machine be included in the company's statement of financial position?

Under non-current assets	
Under current assets	
Within inventories	
Within receivables	

Task 4.15

Internally generated goodwill should be measured at fair value.

Is this statement true or false?

True	
False	

Task 4.16

An asset has a carrying amount of £125,000. Its fair value less costs to sell is £120,000 and its value in use is £130,000, so the asset should be measured at £120,000.

Is this statement true or false?

True	
False	

Task 4.17

During June 20X6, a company made the following purchases of inventory.

1 June	25 units @	£140 per unit
15 June	15 units @	£160 per unit

On 30 June it sold 30 units at a price of £150 per unit. The company uses the first-in, first-out (FIFO) method of valuation.

What is the value of closing inventories at 30 June 20X6?

£1,400	
£1,475	
£1,500	
£1,600	

Task 4.18

A company estimated that its corporation tax liability for the year ended 30 June 20X1 was £113,000. During the year to 30 June 20X2 the amount actually paid to Her Majesty's Revenue and Customs (HMRC) was £108,000. The estimate for the corporation tax liability for the year ended 30 June 20X2 is £129,000.

What amounts should be recognised in the financial statements for the year ended 30 June 20X2?

Tax expense (profit or loss)	Tax payable (statement of financial position)	
£124,000	£124,000	
£124,000	£129,000	
£129,000	£129,000	
£134,000	£129,000	

Task 4.19

An asset with a fair value of £15,400 is acquired under a finance lease on 1 January 20X1 with a deposit on that date of £4,000 and four further annual payments on 31 December each year. The interest rate implicit in the lease is 15% and the actuarial method is used to allocate interest to accounting periods over the lease term.

What is the total lease obligation (liability) at 31 December 20X1?

£7,400	
£9,110	
£10,250	
£13,110	

Task 4.20

Trent Ltd entered into a finance lease agreement on 1 April 20X5. The fair value of the asset was £76,000 and Trent Ltd agreed to make four annual payments of £25,000 starting on 31 March 20X6. The rate of interest implicit in the lease is 12%. Trent Ltd uses the actuarial method to account for finance lease interest.

What is the finance charge to profit or loss relating to the lease for the year ended 31 March 20X6?

£6,120	
£9,120	
£9,600	
£25,000	

Task 4.21

At 30 April 20X7 Ellison Ltd has the following two legal claims outstanding:

1   A legal action against the company filed in February 20X7. Ellison Ltd has been advised that it is probable that the liability will materialise.

2   A legal action taken by the company against another entity, started in March 20X4. Ellison Ltd has been advised that it is probable that it will win the case.

According to IAS 37 *Provisions, contingent liabilities and contingent assets*, how should the company report these legal actions in its financial statements for the year ended 30 April 20X7?

Legal action 1	Legal action 2	
Disclose in a note to the financial statements	No disclosure	
Recognise a provision	No disclosure	
Recognise a provision	Disclose in a note to the financial statements	
Recognise a provision	Recognise the income	

Task 4.22

Which of the following events after the end of the reporting period would normally be classified as adjusting, according to IAS 10 *Events after the reporting period*?

Destruction of a major non-current asset	
Discovery of error or fraud	
Issue of shares	
Purchases of a major non-current asset	

Task 4.23

On 1 September 20X9 Usk Ltd sold goods to Chertsey Ltd. The two companies have agreed that Chertsey Ltd can return any items that are still unsold at 30 November 20X9. All the goods remained in the inventories of Chertsey Ltd at 30 September 20X9.

Usk Ltd should not recognise any revenue from this transaction in its financial statements for the year ended 30 September 20X9.

Is this statement true or false?

True	
False	

Task 4.24

On 1 January 20X5 Stanton Ltd received a government grant of £180,000 in respect of the purchase of new plant costing £750,000 on the same date. The plant is depreciated over 10 years using the straight line method.

According to IAS 20 *Accounting for government grants and disclosure of government assistance*, what is the net amount recognised in profit or loss for the year ended 31 December 20X5 in respect of the purchase of the plant and the receipt of the grant?

Expense of £57,000	
Expense of £93,000	
Income of £105,000	
Income of £180,000	

Task 4.25

At 1 April 20X1 a company had 1 million 50 pence ordinary shares in issue. On 1 August a further 400,000 50 pence ordinary shares were issued. Profit for the year was £680,000.

What is the earnings per share for the year ended 31 March 20X2?

48.6p	
53.7p	
68.0p	
107.4p	

Task 4.26

According to IFRS 8 *Operating segments*, an entity should only report information about an operating segment if its reported revenue is 10 per cent or more of the combined revenue, internal and external, of all operating segments.

Is this statement true or false?

True	
False	

Task 4.27

Wensley plc holds 25% of the voting power in Hawes Ltd and appoints one of its four directors.

The consolidated statement of comprehensive income of Wensley plc should include 25% of Hawes Ltd's profit or loss for the year as a separate line item.

Is this statement true or false?

True	
False	

Question bank

Task 4.28

Erewash Ltd has the power to govern the financial and operating policies of Amber Ltd so as to obtain benefits from its activities. In relation to Erewash Ltd, Amber Ltd is:

An associate	
A parent	
A simple investment	
A subsidiary	

The consolidated statement of financial position

Task 5.1

On 1 January 20X1 X plc purchased 75% of the ordinary share capital of Y Ltd when the retained earnings of Y Ltd stood at £240,000. At 31 December 20X1 the summarised statements of financial position of the two companies were as follows.

	X plc £'000	Y Ltd £'000
Assets		
Property, plant and equipment	800	400
Investment in Y Ltd	350	–
Current assets	170	130
	1,320	530
Equity and liabilities		
Share capital	800	200
Retained earnings	420	280
	1,220	480
Current liabilities	100	50
	1,320	530

Draft a consolidated statement of financial position for X plc and its subsidiary as at 31 December 20X1.

Consolidated statement of financial position as at 31 December 20X1

	£'000
Assets	
Goodwill	
Property, plant and equipment	
Current assets	
Equity and liabilities	
Share capital	
Retained earnings	
Non-controlling interest	
Current liabilities	

Workings

Goodwill	£'000
Price paid	
Share capital – attributable to X plc	
Retained earnings – attributable to X plc	

Retained earnings	£'000
X plc	
Y Ltd – attributable to X plc	

Non-controlling interest (NCI)	£'000
Share capital – attributable to NCI	
Retained earnings – attributable to NCI	

Task 5.2

Fertwrangler Ltd has one subsidiary, Voncarryon Ltd, which it acquired on 1 April 20X2. The statement of financial position of Voncarryon Ltd as at 31 March 20X3 is set out below.

Voncarryon Ltd
Summarised statement of financial position as at 31 March 20X3

	£'000
Non-current assets	3,855
Current assets	4,961
Total assets	8,816
Equity	
Share capital	2,000
Share premium	1,000
Retained earnings	1,770
	4,770
Non-current liabilities	1,500
Current liabilities	2,546
Total equity and liabilities	8,816

Further information

(a) The share capital of Voncarryon Ltd consists of ordinary shares of £1 each. There have been no changes to the balances of share capital and share premium during the year. No dividends were paid by Voncarryon Ltd during the year.

(b) Fertwrangler acquired 1,200,000 shares in Voncarryon Ltd on 1 April 20X2 at a cost of £3,510,000.

(c) At 1 April 20X2 the balance on the retained earnings reserve of Voncarryon Ltd was £1,350,000.

(d) The fair value of the non-current assets of Voncarryon Ltd at 1 April 20X2 was £4,455,000. The book value of the assets at 1 April 20X2 was £4,055,000. The revaluation has not been reflected in the books of Voncarryon Ltd.

(e) Goodwill arising on consolidation had suffered an impairment loss of £66,000 by 31 March 20X3.

(f) At 31 March 20X3 the balance on the retained earnings reserve of Fertwrangler Ltd was £5,610,000.

(g) Non-controlling interest is measured at the proportionate share of the fair value of Voncarryon's net assets.

(a) **Calculate the goodwill figure relating to the acquisition of Voncarryon Ltd that will appear in the consolidated statement of financial position of Fertwrangler Ltd as at 31 March 20X3.**

£ ☐

(b) **Calculate the non-controlling interest figure that will appear in the consolidated statement of financial position of Fertwrangler Ltd at 31 March 20X3.**

£ ☐

(c) **Calculate the balance on the consolidated retained earnings reserve that will appear in the consolidated statement of financial position of Fertwrangler Ltd at 31 March 20X3.**

£ ☐

Task 5.3

Bell plc has one subsidiary, Clive Ltd, and one investment in an associate company, Grant Ltd. The summarised statements of financial position of Clive Ltd and Grant Ltd as at 31 March 20X5 are set out below.

Statements of financial position as at 31 March 20X5

	Clive Ltd £'000	Grant Ltd £'000
Assets		
Property, plant and equipment	32,504	18,465
Current assets	11,585	4,852
Total assets	44,089	23,317
Equity and liabilities		
Equity		
Share capital	20,000	10,000
Share premium	5,000	–
Retained earnings	12,930	9,000
Total equity	37,930	19,000
Current liabilities	6,159	4,317
Total equity and liabilities	44,089	23,317

Further information

- The share capital of Clive Ltd consists of ordinary shares of £1 each. There have been no changes to the balances of share capital and share premium during the year. No dividends were paid by Clive Ltd during the year.

- Bell plc acquired 12,000,000 shares in Clive Ltd on 1 April 20X4 at a cost of £25,160,000.

- At 1 April 20X4 the balance on the retained earnings reserve of Clive Ltd was £10,600,000.

- The fair value of the property, plant and equipment of Clive Ltd at 1 April 20X4 was £33,520,000. The book value of the property, plant and equipment at 1 April 20X4 was £30,520,000. The revaluation has not been reflected in the books of Clive Ltd. There were no other differences between fair values and book values as at 1 April 20X4.

- The share capital of Grant Ltd consists of ordinary shares of £1 each. There have been no changes to the balance of share capital during the year. No dividends were paid by Grant Ltd during the year.

- Bell plc acquired 2,500,000 shares in Grant Ltd on 1 April 20X4 at a cost of £5,000,000.

- At 1 April 20X4 the balance on the retained earnings reserve of Grant Ltd was £8,000,000.

- The fair value of the net assets of Grant Ltd was £18,000,000, the same as the book value as at this date.

- Goodwill arising on the acquisition of both investments was reviewed for impairment at 31 March 20X5. The directors estimate that the impairment loss amounted to £200,000 for Clive Ltd and £50,000 for Grant Ltd.

- Non-controlling interests are measured as the proportionate share of the fair value of the subsidiary's net assets.

(a) **Calculate the goodwill figure relating to the acquisition of Clive Ltd that will appear in the consolidated statement of financial position of Bell plc as at 31 March 20X5.**

£ [   ]

(b) **Calculate the amount of the investment in the associate, Grant Ltd, that will appear in the consolidated statement of financial position of Bell plc as at 31 March 20X5.**

£ [   ]

(c) **Define an 'associate' making reference to relevant accounting standards.**

Task 5.4

The Managing Director of Dumyat plc has asked you to prepare the statement of financial position for the group. Dumyat plc has one subsidiary, Devon Ltd. The statements of financial position of the two companies as at 31 October 20X7 are set out below.

Statements of financial position as at 31 October 20X7

	Dumyat plc £'000	Devon Ltd £'000
Assets		
Non-current assets		
Property, plant and equipment	65,388	31,887
Investment in Devon Ltd	26,000	
	91,388	31,887
Current assets		
Inventories	28,273	5,566
Trade and other receivables	11,508	5,154
Receivable from Devon Ltd	4,000	0
Cash and cash equivalents	2,146	68
	45,927	10,788
Total assets	137,315	42,675

EQUITY AND LIABILITIES

Equity

Share capital	25,000	12,000
Share premium	12,000	4,000
Retained earnings	55,621	17,092
Total equity	92,621	33,092
Non-current liabilities		
Long-term loans	25,000	4,000
Current liabilities		
Trade and other payables	13,554	1,475
Payable to Dumyat plc	0	4,000
Tax liabilities	6,140	108
	19,694	5,583
Total liabilities	44,694	9,583
Total equity and liabilities	137,315	42,675

You have been given the following further information.

- The share capital of Devon Ltd consists of ordinary shares of £1 each. Ownership of these shares carries voting rights in Devon Ltd. There have been no changes to the balances of share capital and share premium during the year. No dividends were paid or proposed by Devon Ltd during the year.

- Dumyat plc acquired 9,000,000 shares in Devon Ltd on 1 November 20X6.

- At 1 November 20X6 the balance of retained earnings of Devon Ltd was £12,052,000.

- The fair value of the non-current assets of Devon Ltd at 1 November 20X6 was £28,800,000. The book value of the non-current assets at 1 November 20X6 was £25,800,000. The revaluation has not been recorded in the books of Devon Ltd (ignore any effect on the depreciation for the year).

- The directors of Dumyat plc have concluded that goodwill has not been impaired during the year.

- The non-controlling interest is measured at the proportionate share of the fair value of Devon Ltd's net assets.

Draft a consolidated statement of financial position for Dumyat plc and its subsidiary as at 31 October 20X7.

Dumyat plc

(Complete the left hand column by writing in the correct line item from the list provided.)

Consolidated statement of financial position as at 31 October 20X7

	£'000
Assets	
Non-current assets:	
▼	
▼	
Current assets:	
▼	
▼	
▼	
Total assets	
Equity and liabilities	
Equity attributable to owners of the parent	
▼	
▼	
▼	
Non-controlling interest	
Total equity	
Non-current liabilities:	
▼	
Current liabilities:	
▼	
▼	
Total liabilities	
Total equity and liabilities	

Picklist for line items:

Cash and cash equivalents
Goodwill
Inventories
Long term loans
Property, plant and equipment
Retained earnings
Share capital
Share premium
Tax payable
Trade and other payables
Trade and other receivables

Workings

(Complete the left hand column by writing in the correct narrative from the list provided.)

Goodwill		£'000
	▼	
	▼	
	▼	
	▼	
	▼	

Picklist for narratives:

Price paid
Retained earnings – attributable to Dumyat plc
Revaluation reserve – attributable to Dumyat plc
Share capital – attributable to Dumyat plc
Share premium – attributable to Dumyat plc

Retained earnings		£'000
	▼	
	▼	

Picklist for narratives:

Devon Ltd – attributable to Dumyat plc
Dumyat plc
Revaluation

Non-controlling interest (NCI)		£'000
	▼	
	▼	
	▼	
	▼	

Picklist for narratives:

Current assets – attributable to NCI
Non-current assets – attributable to NCI
Price paid
Retained earnings – attributable to NCI
Revaluation reserve – attributable to NCI
Share capital – attributable to NCI
Share premium – attributable to NCI

Task 5.5

The Managing Director of Tolsta plc has asked you to prepare the statement of financial position for the group. Tolsta plc has one subsidiary, Balallan Ltd. The statements of financial position of the two companies as at 31 October 20X8 are set out below.

Statements of financial position as at 31 October 20X8

	Tolsta plc	Balallan Ltd
Assets	£'000	£'000
Non-current assets		
Property, plant and equipment	47,875	31,913
Investment in Balallan Ltd	32,000	
	79,875	31,913
Current assets		
Inventories	25,954	4,555
Trade and other receivables	14,343	3,656
Cash and cash equivalents	1,956	47
	42,253	8,258
Total assets	122,128	40,171
Equity and liabilities		
Equity		
Share capital	45,000	12,000
Share premium	12,000	6,000
Retained earnings	26,160	11,340
Total equity	83,160	29,340
Non-current liabilities		
Long-term loans	20,000	7,000
Current liabilities		
Trade and other payables	14,454	3,685
Tax liabilities	4,514	146
	18,968	3,831
Total liabilities	38,968	10,831
Total equity and liabilities	122,128	40,171

Further information

- The share capital of Balallan Ltd consists of ordinary shares of £1 each. Ownership of these shares carries voting rights in Balallan Ltd. There have been no changes to the balances of share capital and share premium during the year. No dividends were paid or proposed by Balallan Ltd during the year.

- Tolsta plc acquired 8,000,000 shares in Balallan Ltd on 1 November 20X7.

- At 1 November 20X7 the balance of retained earnings of Balallan Ltd was £9,750,000.

- The fair value of the non-current assets of Balallan Ltd at 1 November 20X7 was £31,100,000. The book value of the non-current assets at 1 November 20X7 was £26,600,000. The revaluation has not been recorded in the books of Balallan Ltd (ignore any effect on the depreciation for the year).

- Included in Trade and other receivables for Tolsta plc and in Trade and other payables for Balallan Ltd is an inter-company transaction for £2,000,000 that took place in early October 20X8.

- The directors of Tolsta plc have concluded that goodwill has been impaired by £2,100,000 during the year.

- The non-controlling interest is measured as the proportionate share of the fair value of Balallan Ltd's net assets.

Draft a consolidated statement of financial position for Tolsta plc and its subsidiary as at 31 October 20X8.

Tolsta plc

Consolidated statement of financial position as at 31 October 20X8

	£'000
Assets	
Non-current assets:	
Intangible assets: goodwill	
Property, plant and equipment	_____
	_____
Current assets:	
Inventories	
Trade and other receivables	
Cash and cash equivalents	_____
	_____
Total assets	_____
Equity and liabilities	
Equity attributable to owners of the parent:	
Share capital	
Share premium	
Retained earnings	_____
Non-controlling interest	_____
Total equity	_____
Non-current liabilities:	
Long-term loan	_____
Current liabilities:	
Trade and other payables	
Tax liabilities	_____
	_____
Total liabilities	_____
Total equity and liabilities	_____

Workings

(Complete the left hand column by writing in the correct narrative from the list provided.)

Goodwill		£'000
	▼	
	▼	
	▼	
	▼	
	▼	
	▼	

Picklist for narratives:

Impairment
Price paid
Retained earnings – attributable to Tolsta plc
Revaluation reserve – attributable to Tolsta plc
Share capital – attributable to Tolsta plc
Share premium – attributable to Tolsta plc

Retained earnings		£'000
	▼	
	▼	
	▼	

Picklist for narratives:

Balallan Ltd – attributable to Tolsta plc
Impairment
Revaluation
Tolsta plc

Non-controlling interest (NCI)		£'000
	▼	
	▼	
	▼	
	▼	

Picklist for narratives:

Current assets – attributable to NCI
Impairment
Non-current assets – attributable to NCI
Price paid
Retained earnings – attributable to NCI
Revaluation reserve – attributable to NCI
Share capital – attributable to NCI
Share premium – attributable to NCI

Task 5.6

Ard plc has one subsidiary, Ledi Ltd. The summarised statements of financial position of the two companies as at 31 March 20X9 are set out below.

Summarised statements of financial position as at 31 March 20X9

	Ard plc	Ledi Ltd
Assets	£'000	£'000
Non-current assets		
Property, plant and equipment	45,210	27,480
Investment in Ledi Ltd	23,000	
	68,210	27,480
Current assets	32,782	10,835
Total assets	100,992	38,315
Equity and liabilities		
Equity		
Share capital	50,000	20,000
Retained earnings	21,526	9,740
Total equity	71,526	29,740
Non-current liabilities	14,000	4,000
Current liabilities	15,466	4,575
Total equity and liabilities	100,992	38,315

Further information

- The share capital of Ledi Ltd consists of ordinary shares of £1 each. Ownership of these shares carries voting rights in Ledi Ltd. There have been no changes to the balances of share capital and share premium during the year. No dividends were paid or proposed by Ledi Ltd during the year.

- Ard plc acquired 12,000,000 shares in Ledi Ltd on 1 April 20X8.

- On 1 April 20X8 the balance of retained earnings of Ledi Ltd was £7,640,000.

- Included in Trade and other receivables for Ard plc and in Trade and other payables for Ledi Ltd is an inter-company transaction for £3,000,000 that took place in early March 20X9.

- The directors of Ard plc have concluded that goodwill has been impaired by £1,600,000 during the year.

Draft a consolidated statement of financial position for Ard plc and its subsidiary as at 31 March 20X9.

Ard plc

Consolidated statement of financial position as at 31 March 20X9

	£'000
Assets	
Non-current assets:	
Intangible assets: goodwill	
Property, plant and equipment	
Current assets	
Total assets	
Equity and liabilities	
Equity attributable to owners of the parent	
Share capital	
Retained earnings	
Non-controlling interest	
Total equity	
Non-current liabilities	
Current liabilities	
Total liabilities	
Total equity and liabilities	

Workings

(Complete the left hand column by writing in the correct narrative from the list provided).

Goodwill		£'000
	▼	
	▼	
	▼	
	▼	

Picklist for narratives:

Impairment
Price paid
Retained earnings – attributable to Ard plc
Share capital – attributable to Ard plc

Retained earnings		£'000
	▼	
	▼	
	▼	

Picklist for narratives:

Ard plc
Impairment
Ledi Ltd – attributable to Ard plc

Non-controlling interest (NCI)		£'000
	▼	
	▼	

Picklist for narratives:

Current assets – attributable to NCI
Impairment
Non-current assets – attributable to NCI
Price paid
Retained earnings – attributable to NCI
Share capital – attributable to NCI

Task 5.7

The Managing Director of Glebe plc has asked you to prepare the statement of financial position for the group. Glebe plc acquired 70% of the issued share capital of Starks Ltd on 1 April 20X0. At that date Starks Ltd had issued share capital of £10,000,000 and retained earnings of £11,540,000.

The summarised statements of financial position of the two companies as at 31 March 20X1 are set out below.

	Glebe plc	Starks Ltd
	£'000	£'000
ASSETS		
Investment in Starks Ltd	18,000	
Non-current assets	36,890	25,600
Current assets	22,364	7,835
Total assets	77,254	33,435
EQUITY AND LIABILITIES		
Equity		
Share capital	40,000	10,000
Retained earnings	12,249	16,650
Total equity	52,249	26,650
Non-current liabilities	13,000	5,000
Current liabilities	12,005	1,785
Total liabilities	25,005	6,785
Total equity and liabilities	77,254	33,435

Additional data

- The fair value of the non-current assets of Starks Ltd at 1 April 20X0 was £26,300,000. The book value of the non-current assets at 1 April 20X0 was £23,900,000. The revaluation has not been recorded in the books of Starks Ltd (ignore any effect on the depreciation for the year).

- The directors of Glebe plc have concluded that goodwill has been impaired by £400,000 during the year.

- Glebe plc has decided non-controlling interests will be valued at their proportionate share of net assets.

Draft a consolidated statement of financial position for Glebe plc and its subsidiary as at 31 March 20X1.

Glebe plc

Consolidated statement of financial position as at 31 March 20X1

	£'000
Assets	
Non-current assets:	
Intangible assets: goodwill	
Property, plant and equipment	
Current assets:	
Total assets	
Equity and liabilities	
Equity attributable to owners of the parent	
Share capital	
Retained earnings	
Non-controlling interest	
Total equity	
Non-current liabilities:	
Current liabilities:	
Total liabilities	
Total equity and liabilities	

Workings

(Complete the left hand column by writing in the correct narrative from the list provided.)

Goodwill		£'000
	▼	
	▼	
	▼	
	▼	
	▼	

Picklist for narratives:

Impairment
Price paid
Retained earnings – attributable to Glebe plc
Revaluation reserve – attributable to Glebe plc
Share capital – attributable to Glebe plc

Retained earnings		£'000
	▼	
	▼	
	▼	

Picklist for narratives:

Glebe plc
Impairment
Revaluation
Starks Ltd – attributable to Glebe plc

Non-controlling interest (NCI)		£'000
	▼	
	▼	
	▼	

Picklist for narratives:

Current assets – attributable to NCI
Impairment
Non-current assets – attributable to NCI
Price paid
Retained earnings – attributable to NCI
Revaluation reserve – attributable to NCI
Share capital – attributable to NCI

The consolidated statement of comprehensive income

Task 6.1

P plc has owned 7,000 of the 10,000 ordinary shares in S Ltd since 1 April 20X0. The statements of comprehensive income for each company for the year ended 31 March 20X2 are given below.

Statements of comprehensive income for the year ended 31 March 20X2

	P plc £'000	S Ltd £'000
Continuing operations		
Revenue	4,600	2,210
Cost of sales	(2,700)	(1,320)
Gross profit	1,900	890
Other income – dividend from S Ltd	70	–
Operating expenses	(870)	(430)
Profit before tax	1,100	460
Tax	(300)	(120)
Profit for the period from continuing operations	800	340

Draft a consolidated statement of comprehensive income for P plc and its subsidiary for the year ended 31 March 20X2.

Consolidated statement of comprehensive income for the year ended 31 March 20X2

	£'000
Continuing operations	
Revenue	
Cost of sales	
Gross profit	
Other income	
Operating expenses	
Profit before tax	
Tax	
Profit for the period from continuing operations	

	£'000
Attributable to:	
Equity holders of the parent	
Non-controlling interests	

Task 6.2

C plc purchased 60% of the shares in D Ltd a number of years ago. The statements of comprehensive income for each company for the year ended 31 December 20X1 are given below.

	C plc £'000	D Ltd £'000
Continuing operations		
Revenue	38,600	14,700
Cost of sales	(25,000)	(9,500)
Gross profit	13,600	5,200
Other income – dividend from D Ltd	300	–
Operating expenses	(7,700)	(2,900)
Profit before tax	6,200	2,300
Tax	(1,600)	(600)
Profit for the period from continuing operations	4,600	1,700

You are also given the following information.

- During the year C plc sold goods which had cost £4,000,000 to D Ltd for £5,000,000. All of the goods were still in the inventory of D Ltd at the year-end.

Draft a consolidated statement of comprehensive income for C plc and its subsidiary for the year ended 31 December 20X1.

Consolidated statement of comprehensive income for the year ended 31 December 20X1

	£'000
Continuing operations	
Revenue	
Cost of sales	
Gross profit	
Other income	
Operating expenses	
Profit before tax	
Tax	
Profit for the period from continuing operations	
Attributable to:	
Equity holders of the parent	
Non-controlling interests	

Workings

Revenue	£'000
C plc	
D Ltd	
Total inter-company adjustment	

Cost of sales	£'000
C plc	
D Ltd	
Total inter-company adjustment	

Task 6.3

The managing director of Aswall plc has asked you to prepare the draft consolidated statement of comprehensive income for the group. The company has one subsidiary, Unsafey Ltd. The statements of comprehensive income for the two companies for the year ended 31 March 20X4 are set out below.

Statements of comprehensive income for the year ended 31 March 20X4

	Aswall plc £'000	Unsafey Ltd £'000
Continuing operations		
Revenue	32,412	12,963
Cost of sales	(14,592)	(5,576)
Gross profit	17,820	7,387
Other income – dividend from Unsafey Ltd	1,500	–
Distribution costs	(5,449)	(1,307)
Administrative expenses	(3,167)	(841)
Profit from operations	10,704	5,239
Finance costs	(1,960)	(980)
Profit before tax	8,744	4,259
Tax	(2,623)	(1,063)
Profit for the period from continuing operations	6,121	3,196

Further information:

- Aswall plc owns 75% of the ordinary share capital of Unsafey Ltd.

- During the year Unsafey Ltd sold goods which had cost £1,200,000 to Aswall plc for £1,860,000. None of the goods had been sold by Aswall plc by the end of the year.

Draft a consolidated statement of comprehensive income for Aswall plc and its subsidiary for the year ended 31 March 20X4.

Aswall plc

Consolidated statement of comprehensive income for the year ended 31 March 20X4

	£'000
Continuing operations	
Revenue	
Cost of sales	
Gross profit	
Other income	
Distribution costs	
Administrative expenses	
Profit from operations	
Finance costs	
Profit before tax	
Tax	
Profit for the period from continuing operations	
Attributable to:	
Equity holders of the parent	
Non-controlling interest	

Workings

Revenue	£'000
Aswall plc	
Unsafey Ltd	
Total inter-company adjustment	

Cost of sales	£'000
Aswall plc	
Unsafey Ltd	
Total inter-company adjustment	

Non-controlling interest (NCI)	£'000
Profit for the period attributable to NCI	
Unrealised profit attributable to NCI	

Task 6.4

Danube plc has one subsidiary, Inn Ltd.

Extracts from their statements of comprehensive income for the year ended 31 March 20X2 are shown below:

	Danube plc £'000	Inn Ltd £'000
Continuing operations		
Revenue	15,800	5,400
Cost of sales	(8,500)	(2,800)
Gross profit	7,300	2,600
Other income	300	–
Operating expenses	(3,300)	(1,230)
Profit from operations	4,300	1,370

Additional data

- Danube Plc acquired 75% of the ordinary share capital of Inn Ltd on 1 April 20X1

- During the year Inn Ltd sold goods which had cost £600,000 to Danube plc for £1,000,000. Half of these goods still remain in the inventories of Danube plc at the end of the year.

- Other income of Danube plc included a dividend received from Inn Ltd

- Inn ltd had paid a dividend of 400,000 on 1 March 20X2

Draft the consolidated statement of comprehensive income for Danube plc and its subsidiary up to and including the profit from operations line for the year ended 31 March 20X2.

Danube plc

Consolidated statement of comprehensive income for the year ended 31 March 20X2

	£'000
Continuing operations	
Revenue	
Cost of sales	
Gross profit	
Other income	
Operating expenses	
Profit from operations	

Workings

Revenue	£'000
Danube plc	
Inn Ltd	
Total inter-company adjustment	

Cost of sales	£'000
Danube plc	
Inn Ltd	
Total inter-company adjustment	

Task 6.5

The managing director of Wewill plc has asked you to prepare the draft consolidated statement of comprehensive income for the group. The company has one subsidiary, Rokyu Ltd. The statements of comprehensive income for the two companies for the year ended 31 March 20X4 are set out below.

Statements of comprehensive income for the year ended 31 March 20X4

	Wewill plc	Rokyu Ltd
	£'000	£'000
Continuing operations		
Revenue	36,400	14,600
Cost of sales	(20,020)	(6,935)
Gross profit	16,830	7,665
Other income – dividend from Rokyu Ltd	860	–
Distribution costs	(6,552)	(3,358)
Administrative expenses	(4,004)	(1,898)
Profit from operations	6,684	2,409
Finance costs	(675)	(154)
Profit before tax	6,009	2,255
Tax	(1,468)	(445)
Profit for the period from continuing operations	4,541	1,810

Additional data:

- Wewill plc acquired 80% of the ordinary share capital of Rokyu Ltd on 1 April 20X3.

- During the year Wewill plc sold goods which had cost £1,000,000 to Rokyu Ltd for £1,400,000. None of the goods had been sold by Rokyu Ltd by the end of the year.

Draft a consolidated statement of comprehensive income for Wewill plc and its subsidiary for the year ended 31 March 20X4.

Wewill plc

Consolidated statement of comprehensive income for the year ended 31 March 20X4

	£'000
Continuing operations	
Revenue	
Cost of sales	
Gross profit	
Other income	
Distribution costs	
Administrative expenses	
Profit from operations	
Finance costs	
Profit before tax	
Tax	
Profit for the period from continuing operations	
Attributable to:	
Equity holders of the parent	
Non-controlling interest	

Workings

Revenue	£'000
Wewill plc	
Rokyu Ltd	
Total inter-company adjustment	

Cost of sales	£'000
Wewill plc	
Rokyu Ltd	
Total inter-company adjustment	

Calculating ratios

Task 7.1

Given below is a summarised statement of comprehensive income and a summarised statement of financial position for a company.

Statement of comprehensive income for the year ended 30 April 20X2

	£'000
Continuing operations	
Revenue	989
Cost of sales	(467)
Gross profit	522
Operating expenses	(308)
Profit from operations	214
Interest payable	(34)
Profit before tax	180
Tax	(48)
Profit for the period from continuing operations	132

Statement of financial position as at 30 April 20X2

	£'000
Non-current assets	1,200
Current assets	700
	1,900
Share capital and reserves	1,000
Non-current liabilities: Long-term loan	400
Current liabilities	500
	1,900

Calculate the following ratios to the nearest ONE DECIMAL PLACE:

(a)	Gross profit percentage	%
(b)	Operating profit percentage	%
(c)	Return on capital employed	%
(d)	Asset turnover (net assets)	times
(e)	Interest cover	times
(f)	Gearing	%

Task 7.2

Given below are extracts from a company's statement of comprehensive income and statement of financial position.

Statement of comprehensive income for the year ended 30 June 20X2 – extract

	£
Revenue	772,400
Cost of sales	507,400
Gross profit	265,000

Statement of financial position as at 30 June 20X2 – extract

	£
Inventories	58,600
Trade receivables	98,400
Trade payables	86,200
Bank overdraft	6,300

Calculate the following ratios to the nearest ONE DECIMAL PLACE.

(a)	Current ratio		:1
(b)	Quick (acid test) ratio		:1
(c)	Trade receivables collection period		days
(d)	Inventory turnover		times
(e)	Inventory holding period		days
(f)	Trade payables payment period		days

Task 7.3

You have been asked to calculate ratios for Midsummer Ltd in respect of its financial statements for the year ending 31 March 20X4 to assist a shareholder in his analysis of the company. He has given you Midsummer's statement of comprehensive income and the summarised statement of financial position prepared for internal purposes. These are set out below.

Midsummer Ltd

Statement of comprehensive income for the year ended 31 March 20X4

	£'000
Continuing operations	
Revenue	8,420
Cost of sales	(3,536)
Gross profit	4,884
Distribution costs	(1,471)
Administrative expenses	(1,224)
Profit from operations	2,189
Finance costs	(400)
Profit before tax	1,789
Tax	(465)
Profit for the period from continuing operations	1,324

Midsummer Ltd

Summarised statement of financial position as at 31 March 20X4

	£'000
Assets	
Non-current assets	15,132
Current assets	4,624
Total assets	19,756
EQUITY AND LIABILITIES	
Equity	
Share capital	6,000
Share premium	2,000
Retained earnings	4,541
Total equity	12,541
Non-current liabilities: long term loan	5,000
Current liabilities	2,215
Total liabilities	7,215
Total equity plus liabilities	19,756

(a) **State the formulae that are used to calculate each of the following ratios:**

(Write in the correct formula from the list provided)

(i) Return on capital employed	▼

Formulae:

Profit after tax/Total equity × 100

Profit from operations/Total equity × 100

Profit after tax/Total equity + Non-current liabilities × 100

Profit from operations/Total equity + Non-current liabilities × 100

(ii) Operating profit percentage	▼

Formulae:

Profit from operations/Revenue × 100

Profit from operations/Total assets × 100

Profit from operations/Total equity + Non-current liabilities × 100

Profit from operations/Finance costs × 100

(iii) Gross profit percentage	▼

Formulae:

Gross profit/Total equity × 100

Gross profit/Revenue × 100

Gross profit/Total assets × 100

Gross profit/Total assets – current liabilities

(iv) Asset turnover (net assets)	▼

Formulae:

Revenue/Total assets – current liabilities

Revenue/Total assets – total liabilities

Total assets – current liabilities/Revenue

Total assets – total liabilities/Revenue

(v) Gearing	▼

Formulae:

Current assets/Current liabilities

Revenue/Total assets – current liabilities

Non-current liabilities/Total equity + non-current liabilities

Profit after tax/Number of issued ordinary shares

(vi) Interest cover	▼

Formulae:

Finance costs/profit from operations

Finance costs/revenue

Profit from operations/finance costs

Revenue/finance costs

(b) **Calculate the ratios to the nearest ONE DECIMAL PLACE.**

(i) Return on capital employed		%
(ii) Operating profit percentage		%
(iii) Gross profit percentage		%
(iv) Asset turnover (net assets)		times
(v) Gearing		%
(vi) Interest cover		%

Task 7.4

A shareholder in Drain Ltd has asked you to help her by analysing the financial statements of the company for the year ended 31 March 20X6. These are set out below.

Drain Ltd
Statement of comprehensive Income for the year ended 31 March 20X6

	£'000
Continuing operations	
Revenue	21,473
Cost of sales	(9,878)
Gross profit	11,595
Distribution costs	(4,181)
Administrative expenses	(3,334)
Profit from operations	4,080
Finance costs	(350)
Profit before tax	3,730
Tax	(858)
Profit for the period from continuing operations	2,872

Drain Ltd
Statement of financial position as at 31 March 20X6

	£'000
ASSETS	
Non-current assets	
Property, plant and equipment	27,781
Current assets	
Inventories	1,813
Trade receivables	3,000
Cash and cash equivalents	62
	4,875
Total assets	32,656
EQUITY AND LIABILITIES	
Equity	
Share capital	5,000
Retained earnings	20,563
	25,563
Non-current liabilities	
Bank loans	5,000
Current liabilities	
Trade and other payables	1,235
Tax liabilities	858
	2,093
Total liabilities	7,093
Total equity and liabilities	32,656

(a) **State the formulae that are used to calculate each of the following ratios:**

(Write in the correct formula from the list provided)

(i) Gross profit percentage	▼

Formulae:

Gross profit/Total equity × 100

Gross profit/Revenue × 100

Gross profit/Total assets × 100

Gross profit/Total assets − current liabilities

(ii) Operating profit percentage	▼

Formulae:

Profit from operations/Revenue × 100

Profit from operations/Total assets × 100

Profit from operations/Total equity + Non-current liabilities × 100

Profit from operations/Finance costs × 100

(iii) Current ratio	▼

Formulae:

Total assets/Total liabilities

Current assets − inventories/Current liabilities

Current assets/Current liabilities

Total assets − inventories/Total liabilities

(iv) Quick (acid test) ratio	▼

Formulae:

Current assets/Current liabilities

Total assets − inventories/Total liabilities

Total assets/Total liabilities

Current assets − inventories/Current liabilities

(v) Inventory holding period	▼

Formulae:

Inventories/cost of sales × 365

Inventories/revenue × 365

Cost of sales/inventories × 365

Revenue/inventories × 365

(vi) Trade receivables collection period	▼

Formulae:

Trade payables/Cost of sales × 365

Trade receivables/Cost of sales × 365

Revenue/Trade receivables × 365

Trade receivables/Revenue × 365

(b) **Calculate the ratios to the nearest ONE DECIMAL PLACE.**

(i) Gross profit percentage		%
(ii) Operating profit percentage		%
(iii) Current ratio		:1
(iv) Quick (acid test) ratio		:1
(v) Inventory holding period		days
(vi) Trade receivables collection period		days

Task 7.5

You have been asked to calculate ratios for Route Ltd in respect of its financial statements for the year ending 31 March 20X7.

Route Ltd's statement of comprehensive income and statement of financial position are set out below.

Route Ltd

Statement of comprehensive income for the year ended 31 March 20X7

	£'000
Continuing operations	
Revenue	20,562
Cost of sales	(11,309)
Gross profit	9,253
Distribution costs	(4,841)
Administrative expenses	(3,007)
Profit from operations	1,405
Finance costs – interest on bank loan	(800)
Profit before tax	605
Tax	(133)
Profit for the period from continuing operations	472

Route Ltd

Statement of financial position as at 31 March 20X7

Assets	£'000
Non-current assets	
Property, plant and equipment	23,982
Current assets	
Inventories	4,012
Trade and other receivables	2,241
Cash and cash equivalents	84
	6,337
Total assets	30,319

Equity and liabilities

Equity

Share capital	4,000
Retained earnings	9,413
Total equity	13,413
Non-current liabilities	
Bank loans	14,000
Current liabilities	
Trade and other payables	2,773
Tax liabilities	133
	2,906
Total liabilities	16,906
Total equity and liabilities	30,319

(a) **State the formulae that are used to calculate each of the following ratios:**

(Write in the correct formula from the list provided)

(i) Return on total assets	▼

Formulae:

Profit after tax/Total assets × 100

Profit from operations/Total assets × 100

Profit from operations/Total equity × 100

Profit from operations/Total equity + Non-current liabilities × 100

(ii) Operating expenses/revenue percentage	▼

Formulae:

Administrative expenses/Revenue × 100

Distribution costs + administrative expenses/Revenue × 100

Distribution costs/Revenue × 100

Revenue/Distribution costs + administrative expenses × 100

(iii) Current ratio	▼

Formulae:

Total assets/Total liabilities

Current assets – inventories/Current liabilities

Current assets/Current liabilities

Total assets – inventories/Total liabilities

(iv) Quick (acid test) ratio	▼

Formulae:

Current assets/Current liabilities

Total assets – inventories/Total liabilities

Total assets/Total liabilities

Current assets – inventories/Current liabilities

(v) Gearing ratio	▼

Formulae:

Current assets/Current liabilities

Revenue/Total assets – current liabilities

Non-current liabilities/Total equity + non-current liabilities

Profit after tax/Number of issued ordinary shares

(vi) Interest cover	▼

Formulae:

Finance costs/profit from operations

Finance costs/revenue

Profit from operations/finance costs

Revenue/finance costs

(b) **Calculate the ratios to the nearest ONE DECIMAL PLACE.**

(i)	Return on total assets		%
(ii)	Operating expenses/revenue percentage		%
(iii)	Current ratio		:1
(iv)	Quick (acid test) ratio		:1
(v)	Gearing ratio		%
(vi)	Interest cover		times

Task 7.6

You have been asked to calculate ratios for Orford Ltd in respect of its financial statements for the year ending 31 October 20X8.

Orford Ltd's statement of comprehensive income and statement of financial position are set out below.

Orford Ltd

Statement of comprehensive income for the year ended 31 October 20X8

	£'000
Continuing operations	
Revenue	4,900
Cost of sales	(2,597)
Gross profit	2,303
Distribution costs	(1,225)
Administrative expenses	(490)
Profit from operations	588
Finance costs	(161)
Profit before tax	427
Tax	(64)
Profit for the period from continuing operations	363

BPP LEARNING MEDIA

Orford Ltd

Statement of financial position as at 31 October 20X8

Assets	£'000
Non-current assets	
Property, plant and equipment	8,041
Current assets	
Inventories	649
Trade receivables	392
Cash and cash equivalents	0
	1,041
Total assets	9,082
Equity and liabilities	
Equity	
Share capital	2,500
Retained earnings	3,741
Total equity	6,241
Non-current liabilities	
Bank loans	2,300
Current liabilities	
Trade payables	286
Tax liabilities	64
Bank overdraft	191
	541
Total liabilities	2,841
Total equity and liabilities	9,082

(a) **State the formulae that are used to calculate each of the following ratios:**

(Write in the correct formula from the list provided)

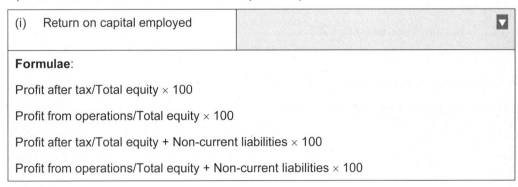

(i) Return on capital employed	▼

Formulae:

Profit after tax/Total equity × 100

Profit from operations/Total equity × 100

Profit after tax/Total equity + Non-current liabilities × 100

Profit from operations/Total equity + Non-current liabilities × 100

(ii) Return on equity	▼

Formulae:

Profit after tax/Total equity × 100

Profit before tax/Total equity × 100

Profit from operations/Total equity × 100

Profit from operations/Total equity + Non-current liabilities × 100

(iii) Inventory holding period	▼

Formulae:

Inventories/cost of sales × 365

Inventories/revenue × 365

Cost of sales/inventories × 365

Revenue/inventories × 365

(iv) Trade receivables collection period	▼

Formulae:

Trade payables/Cost of sales × 365

Trade receivables/Cost of sales × 365

Revenue/Trade receivables × 365

Trade receivables/Revenue × 365

(v) Trade payables payment period	▼

Formulae:

Trade payables/Revenue × 365

Trade payables/Cost of sales × 365

Revenue/Trade payables × 365

Cost of sales/Trade payables × 365

(vi) Working capital cycle		▼

Formulae:

Current assets/Current liabilities

Current assets – inventories/Current liabilities

Inventory days + Receivable days – Payable days

Inventory days + Receivable days + Payable days

(vii) Asset turnover (total assets)		▼

Formulae:

Revenue/Total assets

Revenue/Total assets – current liabilities

Revenue/Total assets – total liabilities

Total assets – total liabilities/Revenue

(b) **Calculate the ratios to the nearest ONE DECIMAL PLACE.**

(i)	Return on capital employed		%
(ii)	Return on equity		%
(iii)	Inventory holding period		days
(iv)	Trade receivables collection period		days
(v)	Trade payables payment period		days
(vi)	Working capital cycle		days
(vii)	Asset turnover (total assets)		times

Task 7.7

You have been asked to calculate ratios for Tower Ltd in respect of its financial statements for the year ending 31 October 20X9.

Tower Ltd's statement of comprehensive income and statement of financial position as follows:

Tower Ltd

Statement of comprehensive income for the year ended 31 October 20X9

	£'000
Continuing operations	
Revenue	27,800
Cost of sales	(14,178)
Gross profit	13,622
Distribution costs	(6,950)
Administrative expenses	(3,892)
Profit from operations	2,780
Finance costs	(840)
Profit before tax	1,940
Tax	(894)
Profit for the period from continuing operations	1,046

Tower Ltd

Statement of financial position as at 31 October 20X9

Assets	£'000
Non-current assets	
Property, plant and equipment	23,016
Current assets	
Inventories	3,261
Trade receivables	1,946
Cash and cash equivalents	-
	5,207
Total assets	28,223
Equity and liabilities	
Equity	
Share capital	8,500
Retained earnings	5,037
Total equity	13,537
Non-current liabilities	
Bank loans	12,000
Current liabilities	
Trade payables	1,276
Tax liabilities	894
Bank overdraft	516
	2,686
Total liabilities	14,686
Total equity and liabilities	28,223

(a) **State the formulae that are used to calculate each of the following ratios:**

(Write in the correct formula from the list provided)

(i) Gross profit percentage	▼

Formulae:

Gross profit/Total equity $\times$ 100

Gross profit/Revenue $\times$ 100

Gross profit/Total assets $\times$ 100

Gross profit/Total assets – current liabilities

(ii) Operating profit percentage	▼

Formulae:

Profit from operations/Revenue $\times$ 100

Profit from operations/Total assets $\times$ 100

Profit from operations/Total equity + Non-current liabilities $\times$ 100

Profit from operations/Finance costs $\times$ 100

(iii) Gearing	▼

Formulae:

Current assets/Current liabilities

Revenue/Total assets – current liabilities

Non-current liabilities/Total equity + non-current liabilities

Profit after tax/Number of issued ordinary shares

(iv) Interest cover	▼

Formulae:

Finance costs/profit from operations

Finance costs/revenue

Profit from operations/finance costs

Revenue/finance costs

(v) Current ratio	 ▼

Formulae:

Total assets/Total liabilities

Current assets – inventories/Current liabilities

Current assets/Current liabilities

Total assets – inventories/Total liabilities

(vi) Quick (acid test) ratio	▼

Formulae:

Current assets/Current liabilities

Total assets – inventories/Total liabilities

Total assets/Total liabilities

Current assets – inventories/Current liabilities

(vii) Trade receivables collection period	▼

Formulae:

Trade payables/Cost of sales × 365

Trade receivables/Cost of sales × 365

Revenue/Trade receivables × 365

Trade receivables/Revenue × 365

(viii) Trade payables payment period	▼

Formulae:

Trade payables/Revenue × 365

Trade payables/Cost of sales × 365

Revenue/Trade payables × 365

Cost of sales/Trade payables × 365

(b) **Calculate the ratios to the nearest ONE DECIMAL PLACE.**

(i)	Gross profit percentage		%
(ii)	Operating profit percentage		%
(iii)	Gearing		%
(iv)	Interest cover		times
(v)	Current ratio		:1
(vi)	Quick (acid test) ratio		:1
(vii)	Trade receivables collection period		days
(viii)	Trade payables payment period		days

Task 7.8

You have been asked to calculate ratios for Jewel Ltd in respect of its financial statements for the year ending 31 March 20X1 to assist your manager in his analysis of the company.

Jewel Ltd's statement of comprehensive income and statement of financial position are set out below.

Jewel Ltd – Statement of comprehensive income for the year ended 30 September 20X1

	£'000
Continuing operations	
Revenue	36,000
Cost of sales	(19,800)
Gross profit	16,200
Distribution costs	(6,840)
Administrative expenses	(6,120)
Profit from operations	3,240
Finance costs	(280)
Profit before tax	2,960
Tax	(2,094)
Profit for the period from continuing operations	866

Jewel Ltd – Statement of financial position as at 30 September 20X1

	£'000
ASSETS	
Non-current assets	
Property, plant and equipment	26,908
Current assets	
Inventories	2,376
Trade receivables	3,960
Cash and cash equivalents	787
	7,123
Total assets	34,031
EQUITY AND LIABILITIES	
Equity	
Share capital	12,000
Retained earnings	14,155
Total equity	26,155
Non-current liabilities	
Bank loans	4,000
	4,000
Current liabilities	
Trade payables	1,782
Tax liabilities	2,094
	3,876
Total liabilities	7,876
Total equity and liabilities	34,031

(a) **State the formulae that are used to calculate each of the following ratios**

(Write in the correct formula from the list provided)

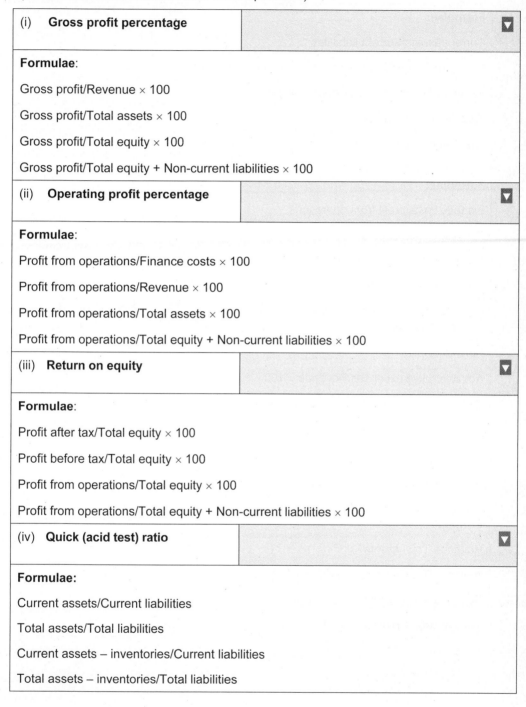

| (i) **Gross profit percentage** | ▼ |

Formulae:

Gross profit/Revenue × 100

Gross profit/Total assets × 100

Gross profit/Total equity × 100

Gross profit/Total equity + Non-current liabilities × 100

| (ii) **Operating profit percentage** | ▼ |

Formulae:

Profit from operations/Finance costs × 100

Profit from operations/Revenue × 100

Profit from operations/Total assets × 100

Profit from operations/Total equity + Non-current liabilities × 100

| (iii) **Return on equity** | ▼ |

Formulae:

Profit after tax/Total equity × 100

Profit before tax/Total equity × 100

Profit from operations/Total equity × 100

Profit from operations/Total equity + Non-current liabilities × 100

| (iv) **Quick (acid test) ratio** | ▼ |

Formulae:

Current assets/Current liabilities

Total assets/Total liabilities

Current assets – inventories/Current liabilities

Total assets – inventories/Total liabilities

(v) Gearing	▼

Formulae:

Current assets/Current liabilities

Non-current liabilities/Total equity + non current liabilities

Revenue/Total assets – current liabilities

Total liabilities/total assets

(vi) Interest cover	▼

Formulae:

Finance costs/profit from operations

Finance costs/revenue

Profit from operations/finance costs

Revenue/finance costs

(vii) Operating expenses/revenue percentage	▼

Formulae:

Administrative expenses/Revenue × 100

Distribution costs + administrative expenses/Revenue × 100

Distribution costs/Revenue × 100

Revenue/Distribution costs + administrative expenses × 100

(viii) Asset turnover (total assets)	▼

Formulae:

Revenue/Total assets

Revenue/Total assets – current liabilities

Revenue/Total assets – total liabilities

Total assets – total liabilities/Revenue

(b) Calculate the ratios to the nearest ONE DECIMAL PLACE.

(i)	Gross profit percentage		%
(ii)	Operating profit percentage		%
(iii)	Return on equity		%
(iv)	Quick (acid test) ratio		:1
(v)	Gearing		%
(vi)	Interest cover		times
(vii)	Operating expenses/revenue percentage		%
(viii)	Asset turnover (total assets)		times

Interpreting financial statements

Task 8.1

Given below is a range of financial ratios for two companies that both operate in the retail trade.

	Rigby Ltd	Rialto Ltd
Gross profit percentage	60%	32%
Operating profit percentage	28%	10%
Asset turnover	0.80 times	2.2 times
ROCE	22%	22%
Current ratio	2.0	1.8
Quick ratio	1.2	0.4
Inventory turnover	4.8 times	10.3 times
Trade receivables collection period	41 days	3 days
Trade payables payment period	62 days	70 days
Gearing	33%	50%
Interest cover	16 times	5 times

(a) **Comment upon what the ratios indicate about each business.**

(b) **One of the businesses is a supermarket and the other is a jeweller who supplies some goods on credit to long standing customers. Identify which business is which.**

··

Task 8.2

Duncan Tweedy wishes to invest some money in one of two private companies. He has obtained the latest financial statements for Byrne Ltd and May Ltd prepared for internal purposes. As part of his decision making process he has asked you to assess the relative profitability of the two companies, based on the following ratios.

	Byrne Ltd	May Ltd
Return on capital employed	21.5%	32.1%
Gross profit percentage	59.0%	67.0%
Operating profit percentage	25.0%	36.0%
Earnings per share	47p	82p

Prepare a report for Duncan Tweedy that:

(a) **Uses each ratio to comment on the relative profitability of the companies, and**
(b) **Concludes, with reasons, which company is the more profitable.**

··

Task 8.3

A colleague has asked you to take over an assignment. He has been helping a shareholder of Youngernst Ltd to understand the financial statements of the company for the past two years. The shareholder is interested in finding out how well the company has managed working capital. Your colleague has obtained the financial statements of Youngernst Ltd for the past two years and has calculated the following ratios:

Ratio	20X3	20X2
Current ratio	2.8:1	2.3:1
Quick (acid test) ratio	0.6:1	1.1:1
Trade receivables collection period	48 days	32 days
Trade payables payment period	27 days	30 days
Inventory holding period	84 days	67 days

Prepare notes for a meeting with the shareholder that include

(a) **Your comments on the change in the ratios of Youngernst Ltd over the two years, including an analysis of whether the change in each of the ratios shows that the management of the components of working capital has improved or deteriorated.**

(b) **A brief overall conclusion, based on the ratios above.**

Task 8.4

Madge Keygone is the managing director of Asbee Ltd. She has just returned from a meeting with one of the company's major shareholders. The shareholder was concerned about the current ratio, quick ratio, inventory holding period and trade receivables collection period and how they compared with the industry averages. Madge did not understand the shareholder's concern and has asked you to help her. She has calculated these ratios from the summarised financial statements of Asbee Ltd and has obtained the industry averages from computerised databases. These are set out below.

	Asbee Ltd	Industry average
Current ratio	2.3:1	1.9:1
Quick (acid test) ratio	0.8:1	0.9:1
Inventory holding period	176 days	98 days
Trade receivables collection period	51 days	47 days

Prepare a letter for Madge Keygone that includes the following.

(a) **Comments about how the ratios for Asbee Ltd compare with the industry averages and what this tells you about the company**

(b) **A conclusion, based on the ratios above, as to whether the shareholder is right to be concerned.**

Task 8.5

Leopold Scratchy plans to invest in shares in a private company. He has identified two companies that might be suitable, Partridge Ltd and Carington Ltd. He has obtained the latest financial statements of the companies in order to learn more about the risk inherent in, and return provided by, a potential investment in these companies. You have used these financial statements to compute the following ratios:

	Partridge Ltd	Carington Ltd
Gross profit percentage	59%	59%
Return on equity	38%	29%
Earnings per share	53p	41p
Gearing	45%	5%

Both companies have the same number of £1 ordinary shares and approximately the same amount of shareholders' equity (share capital and reserves).

Prepare a report for Leopold Scratchy that includes:

(a) **Comments on the relative return and risk of the two companies based on the ratios above.**

(b) **A conclusion, with reasons based on the ratios above, as to which of the two companies would provide Leopold with the best return on his investment and which of the two companies would be the safer investment.**

Task 8.6

Peter Stewart is a shareholder in Hillhead Ltd. He wishes to assess the efficiency and effectiveness of the management of the company. He has asked you to assist him by analysing the financial statements of the company for the last two years. You have computed the following ratios to assist you in your analysis.

	20X2	20X1
Gross profit percentage	40.0%	45.0%
Operating profit percentage	9.5%	7.5%
Inventory holding period	86.7 days	65.7 days
Trade receivables collection period	55.9 days	40.2 days

The financial statements show that sales have risen by 14% in the period.

Prepare a report for Peter Stewart that includes:

(a) **A comment on the relative performance of the company for the two years based on the ratios calculated and what this tells you about the company**

(b) **ONE suggestion as to how EACH of the ratios might be improved.**

Task 8.7

You have been asked to interpret the statement of cash flows for Bateoven Ltd for the year ended 30 September 20X5. The statement of cash flows and the reconciliation of operating profit to net cash from operating activities for Bateoven Ltd are set out below.

(a) **Bateoven Ltd**

Reconciliation of profit from operations to net cash from operating activities

	£'000
Profit from operations	312
Adjustments:	
Depreciation	3,570
Increase in inventories	(508)
Increase in trade receivables	(471)
Decrease in trade payables	(329)
Cash generated from operations	2,574
Interest paid	(560)
Tax paid	(1,284)
Net cash from operating activities	730

(b) **Bateoven Ltd**

Statement of cash flows for the year ended 30 September 20X5

	£'000	£'000
Net cash from operating activities		730
Investing activities		
Purchases of property, plant and equipment	(9,138)	
Net cash used in investing activities		(9,138)
Financing activities		
Proceeds from issue of share capital	5,000	
Increase in long term loans	4,100	
Dividends paid	(2,000)	
Net cash from financing activities		7,100
Net decrease in cash and cash equivalents		(1,308)
Cash and cash equivalents at the beginning of the year		1,401
Cash and cash equivalents at the end of the year		93

Draft a letter to the directors of Bateoven Ltd commenting on the sources and uses of cash during the year ended 30 September 20X5 as indicated by the statement of cash flows and the reconciliation note.

139

Task 8.8

The directors of Knole Ltd are concerned about the company's liquidity and cash flow. At the beginning of the current year the company had a positive cash balance of nearly £500,000 but by the year end this had become an overdraft of just over £1,500,000. The directors cannot understand how this has happened.

The company purchased new plant and equipment during the year, but there should have been enough cash available to cover this expenditure. Knole Ltd is highly profitable and has been able to raise finance by increasing its bank loans and by issuing new share capital during the year.

The directors have given you the financial statements for the past two years. You have used these to prepare a reconciliation of the profit from operations to net cash from operating activities. You have also calculated some ratios. The reconciliations and the ratios are set out below.

Knole Ltd

Reconciliation of profit from operations to net cash inflow from operating activities for the year ended 31 October

	20X8	20X7
	£'000	£'000
Profit from operations	13,200	11,060
Adjustments for:		
Depreciation	4,777	3,745
Gain on disposal of property, plant and equipment	(880)	(570)
Decrease/(Increase) in inventories	(4,840)	(3,606)
Decrease/(Increase) in trade receivables	(2,640)	(1,208)
(Decrease)/Increase in trade payables	(2,420)	(1,320)
Cash generated by operations	7,197	8,101
Tax paid	(944)	(885)
Interest paid	(280)	(105)
Net cash from operating activities	5,973	7,111

Ratios	20X8	20X7
Current ratio	3.6:1	2.5:1
Quick (acid test) ratio	1.7:1	1.3:1
Gearing	7.2%	4.1%

Prepare a report for the Directors of Knole Ltd that includes:

(a) Comments upon the change in net cash from operating activities between 20X7 and 20X8

(b) A comment on the relative liquidity and financial position of the company for the two years based on the ratios calculated and what this tells you about the company.

Answer bank

Answer bank

Answers to drafting financial statements

Task 1.1

(a) **Paparazzi Ltd**

Statement of comprehensive income for the year ended 30 June 20X2

Continuing operations	£'000
Revenue	14,700
Cost of sales (W)	(10,760)
Gross profit	3,940
Distribution costs	(1,200)
Administrative expenses	(2,120)
Profit/(loss) from operations	620
Finance costs	(84)
Profit/(loss) before tax	536
Tax	(130)
Profit/(loss) for the period from continuing operations	406

Workings

Cost of sales	£'000
Opening inventories	690
Purchases	10,780
Closing inventories	(710)
	10,760

(b) **Paparazzi Ltd**

Statement of financial position as at 30 June 20X2

	£'000
Assets	
Non-current assets:	
Property, plant and equipment (W)	3,272
Current assets:	
Inventories	710
Trade and other receivables (W)	2,448
Cash and cash equivalents	567
	3,725
Total assets	6,997
Equity and liabilities	
Equity:	
Share capital	2,500
Share premium	300
Retained earnings (W)	1,417
Total equity	4,217
Non-current liabilities:	
Bank loan	1,200
Current liabilities:	
Trade and other payables (W)	1,450
Tax liabilities	130
	1,580
Total liabilities	2,780
Total equity and liabilities	6,997

Workings

Property, plant and equipment	£'000
Land and buildings – Cost	2,100
Plant and equipment – Cost	1,050
Motor vehicles: – Cost	1,000
Accumulated depreciation – land and buildings	(280)
Accumulated depreciation – plant and equipment	(194)
Accumulated depreciation – motor vehicles	(404)
	3,272

Trade and other receivables	£'000
Trade and other receivables	2,500
Allowance for doubtful debts	(92)
Prepayments	40
	2,448

Retained earnings	£'000
Retained earnings at 1 July 20X1	1,131
Total profit for the year	406
Dividends paid	(120)
	1,417

Trade and other payables	£'000
Trade payables	1,400
Accruals	50
	1,450

Task 1.2

(a) **Bathlea Limited**

Statement of comprehensive income for the year ended 30 September 20X8

	£'000
Continuing operations	
Revenue	3,509
Cost of sales (W)	(1,641)
Gross profit	1,868
Distribution costs	(857)
Administrative expenses (W)	(902)
Profit/(loss) from operations	109
Finance cost (11 + 1)	(12)
Profit/(loss) before tax	97
Tax	(11)
Profit/(loss) for the period from continuing operations	86

Workings

Cost of sales	£'000
Opening inventories	200
Purchases	1,691
Closing inventories	(250)
	1,641

Administrative expenses	£'000
Administrative expenses	892
Bad debts	10
	902

(b) **Bathlea Limited**

Statement of financial position as at 30 September 20X8

	£'000
Assets	
Non-current assets	
Property, plant and equipment (W)	500
Current assets	
Inventories	250
Trade and other receivables (W)	365
	615
Total assets	1,115
Equity and liabilities	
Equity	
Share capital	500
Retained earnings (W)	141
Total equity	641
Non-current liabilities	
Long-term loan	100
Current liabilities	
Trade and other payables (W)	360
Tax liabilities	11
Bank overdraft	3
	374
Total liabilities	474
Total equity and liabilities	1,115

Workings

Property, plant and equipment	£'000
Land and buildings – Cost	300
Fixtures and fittings – Cost	220
Motor vehicles – Cost	70
Office equipment – Cost	80
Land and buildings – Accumulated depreciation	(65)
Fixtures and fittings – Accumulated depreciation	(43)
Motor vehicles – Accumulated depreciation	(27)
Office equipment – Accumulated depreciation	(35)
	500

Trade and other receivables	£'000
Trade and other receivables	370
Allowance for irrecoverable debts	(5)
Bad debt	(10)
Prepayments	10
	365

Retained earnings	£'000
Retained earnings at 1 October 20X7	70
Total profit for the year	86
Dividends paid	(15)
	141

Trade and other payables	£'000
Trade and other payables	350
Accruals: trial balance	9
Additional interest accrual	1
	360

Task 1.3

(a) **Howardsend Ltd**

Statement of comprehensive income for the year ended 30 September 20X6

	£'000
Continuing operations	
Revenue	53,821
Cost of sales (W)	(25,834)
Gross profit	27,987
Distribution costs (W)	(12,273)
Administrative expenses (W)	(9,255)
Profit/(loss) from operations	6,459
Finance costs (7% × 10,000)	(700)
Profit/(loss) before tax	5,759
Tax	(1,382)
Profit/(loss) for the period from continuing operations	4,377
Other comprehensive income	
Gain on revaluation (11,600 – 9,600)	2,000
Total comprehensive income for the year	6,377

Workings

Cost of sales	£'000
Opening inventories	7,158
Purchases (24,407 + 2,403)	26,810
Closing inventories	(8,134)
	25,834

Distribution costs	£'000
Distribution costs	12,216
Accruals	57
	12,273

Answer bank

Administrative expenses	£'000
Administrative expenses	9,176
Allowance for doubtful debts (132 – 53)	79
	9,255

(b) **Howardsend Ltd**

Statement of financial position as at 30 September 20X6

	£'000
Assets	
Non-current assets	
Property, plant and equipment (W)	44,626
Current assets	
Inventories	8,134
Trade and other receivables (W)	6,468
Cash and cash equivalents	579
	15,181
Total assets	59,807
Equity and liabilities	
Equity	
Share capital	8,000
Share premium	1,000
Revaluation reserve	2,000
Retained earnings (W)	31,824
Total equity	42,824
Non-current liabilities	
Long-term loan	10,000
Current liabilities	
Trade and other payables (W)	5,601
Tax liabilities	1,382
	6,983
Total liabilities	16,983
Total equity and liabilities	59,807

Workings

Property, plant and equipment	£'000
Property, plant and equipment – Cost	57,149
Property, plant and equipment – Accumulated depreciation	(14,523)
Revaluation	2,000
	44,626

Trade and other receivables	£'000
Trade receivables	6,600
Allowance for doubtful debts (2% × 6,600)	(132)
	6,468

Retained earnings	£'000
Retained earnings at 1 October 20X5	28,887
Total profit for the year	4,377
Dividends paid	(1,440)
	31,824

Trade and other payables	£'000
Trade payables (2,577 + 2,403)	4,980
Accruals: trial balance	214
Additional distribution costs accrual	57
Additional interest accrual (7% × 10,000 × 6/12)	350
	5,601

Task 1.4

(a) **Benard Ltd**

Statement of comprehensive income for the year ended 31 October 20X7

	£'000
Continuing operations	
Revenue (50,197 + 3,564)	53,761
Cost of sales (W)	(33,462)
Gross profit	20,299
Distribution costs	(6,654)
Administrative expenses (W)	(4,120)
Profit/(loss) from operations	9,525
Finance costs (560 + 560)	(1,120)
Profit/(loss) before tax	8,405
Tax	(1,254)
Profit/(loss) for the period from continuing operations	7,151

Workings

Cost of sales	£'000
Opening inventories	8,456
Purchases	34,792
Closing inventories	(9,786)
	33,462

Administrative expenses	£'000
Administrative expenses	4,152
Prepayments (48 × 8/12)	(32)
	4,120

(b) **Benard Ltd**
Statement of financial position as at 31 October 20X7

	£'000
Assets	
Non-current assets	
Property, plant and equipment (58,463 – 27,974)	30,489
Current assets	
Inventories	9,786
Trade and other receivables (W)	10,286
Cash and cash equivalents	1,184
	21,256
Total assets	51,745
Equity and liabilities	
Equity	
Share capital	12,000
Retained earnings (W)	18,196
Total equity	30,196
Non-current liabilities	
Bank loan	16,000
Current liabilities	
Trade and other payables (W)	4,295
Tax payable	1,254
	5,549
Total liabilities	21,549
Total equity and liabilities	51,745

Workings

Trade and other receivables	£'000
Trade and other receivables	6,690
Credit sales for October 20X7	3,564
Administrative expenses prepaid	32
	10,286

BPP
LEARNING MEDIA

155

Retained earnings	£'000
Retained earnings at 1 November 20X6	12,345
Total profit for the year	7,151
Dividends paid	(1,300)
	18,196

Trade and other payables	£'000
Trade and other payables	3,348
Accruals: trial balance	387
Additional interest accrual	560
	4,295

Task 1.5

(a) **Laxdale Ltd**

Statement of comprehensive income for the year ended 31 October 20X8

	£'000
Continuing operations	
Revenue	58,411
Cost of sales (W)	(43,342)
Gross profit	15,069
Distribution costs (W)	(6,026)
Administrative expenses (W)	(5,073)
Profit/(loss) from operations	3,970
Finance costs (8% × 15,000)	(1,200)
Profit/(loss) before tax	2,770
Tax	(970)
Profit/(loss) for the period from continuing operations	1,800

Workings

Cost of sales	£'000
Opening inventories	9,032
Purchases	41,620
Depreciation (40% × 1,420)	568
Closing inventories	(7,878)
	43,342

Distribution costs	£'000
Distribution costs	5,443
Depreciation (40% × 1,420)	568
Accruals (45 × 1/3)	15
	6,026

Administrative expenses	£'000
Administrative expenses	4,789
Depreciation (20% × 1,420)	284
	5,073

Depreciation

Buildings (2% × 35,152 − 15,152)	400
Plant and equipment (20% × 12,500 − 7,400)	1,020
	1,420

(b) **Laxdale Ltd**

Statement of financial position as at 31 October 20X8

Assets	£'000
Non-current assets	
Property, plant and equipment (W)	31,832
Current assets	
Inventories	7,878
Trade and other receivables	5,436
Cash and cash equivalents	9,774
	23,088
Total assets	54,920
Equity	
Share capital	25,000
Retained earnings (W)	10,101
Total equity	35,101
Non-current liabilities	
Bank loan	15,000
Current liabilities	
Trade and other payables (W)	3,849
Tax liabilities	970
	4,819
Total liabilities	19,819
Total equity and liabilities	54,920

Workings

Property, plant and equipment	£'000
Land and buildings – Cost	35,152
Plant and equipment – Cost	12,500
Accumulated depreciation – land and buildings (7,000 + 400)	(7,400)
Accumulated depreciation – plant and equipment (7,400 + 1,020)	(8,420)
	31,832

Retained earnings	£'000
Retained earnings at 1 November 20X7	9,801
Total profit for the year	1,800
Dividends paid	(1,500)
	10,101

Trade and other payables	£'000
Trade and other payables	2,798
Accruals: trial balance	436
Additional distribution costs accrual	15
Additional interest accrual	600
	3,849

Task 1.6

(a) **Cappielow Ltd**

Statement of comprehensive income for the year ended 31 March 20X0

	£'000
Continuing operations	
Revenue	35,547
Cost of sales (W)	(28,354)
Gross profit	7,193
Distribution costs (W)	(1,933)
Administrative expenses (W)	(2,207)
Profit/(loss) from operations	3,053
Finance costs	(720)
Profit/(loss) before tax	2,333
Tax	(874)
Profit/(loss) for the period from continuing operations	1,459
Other comprehensive income for the year	
Gain on revaluation of land (7,500 – 5,150)	2,350
Total comprehensive income for the year	3,809

Workings

Cost of sales	£'000
Opening inventories	3,790
Purchases	27,481
Closing inventories	(4,067)
Impairment loss (12,750 – 3,100 – 8,500)	1,150
	28,354

Distribution costs	£'000
Distribution costs	1,857
Accruals (114 × 2/3)	76
	1,933

Administrative expenses	£'000
Administrative expenses	2,235
Prepayment (164 × ¾)	(123)
Bad debt	95
	2,207

(b) **Cappielow Ltd**

Statement of financial position as at 31 March 20X0

	£'000
Assets	
Non-current assets:	
Property, plant and equipment (W)	18,104
Current assets:	
Inventories	4,067
Trade and other receivables (W)	2,161
Cash and cash equivalents	7,578
	13,806
Total assets	31,910

	£'000
Equity and liabilities:	
Equity	
Share capital	10,000
Revaluation reserve (W)	4,350
Retained earnings (W)	3,134
Total equity	17,484
Non-current liabilities:	
Bank loan	12,000
Current liabilities:	
Trade and other payables (W)	1,552
Tax payable	874
	2,426
Total liabilities	14,426
Total equity and liabilities	31,910

Workings

Property, plant and equipment	£'000
Property, plant and equipment: Cost/value (36,780 + 2,350)	39,130
Property, plant and equipment: Accumulated depreciation	(19,876)
Impairment loss	(1,150)
	18,104

Trade and other receivables	£'000
Trade and other receivables	2,133
Administrative expenses prepaid	123
Bad debt	(95)
	2,161

Revaluation reserve	£'000
Revaluation reserve at 1 April 20W9	2,000
Other comprehensive income for the year	2,350
	4,350

Retained earnings	£'000
Retained earnings at 1 April 20W9	2,595
Total profit for the year	1,459
Dividends paid	(920)
	3,134

Trade and other payables	£'000
Trade and other payables	1,347
Accruals: trial balance	129
Distribution costs accrued	76
	1,552

Answers to the statement of cash flows and the statement of changes in equity

Task 2.1

(a) **Reconciliation of profit from operations to net cash from operating activities**

	£
Profit from operations	100,000
Depreciation	20,000
Increase in inventories (30,000 – 25,000)	(5,000)
Decrease in trade receivables (40,000 – 42,000)	2,000
Decrease in trade payables (28,000 – 32,000)	(4,000)
Cash generated from operations	113,000
Interest paid	(10,000)
Tax paid	(25,000)
Net cash from operating activities	78,000

(b) **Net cash from operating activities using the direct method**

	£
Operating activities	
Cash receipts from customers (W)	562,000
Cash paid to suppliers and employees (W)	(449,000)
Cash generated from operations	113,000
Interest paid	(10,000)
Tax paid	(25,000)
Net cash from operating activities	78,000

Workings

Cash receipts from customers	£
Opening trade receivables	42,000
Revenue	560,000
Closing trade receivables	(40,000)
	562,000

Cash paid to suppliers and employees	£
Opening trade payables	32,000
Total purchases (W)	445,000
Closing trade payables	(28,000)
	449,000

Total purchases	£
Cost of sales	300,000
Opening inventories	(25,000)
Closing inventories	30,000
Other expenses	160,000
Depreciation	(20,000)
	445,000

Task 2.2

(a)

£	37,400

	£
Opening balance	13,000
Profit or loss	32,400
Closing balance	(8,000)
	37,400

(b)

£	92,000

	£
Opening balance	94,000
Profit or loss	98,000
Closing balance	(100,000)
	92,000

Task 2.3

(a)

£	230,000

	£'000
Opening balance	1,250
Disposals	(140)
Closing balance	(1,340)
Proceeds from sale	(230)

(b)

£	75,000

	£'000
Net carrying amount	98
Loss on disposal	(23)
	75

(c)

£	122,000

	£'000
Opening balance	480
Disposals (140 – 98)	(42)
Closing balance	(560)
	(122)

Task 2.4

Statement of changes in equity for the year ended 30 April 20X2

	Share capital £	Share premium £	Revaluation reserve £	Retained earnings £	Total equity £
Balance at 1 May 20X1	500,000	100,000	30,000	180,000	810,000
Changes in equity for 20X2					
Total comprehensive income	0	0	70,000	110,000	180,000
Dividends	0	0	0	(35,000)	(35,000)
Issue of share capital (200,000 × 1.4)	200,000	80,000	0	0	280,000
Balance at 30 April 20X2	700,000	180,000	100,000	255,000	1,235,000

Task 2.5

(a) **Evans**

Reconciliation of profit from operations to net cash from operating activities for the year ended 31 October 20X1

	£'000
Profit from operations	441
Adjustments for:	
Depreciation	190
Gain on disposal of property, plant and equipment	(10)
Adjustment in respect of inventories (505 – 486)	19
Adjustment in respect of trade receivables (945 – 657)	(288)
Adjustment in respect of trade payables (560 – 546)	14
Cash generated by operations	366
Interest paid	(23)
Tax paid	(106)
Net cash from operating activities	237

(b) **Evans Ltd**

Statement of cash flows for the year ended 31 October 20X1

	£'000	£'000
Net cash from operating activities		237
Investing activities		
Purchase of property, plant and equipment (W)	(425)	
Proceeds on disposal of property, plant and equipment (W)	75	
Net cash used in investing activities		(350)
Financing activities		
Proceeds of share issue (1,200 – 1,000) + (315 – 270)	245	
Repayment of bank loan (150 – 50)	(100)	
Dividends paid	(40)	
Net cash from financing activities		105
Net increase/(decrease) in cash and cash equivalents		(8)
Cash and cash equivalents at the beginning of the year		10
Cash and cash equivalents at the end of the year		2

Workings

Proceeds on disposal of property, plant and equipment (PPE)	£'000
Carrying amount of PPE sold	65
Gain on disposal	10
	75

Purchases of property, plant and equipment (PPE)	£'000
PPE at start of year	1,010
Depreciation charge	(190)
Carrying amount of PPE sold	(65)
PPE at end of year	(1,180)
Total PPE additions	(425)

(c) **Evans Ltd**

Statement of changes in equity for the year ended 31 October 20X1

	Share Capital	Other Reserves	Retained Earnings	Total Equity
	£'000	£'000	£'000	£'000
Balance at 1 November 20X0	1,000	270	110	1,380
Changes in equity for 20X1				
Profit for the year	0	0	293	293
Dividends	0	0	(40)	(40)
Issue of share capital	200	45	–	245
Balance at 31 October 20X1	1,200	315	363	1,878

Task 2.6

(a) **Lochnagar Ltd**

Reconciliation of profit from operations to net cash from operating activities for the year ended 31 October 20X7

	£'000
Profit from operations	3,360
Adjustments for:	
Depreciation	3,545
Gain on disposal of property, plant and equipment	(224)
Adjustment in respect of inventories (3,696 – 2,464)	(1,232)
Adjustment in respect of trade receivables (3,360 – 2,464)	(896)
Adjustment in respect of trade payables (1,232 – 1,848)	(616)
Cash generated by operations	3,937
Interest paid	(91)
Tax paid	(944)
Net cash from operating activities	2,902

(b) **Lochnagar Ltd**

Statement of cash flows for the year ended 31 October 20X7

	£'000	£'000
Net cash from operating activities		2,902
Investing activities		
Purchases of property, plant and equipment (W)	(5,237)	
Proceeds on disposal of property, plant and equipment (W)	845	
Net cash used in investing activities		(4,392)
Financing activities		
Proceeds of share issue	500	
New bank loans	500	
Net cash from financing activities		1,000
Net increase/(decrease) in cash and cash equivalents		(490)
Cash and cash equivalents at the beginning of the year		129
Cash and cash equivalents at the end of the year		(361)

Workings

Proceeds on disposal of property, plant and equipment (PPE)	£'000
Carrying amount of PPE sold	621
Gain on disposal	224
	845

Purchases of property, plant and equipment (PPE)	£'000
PPE at start of year	24,100
Depreciation charge	(3,545)
Carrying amount of PPE sold	(621)
PPE at end of year	(25,171)
Total PPE additions	(5,237)

Task 2.7

(a) **Thehoose Ltd**

Reconciliation of profit from operations to net cash from operating activities for the year ended 31 March 20X9

	£'000
Profit from operations	5,652
Adjustments for:	
Depreciation	3,469
Gain on disposal of property, plant and equipment	(376)
Adjustment in respect of inventories (5,426 – 4,069)	(1,357)
Adjustment in respect of trade receivables (4,145 – 3,768)	377
Adjustment in respect of trade payables (4,069 – 2,261)	(1,808)
Cash generated by operations	5,957
Interest paid	(280)
Tax paid	(887)
Net cash from operating activities	4,790

(b) **Thehoose Ltd**

Statement of cash flows for the year ended 31 March 20X9

	£'000	£'000
Net cash from operating activities		4,790
Investing activities		
Purchases of property, plant and equipment (W)	(10,116)	
Proceeds on disposal of property, plant and equipment (W)	793	
Net cash used in investing activities		(9,323)
Financing activities		
Proceeds of share issue	2,500	
New bank loans	2,500	
Net cash from financing activities		5,000
Net increase/(decrease) in cash and cash equivalents		467
Cash and cash equivalents at the beginning of the year		(132)
Cash and cash equivalents at the end of the year		335

Workings

Proceeds on disposal of property, plant and equipment (PPE)	£'000
Carrying amount of PPE sold	417
Gain on disposal	376
	793

Purchases of property, plant and equipment (PPE)	£'000
PPE at start of year	21,340
Depreciation charge	(3,469)
Carrying amount of PPE sold	(417)
PPE at end of year	(27,570)
Total PPE additions	10,116

Task 2.8

(a) **Reconciliation of profit from operations to net cash from operating activities for the year ended 31 October 20X9**

	£'000
Profit from operations	6,825
Adjustments for:	
Depreciation	4,398
Gain on disposal of property, plant and equipment	(455)
Adjustment in respect of inventories (6,552 – 4,914)	(1,638)
Adjustment in respect of trade receivables (4,641 – 4,550)	91
Adjustment in respect of trade payables (4,368 – 3,822)	(546)
Cash generated by operations	8,675
Tax paid	(658)
Interest paid	(595)
Net cash from operating activities	7,422

(b) **Adlington Ltd**

Statement of cash flows for the year ended 31 October 20X9

	£'000	£'000
Net cash from operating activities		7,422
Investing activities		
Purchases of property, plant and equipment (W)	(14,483)	
Proceeds on disposal of property, plant and equipment (W)	797	
Net cash used in investing activities		(13,686)
Financing activities		
Proceeds of share issue	3,000	
New bank loans	5,500	
Dividends paid	(500)	
Net cash from financing activities		8,000
Net increase/(decrease) in cash and cash equivalents		1,736
Cash and cash equivalents at the beginning of the year		(1,286)
Cash and cash equivalents at the end of the year		450

Workings

Proceeds on disposal of property, plant and equipment (PPE)	£'000
Carrying amount of PPE sold	342
Gain on disposal	455
	797

Purchases of property, plant and equipment (PPE)	£'000
PPE at start of year	22,246
Depreciation charge	(4,398)
Carrying amount of PPE sold	(342)
PPE at end of year	(31,989)
Total PPE additions	14,483

(c) **Adlington Ltd**

Statement of changes in equity for the year ended 31 October 20X9

	Share Capital	Other Reserves	Retained Earnings	Total Equity
	£'000	£'000	£'000	£'000
Balance at 1 November 20X8	8,000	3,000	11,489	22,489
Changes in equity for 20X9				
Profit for the year	0	0	4,473	4,473
Dividends	0	0	(500)	(500)
Issue of share capital	2,000	1,000	0	3,000
Balance at 31 October 20X9	10,000	4,000	15,462	29,462

Task 2.9

(a) **Forthbank Ltd:**

Reconciliation of profit from operations to net cash from operating activities

	£'000
Profit from operations	5,860
Adjustments for:	
Depreciation	3,366
Dividends received	(650)
Loss on disposal of property, plant and equipment	110
Adjustment in respect of inventories (5,832 – 4,860)	(972)
Adjustment in respect of trade receivables (5,400 – 4,320)	(1,080)
Adjustment in respect of trade payables (3,240 – 3,564)	(324)
Cash generated by operations	6,310
Tax paid	(908)
Interest paid	(301)
Net cash from operating activities	5,101

(b) **Forthbank Ltd**

Statement of cash flows for the year ended 31 March 20X1

	£'000	£'000
Net cash from operating activities		5,101
Investing activities		
Purchases of property, plant and equipment (W)	(11,223)	
Proceeds on disposal of property, plant and equipment (W)	227	
Dividends received	650	
Net cash used in investing activities		(10,346)
Financing activities		
Proceeds of share issue (11,000 – 8,000)	3,000	
New bank loans (4,300 – 800)	3,500	
Dividends paid	(460)	
Net cash from financing activities		6,040
Net increase/(decrease) in cash and cash equivalents		795
Cash and cash equivalents at the beginning of the year		(208)
Cash and cash equivalents at the end of the year		587

Workings

Proceeds on disposal of property, plant and equipment (PPE)	£'000
Carrying amount of PPE sold	337
Loss on disposal	(110)
	227

Purchases of property, plant and equipment (PPE)	£'000
PPE at start of year	19,140
Depreciation charge	(3,366)
Carrying amount of PPE sold	(337)
PPE at end of year	(26,660)
Total PPE additions	(11,223)

(c)

Forthbank Ltd

Statement of changes in equity for the year ended 31 March 20X1

	Share Capital £'000	Other Reserves £'000	Retained Earnings £'000	Total Equity £'000
Balance at 1 April 20X0	6,000	2,000	14,840	22,840
Changes in equity for 20X1				
Profit for the year	0	0	4,446	4,446
Dividends	0	0	(460)	(460)
Issue of share capital	2,000	1,000	0	3,000
Balance at 31 March 20X1	8,000	3,000	18,826	29,826

Answers to accounting standards and The Conceptual Framework – written tasks

Note: based on the information available at the time this book was written, we anticipate that the tasks in this section would be human marked in the real assessment.

Task 3.1

(a) Definitions:

- Assets are resources controlled by the entity as a result of past events and from which future economic benefits are expected to flow to the entity.

- Liabilities are present obligations of the entity arising from past events, the settlement of which is expected to result in an outflow of resources embodying economic benefits from the entity.

- Equity is the owners' residual interest in the assets of the entity after deducting all its liabilities.

(b) Transaction 1 would increase inventories, an asset, by £120 and also increase trade payables, a liability, by £120.

Transaction 2 would decrease the asset inventories by £120, but increase the asset cash by £180. Thus there would be a net increase in assets of £60. In the other half of the statement of financial position, equity would increase by £60, being the profit made on the sale.

(c) The accounting equation after the two transactions would be:

ASSETS LESS LIABILITIES = EQUITY

(i) £1,320 – £920   = £400

(ii) £1,380 – £920   = £460

(d) **Income statement**

	£
Sales	180
Cost of sales	(120)
Gross profit	60

Task 3.2

(a) The IASB *Conceptual Framework* states that **existing and potential investors, lenders and other creditors** are the primary users of general purpose financial reports (financial statements).

These are the people who **provide capital** (finance) to an entity, either in the form of share capital (equity) as owners, or in the form of loans.

(b) The statement of financial position shows the current assets and current liabilities of the company for the current year and the preceding year and the notes to the financial statements provide further information (for example, total receivables are analysed into trade receivables, other receivables and prepayments). The user can observe the movements in working capital and can also calculate ratios that measure working capital management. He or she can also interpret this information in the context of the financial statements as a whole. For example, the statement of comprehensive income (with comparative figures) shows whether revenue and expenses are increasing or decreasing, which may help to explain any unusual movements in working capital. The statement of cash flows will provide additional information on liquidity and should help him or her to assess the extent to which the directors' management of working capital is affecting the company's cash flows.

(c) The IASB's *Conceptual Framework* defines equity as the residual amount found by deducting all of the entity's liabilities from all of the entity's assets. It consists of the capital that the owners have invested, plus accumulated profits, less dividends (or other amounts) paid to the owners. This can be expressed as:

Assets less liabilities = equity

Equity = contributions from owners plus income less expenses less distributions to owners

Income (profits or gains) is increases in equity (net assets) other than contributions from owners. Expenses are decreases in equity (net assets) other than distributions to owners.

Task 3.3

(a) The IASB's *Conceptual Framework* defines the elements of financial statements as follows.

(i) Assets are resources controlled by an entity as a result of past events and from which future economic benefits are expected to flow to the entity.

(ii) Liabilities are present obligations of an entity arising from past events, the settlement of which is expected to result in an outflow of resources embodying economic benefits from the entity.

(iii) Equity is the owners' residual interest in the assets of an entity after deducting all its liabilities.

(b) Inventories are an asset because:

- They are the result of a past event (the purchase of goods); and

- The purchase of inventories gives rise to future economic benefits because it results in a future inflow of cash when the inventories are sold.

Task 3.4

(a) The IASB's *Conceptual Framework for Financial Reporting* explains that the objective of general purpose financial reporting (or published financial statements) is to provide financial information about the reporting entity that is useful to existing and potential investors, lenders and other creditors in making decisions about providing resources to the entity.

(b) The financial statements of the two companies are being used by a potential investor in order to make a decision: which one of the companies should he invest in (provide resources to)? He is concerned with the return he can expect from each of the potential investments. He needs to assess the amount, timing and uncertainty of future net cash inflows to the two companies. Therefore he needs information about the economic resources of the companies and the claims against them (the financial position of each company), and changes in these economic resources and claims (which mainly result from each company's financial performance).

Task 3.5

(a) (i) Information is relevant if it is capable of making a difference in the decisions made by users.

(ii) If financial information faithfully represents the economic phenomena that it purports to represent, it is

- complete;
- neutral; and
- free from error.

(b) The four enhancing qualitative characteristics of useful financial information are:

- comparability
- verifiability
- timeliness
- understandability

Task 3.6

(a) Under the going concern basis, a company prepares its financial statements on the assumption that it is a going concern, that is, it will continue in operation for the foreseeable future. This means that assets are measured at amounts that are relevant to the way in which the company will use them in its ongoing operations, rather than at their 'break up' values (the amounts for which they could be sold immediately as individual items).

Under the accruals basis of accounting, the effects of transactions and other events are recognised when they occur rather than when cash is received or paid. They are recorded in the accounting records and reported in the financial statements in the period to which they relate.

(b) Where there is an accounting standard that specifically applies to a transaction, event or other condition, that standard determines the accounting policy.

In the absence of an accounting standard that specifically applies to a transaction, other event or condition, management should use its judgement in developing and applying an accounting policy that results in information that is:

- relevant to the decision making needs of the user; and
- reliable.

Task 3.7

(a) The freehold building has been treated as an investment property and appears to meet the definition in IAS 40 Investment property. This explains why the property is not measured at historic cost and has not been depreciated. IAS 40 allows investment properties to be carried in the statement of financial position at fair value. If the 'fair value model' is adopted, changes in fair value (gains and losses) are recognised in profit or loss (the statement of comprehensive income), but no depreciation is charged.

(b) The treatment of the fire and the subsequent losses is correct. These events arose after the year-end and concern conditions that did not exist at that date. IAS 10 Events after the reporting period would only require adjustments to the financial statements if the fire had occurred during the year (the fire would then be an adjusting event). Where a non-adjusting event after the reporting period is material, non-disclosure could influence decisions taken by users on the basis of the financial statements and therefore IAS 10 requires disclosure of the nature of the event and an estimate of its financial effect.

(c) Deferred tax is not an actual tax. It can be thought of as a way of applying the accruals concept. Recognising a liability for deferred tax attempts to account for the tax charge in the same period as the transactions and events that will give rise to it.

IAS 12 Income taxes requires the company to recognise a deferred tax liability for all taxable temporary differences. A temporary difference is the difference between the carrying amount of an asset or liability in the statement of financial position and its tax base (the amount at which it is valued for tax purposes). For example, suppose that an item of property is revalued. The property is carried in the statement of financial position at fair value and a gain is recognised in the financial statements. Tax is not charged on the gain until the property is sold and the gain is realised. Therefore there is a temporary difference and deferred tax is provided on this temporary difference.

Task 3.8

(a) IFRS 5 defines a discontinued operation as a component of an entity that has either been disposed of or is held for sale and represents a separate major line of business or geographical area of operations.

A component of an entity has operations and cash flows that can be clearly distinguished, operationally and for financial reporting purposes, from the rest of the entity.

If a discontinued operation has not actually been disposed of during the period, it must be available for immediate sale, the sale must be highly probable and management must be committed to the sale (for example, by taking active steps to find a buyer). The sale must be expected to take place within the next twelve months.

(b) The distinction between continuing operations and discontinued operations provides additional useful information for users and enables the user of accounts to make a better judgement of the company's performance in the current period. Because the results of discontinued operations are presented separately from continuing operations, users may be able to make rough predictions about the company's results in future. For example, if discontinued operations have made losses while the rest of the business is profitable, this suggests that the company's overall results will improve in the following period.

Task 3.9

(a) **Inventories**

(i) Financial statements are prepared on an accruals basis. This means that costs are matched with the revenues to which they relate. In addition, IAS 2 *Inventories* states that the carrying amount of inventories is recognised as an expense in the period in which the related revenue is recognised. Closing inventories are therefore recognised as an asset in the statement of financial position and carried forward to the next period, when they will be sold and the revenue will be recognised.

(ii) Closing inventories are valued at the lower of cost and net realisable value.

(b) **Impairment**

(i) IAS 36 *Impairment of assets* requires an impairment review to be carried out if there is any indication that an asset has become impaired. An asset is impaired if its carrying amount is greater than its recoverable amount. IAS 36 also states that certain assets should be reviewed for impairment annually, even if there is no indication of impairment. These assets are goodwill acquired in a business combination and intangible assets with indefinite lives.

(ii) When an asset is reviewed for impairment, its carrying amount is compared with its recoverable amount. Recoverable amount is the higher of fair value less costs to sell and value in use.

Task 3.10

The treatment of the damages claim is governed by IAS 37 *Provisions, contingent liabilities and contingent assets*. According to IAS 37 a provision should be recognised when:

(a) An entity has a present obligation (legal or constructive) as a result of a past event.

(b) It is probable that a transfer of economic benefits will be required to settle the obligation.

(c) A reliable estimate can be made of the obligation.

For a provision to be recognised, the circumstances must meet each of these three criteria. In the case of the damages claim there is a present obligation (a) to pay damages. The lawyer has stated that this transfer of economic benefits is probable (b). In addition the amount of the claim has been estimated reliably (c) at £250,000, so a provision for this amount should be recognised in the financial statements.

Task 3.11

(a) IAS 37 *Provisions, contingent liabilities and contingent assets* states that a provision should be recognised when:

- an entity has a present obligation as a result of a past event. The obligation can be either legal or constructive; and

- it is probable that an outflow of resources embodying economic benefits will be required to settle the obligation; and

- a reliable estimate can be made of the amount of the obligation.

(b) Houghton Ltd has a constructive obligation to make the refunds because it has publicised its policy, leading its customers to expect that it will refund purchases. (The past obligating event is the sale of the product).

It is also probable that the company will actually have to make some refunds (an outflow of resources embodying economic benefits) in the next reporting period (refunds have already been claimed).

Although the precise amount of future claims is unknown it should be possible to make a reasonable estimate based on past experience. (IAS 37 explains that it is almost always possible to make a reliable estimate.)

Therefore Houghton Ltd should recognise a provision, based on its best estimate of the cost of refunds relating to goods sold in the last three months of the year.

(c) IAS 37 requires disclosure of the following information for each class of provision:

- The carrying amount at the beginning and end of the period
- Additional provisions made in the period
- Amounts used during the period
- Unused amounts reversed during the period

There should also be a narrative note giving:

- A brief description of the nature of the obligation and expected timing of any resulting transfers of economic benefit

- An indication of the uncertainties about the amount or timing of those transfers of economic benefit

Task 3.12

(a) IAS 27 *Consolidated and separate financial statements* explains that a parent controls a subsidiary. Control is the power to govern the financial and operating policies of an entity so as to obtain benefits from its activities.

Control is presumed to exist when the parent owns more than half the voting power of an entity. Control also exists when the parent owns half or less of the voting power of an entity when there is:

- Power over more than half of the voting rights by virtue of an agreement with other investors

- Power to govern the financial and operating policies of the entity under a statute or an agreement

- Power to appoint or remove the majority of the members of the board of directors or

- Power to cast the majority of votes at meetings of the board of directors.

(b) IFRS 3 *Business combinations* states that goodwill acquired in a business combination should be carried in the statement of financial position at cost less any impairment losses. The cost of goodwill is the difference between the cost of the investment and the fair value of the identifiable assets and liabilities acquired. Goodwill is not amortised, but must be reviewed for impairment annually. Therefore the directors of Lavendar cannot write off the goodwill on acquisition immediately.

Answers to accounting standards and regulation – objective test questions

Task 4.1

International Financial Reporting Standards Foundation	✓
International Accounting Standards Board	
International Financial Reporting Standards Interpretations Committee	
International Financial Reporting Standards Advisory Council	

Task 4.2

True	
False	✓

The IASB develops and issues international financial reporting standards (IFRSs); the IFRS Foundation oversees the standard setting process.

Task 4.3

1 and 4	
3 and 5	
2 and 3	
2 and 4	✓

Task 4.4

True	✓
False	

This is a change in accounting estimate.

Task 4.5

Adjust opening retained earnings and comparative figures	✓
Adjust the financial statements for the current period	

IAS 8 *Accounting policies, changes in accounting estimates and errors* requires the financial statements to be corrected retrospectively (a prior period adjustment).

Task 4.6

True	
False	✓

A decrease in trade receivables means that less cash has been 'tied up' in working capital.

Task 4.7

1 only	
2 only	✓
Both 1 and 2	
Neither 1 nor 2	

Task 4.8

£888,000	
£897,000	
£955,000	✓
£1,005,000	

General overheads should not be included in the cost of an item of property, plant and equipment.

Task 4.9

£4,000	
£4,211	
£5,000	
£5,263	✓

£200,000 ÷ 38 = £5,263

Task 4.10

£9,143	
£11,429	
£12,800	✓
£18,286	

Carrying amount at 1 January 20X2	=	£80,000 – (2 × 8,000)
	=	£64,000
Remaining useful life at 1 January 20X2	=	7 – 2 years
	=	5 years
Depreciation charge y/e 31 December 20X2	=	$\dfrac{£64,000}{5}$
	=	£12,800

Task 4.11

£40,000	
£58,400	
£60,000	✓
£288,800	

	£
Carrying amount at 31 December 20X5	
£460,000 – (2 × £460,000/46 years)	440,000
Disposal proceeds	500,000
Profit on disposal	60,000

Task 4.12

True	✓
False	

IAS 23 *Borrowing costs* states that borrowing costs that are directly attributable to the acquisition, construction or production of a **qualifying asset** should be capitalised as part of the cost of that asset. Assets that are ready for their intended use or sale when they are acquired are not qualifying assets.

Other borrowing costs must be recognised as an expense in the period in which they are incurred.

Task 4.13

Loss of £250,000 in other comprehensive income	
Loss of £200,000 in profit or loss	
Loss of £250,000 in profit or loss	✓
Loss of £50,000 in profit or loss; loss of £200,000 in other comprehensive income	

Under the fair value model for investment property, all gains and losses on remeasurement are recognised in profit or loss. (This is different from the revaluation model in IAS 16.)

Task 4.14

Under non-current assets	
Under current assets	✓
Within inventories	
Within receivables	

Non-current assets held for sale are shown separately under the 'current assets' heading.

Task 4.15

True	
False	✓

IAS 38 *Intangible assets* prohibits the recognition of internally generated goodwill.

Task 4.16

True	
False	✓

According to IAS 36 *Impairment of assets*, an asset is impaired if its recoverable amount is lower than its carrying amount. An asset's recoverable amount is the higher of fair value less costs to sell or value in use. This asset has a recoverable amount of £130,000, so it is not impaired and should continue to be measured at its carrying amount of £125,000.

Task 4.17

£1,400	
£1,475	
£1,500	✓
£1,600	

- The items sold are assumed to be the 25 units purchased on 1 June and 5 units purchased on 15 June.

- Therefore the items in inventory are 10 units purchased on 15 June.

- Net realisable value is lower than cost, so the value of inventories is: 10 × 150 = £1,500

Task 4.18

Tax expense (profit or loss)	Tax payable (statement of financial position)	
£124,000	£124,000	
£124,000	£129,000	✓
£129,000	£129,000	
£134,000	£129,000	

	£
Expense for current year	129,000
Less: adjustment in respect of prior period	(5,000)
Tax expense in profit or loss	124,000
Tax payable (liability)	129,000

Task 4.19

£7,400	
£9,110	✓
£10,250	
£13,110	

Using the actuarial method, the liability at 31 December 20X1 is:

	£
Fair value	15,400
Less: deposit	(4,000)
	11,400
Interest (11,400 × 15%)	1,710
Payment 31 December 20X1	(4,000)
	9,110

Task 4.20

£6,120	
£9,120	✓
£9,600	
£25,000	

Finance charge of £9,120 (76,000 × 12%)

Task 4.21

Legal action 1	Legal action 2	
Disclose in a note to the financial statements	No disclosure	
Recognise a provision	No disclosure	
Recognise a provision	Disclose in a note to the financial statements	✓
Recognise a provision	Recognise the income	

Task 4.22

A	Destruction of a major non-current asset	
B	Discovery of error or fraud	✓
C	Issue of shares	
D	Purchases of a major non-current asset	

....

Task 4.23

True	✓
False	

Usk Ltd has not yet transferred the significant risks and rewards of ownership of the goods and cannot recognise revenue (IAS 18 *Revenue*).

....

Task 4.24

Expense of £57,000	✓
Expense of £93,000	
Income of £105,000	
Income of £180,000	

	£
Depreciation of plant (750,000 ÷ 10)	75,000
Amortisation of grant (180,000 ÷ 10)	(18,000)
	57,000

....

Task 4.25

48.6p	
53.7p	✓
68.0p	
107.4p	

Net profit attributable to ordinary shareholders = £680,000

Number of shares	=	$1,000,000 \times 4/12 + 1,400,000 \times 8/12$
	=	333,333 + 933,333
	=	1,266,666
	=	$\dfrac{680,000}{1,266,666}$
	=	53.7 pence

Task 4.26

True	
False	✓

Information about operating segments that do not meet any of the quantitative thresholds may be disclosed, if management believes that information about the segment would be useful to users of the financial statements.

Task 4.27

True	✓
False	

Hawes Ltd is an associate of Wensley plc.

Task 4.28

An associate	
A parent	
A simple investment	
A subsidiary	✓

Erewash Ltd **controls** Amber Ltd. Control is the power to govern the financial and operating policies of an entity so as to obtain benefits from its activities (IAS 27).

Answers to the consolidated statement of financial position

Task 5.1

Consolidated statement of financial position as at 31 December 20X1

	£'000
Assets	
Goodwill (W)	20
Property, plant and equipment (800 + 400)	1,200
Current assets (170 + 130)	300
	1,520
Equity and liabilities	
Share capital	800
Retained earnings (W)	450
	1,250
Non-controlling interest (W)	120
	1,370
Current liabilities (100 + 50)	150
	1,520

Workings

Goodwill	£'000
Price paid	350
Share capital – attributable to X plc (75% × 200)	(150)
Retained earnings – attributable to X plc (75% × 240)	(180)
	20

Retained earnings	£'000
X plc	420
Y Ltd – attributable to X plc (75% × (280 – 240))	30
	450

Non-controlling interest (NCI)	£'000
Share capital – attributable to NCI (25% × 200)	50
Retained earnings – attributable to NCI (25% × 280)	<u>70</u>
	<u>120</u>

Task 5.2

(a) **Goodwill**

£ | 594,000

	£'000	£'000
Price paid		3,510
Share capital – attributable to parent (60% × 2,000)	1,200	
Share premium – attributable to parent (60% × 1,000)	600	
Retained earnings – attributable to parent (60% × 1,350)	810	
Fair value adjustment – attributable to parent (60% × 400)	<u>240</u>	
		<u>(2,850)</u>
		660
Less: impairment		<u>(66)</u>
		<u>594</u>

Working

Group structure

F Ltd

$$\frac{1,200,000}{2,000,000} \times 100 = 60\% \longrightarrow$$

V Ltd

(b) **Non-controlling interest**

£	2,068,000

	£'000
Share capital – attributable to NCI (40% × 2,000)	800
Share premium –attributable to NCI (40% × 1,000)	400
Retained earnings – attributable to NCI (40% × 1,770)	708
Fair value adjustment – attributable to NCI (40% × 400)	160
	2,068

(c) **Consolidated retained earnings reserve**

£	5,796,000

	£'000	£'000
Fertwrangler Ltd		5,610
Voncarryon Ltd:		
At 31 March 20X3	1,770	
At acquisition	(1,350)	
	420	
Attributable to parent (60%)		252
Impairment of goodwill		(66)
		5,796

....

Task 5.3

(a)

£	1,800,000

Goodwill relating to the acquisition of Clive Ltd at 31 March 20X5

	£'000	£'000
Price paid		25,160
Share capital – attributable to parent (60% × 20,000)	12,000	
Share premium – attributable to parent (60% × 5,000)	3,000	
Retained earnings – attributable to parent (60% × 10,600)	6,360	

	£'000	£'000
Fair value adjustment – attributable to parent (60% × 3,000)	1,800	
		(23,160)
		2,000
Less: impairment		(200)
		1,800

(b)

£	5,200,000

Investment in associate

	£'000
Cost	5,000
Bell plc's share of post-acquisition profit (25% × 1,000)	250
Less: goodwill written off (W)	(50)
	5,200

Alternative calculation (proof)

	£'000
Bell plc's share of net assets at year end (25% × 19,000)	4,750
Add: goodwill (W)	450
	5,200

Working: Goodwill

	£'000
Cost of investment/price paid	5,000
Share capital – attributable to Bell plc (25% × 10,000)	(2,500)
Retained earnings – attributable to Bell plc (25% × 8,000)	(2,000)
	500
Less: impairment loss	(50)
	450

(c) IAS 28 *Investments in associates* defines an associate as an entity over which the investor has significant influence and that is not a subsidiary. Significant influence is the power to participate in the financial and operating policy decisions of the investee but is not control or joint control over those policies.

Task 5.4

Dumyat plc

Consolidated statement of financial position as at 31 October 20X7

	£'000
Assets	
Non-current assets:	
Goodwill (W)	2,711
Property, plant and equipment (65,388 + 31,887 + 3,000)	100,275
	102,986
Current assets:	
Inventories (28,273 + 5,566)	33,839
Trade and other receivables (11,508 + 5,154)	16,662
Cash and cash equivalents (2,146 + 68)	2,214
	52,715
Total assets	155,701
Equity and liabilities	
Equity attributable to owners of the parent	
Share capital	25,000
Share premium	12,000
Retained earnings (W)	59,401
	96,401
Non-controlling interest (W)	9,023
Total equity	105,424
Non-current liabilities:	
Long-term loans (25,000 + 4,000)	29,000
Current liabilities:	
Trade and other payables (13,554 + 1,475)	15,029
Tax payable (6,140 + 108)	6,248
	21,277
Total liabilities	50,277
Total equity and liabilities	155,701

Workings

Note: **Group structure**

Dumyat plc owns 75% of Devon Ltd (9,000,000/12,000,000).

Goodwill	£'000
Price paid	26,000
Share capital – attributable to Dumyat plc (75% × 12,000)	(9,000)
Share premium – attributable to Dumyat plc (75% × 4,000)	(3,000)
Retained earnings – attributable to Dumyat plc (75% × 12,052)	(9,039)
Revaluation reserve – attributable to Dumyat plc (75% × 3,000)	(2,250)
	2,711

Retained earnings	£'000
Dumyat plc	55,621
Devon Ltd – attributable to Dumyat plc (75% ×(17,092 – 12,052))	3,780
	59,401

Non-controlling interest (NCI)	£'000
Share capital – attributable to NCI (25% × 12,000)	3,000
Share premium – attributable to NCI (25% × 4,000)	1,000
Retained earnings – attributable to NCI (25% × 17,092)	4,273
Revaluation reserve – attributable to NCI (25% × 3,000)	750
	9,023

Task 5.5

Tolsta plc

Consolidated statement of financial position as at 31 October 20X8

	£'000
Assets	
Non-current assets:	
Intangible assets: goodwill (W)	8,400
Property, plant and equipment (47,875 + 31,913 + 4,500)	84,288
	92,688
Current assets:	
Inventories	30,509
Trade and other receivables (14,343 + 3,656 – 2,000)	15,999
Cash and cash equivalents	2,003
	48,511
Total assets	141,199
Equity and liabilities	
Equity attributable to owners of the parent:	
Share capital	45,000
Share premium	12,000
Retained earnings (W)	25,120
	82,120
Non-controlling interest (W)	11,280
Total equity	93,400
Non-current liabilities:	
Long-term loan	27,000
Current liabilities:	
Trade and other payables (14,454 + 3,685 – 2,000)	16,139
Tax liabilities	4,660
	20,799
Total liabilities	47,799
Total equity and liabilities	141,199

Workings

Note: **Group structure**

Tolsta plc owns 2/3 of Balallan Ltd (8,000,000/12,000,000).

Goodwill	£'000
Price paid	32,000
Share capital – attributable to Tolsta plc (2/3 × 12,000)	(8,000)
Share premium – attributable to Tolsta plc (2/3 × 6,000)	(4,000)
Retained earnings – attributable to Tolsta plc (2/3 × 9,750)	(6,500)
Revaluation reserve – attributable to Tolsta plc (2/3 × 4,500)	(3,000)
Impairment	(2,100)
	8,400

Retained earnings	£'000
Tolsta plc	26,160
Balallan Ltd – attributable to Tolsta plc (2/3% × (11,340 – 9,750))	1,060
Impairment	(2,100)
	25,120

Non-controlling interest (NCI)	£'000
Share capital – attributable to NCI (1/3 × 12,000)	4,000
Share premium – attributable to NCI (1/3 × 6,000)	2,000
Retained earnings – attributable to NCI (1/3 × 11,340)	3,780
Revaluation reserve – attributable to NCI (1/3 × 4,500)	1,500
	11,280

Task 5.6

Ard plc

Consolidated statement of financial position as at 31 March 20X9

	£'000
Assets	
Non-current assets:	
Intangible assets: goodwill (W)	4,816
Property, plant and equipment	72,690
Current assets (32,782 + 10,835 – 3,000)	40,617
Total assets	118,123
Equity and liabilities	
Equity attributable to owners of the parent	
Share capital	50,000
Retained earnings (W)	21,186
Non-controlling interest (W)	11,896
Total equity	83,082
Non-current liabilities	18,000
Current liabilities (15,466 + 4,575 – 3,000)	17,041
Total liabilities	35,041
Total equity and liabilities	118,123

Workings

Note: **Group structure**

Ard plc owns 60% of Ledi Ltd (12,000,000/20,000,000).

Goodwill	£'000
Price paid	23,000
Share capital – attributable to Ard plc (60% × 20,000)	(12,000)
Retained earnings – attributable to Ard plc (60% × 7,640)	(4,584)
Impairment	(1,600)
	4,816

Retained earnings	£'000
Ard plc	21,526
Ledi Ltd – attributable to Ard plc (60% × (9,740 – 7,640))	1,260
Impairment	(1,600)
	21,186

Non-controlling interest (NCI)	£'000
Share capital – attributable to NCI (40% × 20,000)	8,000
Retained earnings – attributable to NCI (40% × 9,740)	3,896
	11,896

Task 5.7

Glebe plc

Consolidated statement of financial position as at 31 March 20X1

	£'000
Assets	
Non-current assets:	
Intangible assets: goodwill (W)	842
Property, plant and equipment (36,890 + 25,600 + 2,400)	64,890
Current assets:	30,199
Total assets	95,931
Equity and liabilities	
Equity attributable to owners of the parent	
Share capital	40,000
Retained earnings (W)	15,426
Non-controlling interest (W)	8,715
Total equity	64,141
Non-current liabilities:	18,000
Current liabilities:	13,790
Total liabilities	31,790
Total equity and liabilities	95,931

Workings

Goodwill	£'000
Price paid	18,000
Share capital – attributable to Glebe plc (70% × 10,000)	(7,000)
Retained earnings – attributable to Glebe plc (70% × 11,540)	(8,078)
Revaluation reserve – attributable to Glebe plc (70% x 2,400)	(1,680)
Impairment	(400)
	842

Retained earnings	£'000
Glebe plc	12,249
Starks Ltd – attributable to Glebe plc (70% × (16,650 – 11,540))	3,577
Impairment	(400)
	15,426

Non-controlling interest (NCI)	£'000
Share capital – attributable to NCI (30% × 10,000)	3,000
Retained earnings – attributable to NCI (30% × 16,650)	4,995
Revaluation reserve– attributable to NCI (30% x 2,400)	720
	8,715

Answers to the consolidated statement of comprehensive income

Task 6.1

Consolidated statement of comprehensive income for the year ended 31 March 20X2

	£'000
Continuing operations	
Revenue	6,810
Cost of sales	4,020
Gross profit	2,790
Other income	0
Operating expenses	1,300
Profit before tax	1,490
Tax	420
Profit for the period from continuing operations	1,070
Attributable to:	
Equity holders of the parent	968
Non-controlling interests (30% × 340)	102
	1,070

Task 6.2

Consolidated statement of comprehensive income for the year ended 31 December 20X1

	£'000
Continuing operations	
Revenue (W)	48,300
Cost of sales (W)	30,500
Gross profit	17,800
Other income	0
Operating expenses	10,600
Profit before tax	7,200
Tax	2,200
Profit for the period from continuing operations	5,000
Attributable to:	
Equity holders of the parent	4,320
Non-controlling interests (1,700 × 40%)	680
	5,000

Working

Revenue	£'000
C plc	38,600
D Ltd	14,700
Total inter-company adjustment	(5,000)
	48,300

Cost of sales	£'000
C plc	25,000
D Ltd	9,500
Total inter-company adjustment (5,000 – 1,000 unrealised profit)	(4,000)
	30,500

Task 6.3

Aswall plc

Consolidated statement of comprehensive income for the year ended 31 March 20X4

	£'000
Continuing operations	
Revenue (W)	43,515
Cost of sales (W)	(18,968)
Gross profit	24,547
Other income	0
Distribution costs	(6,756)
Administrative expenses	(4,008)
Profit from operations	13,783
Finance costs	(2,940)
Profit before tax	10,843
Tax	(3,686)
Profit for the period from continuing operations	7,157
Attributable to:	
Equity holders of the parent	6,523
Non-controlling interest (W)	634
	7,157

Workings

Revenue	£'000
Aswall plc	32,412
Unsafey Ltd	12,963
Total inter-company adjustment	(1,860)
	43,515

Cost of sales	£'000
Aswall plc	14,592
Unsafey Ltd	5,576
Total inter-company adjustment (1,860 – 660 unrealised profit)	(1,200)
	18,968

Non-controlling interest (NCI)	£'000
Profit for the period attributable to NCI (25% × 3,196)	799
Unrealised profit attributable to NCI (25% × 660)	(165)
	634

Task 6.4

Danube plc

Consolidated statement of comprehensive income for the year ended 31 March 20X2

	£'000
Continuing operations	
Revenue	20,200
Cost of sales	(10,500)
Gross profit	9,700
Other income	0
Operating expenses	(4,530)
Profit from operations	5,170

Workings

Revenue	£'000
Danube plc	15,800
Inn Ltd	5,400
Total inter-company adjustment	(1,000)
	20,200

Cost of sales	£'000
Danube plc	8,500
Inn Ltd	2,800
Total inter-company adjustment (1,000 – 200)	(800)
	10,500

Task 6.5

Wewill plc

Consolidated statement of comprehensive income for the year ended 31 March 20X4

	£'000
Continuing operations	
Revenue (W)	49,600
Cost of sales (W)	(25,955)
Gross profit	23,645
Other income	0
Distribution costs	(9,910)
Administrative expenses	(5,902)
Profit from operations	7,833
Finance costs	(829)
Profit before tax	7,004
Tax	(1,913)
Profit for the period from continuing operations	5,091
Attributable to:	
Equity holders of the parent	4,729
Non-controlling interest (20% × 1,810)	362
	5,091

Workings

Revenue	£'000
Wewill plc	36,400
Rokyu Ltd	14,600
Total inter-company adjustment	(1,400)
	49,600

Cost of sales	£'000
Wewill plc	20,020
Rokyu Ltd	6,935
Total inter-company adjustment (1,400 – 400)	(1,000)
	25,955

Answers to calculating ratios

Task 7.1

(a)	Gross profit percentage $\dfrac{522}{989} \times 100$		52.8	%
(b)	Operating profit percentage $\dfrac{214}{989} \times 100$		21.6	%
(c)	Return on capital employed $\dfrac{214}{1,400} \times 100$		15.3	%
(d)	Asset turnover (net assets) $\dfrac{989}{1,400}$		0.7	times
(e)	Interest cover $\dfrac{214}{34}$		6.3	times
(f)	Gearing $\dfrac{400}{1,400} \times 100$		28.6	%

Task 7.2

(a)	Current ratio $\dfrac{58,600 + 98,400}{86,200 + 6,300}$		1.7	:1
(b)	Quick (acid test) ratio $\dfrac{98,400}{86,200 + 6,300}$		1.1	:1
(c)	Trade receivables collection period $\dfrac{98,400}{772,400} \times 365$		46.5	days
(d)	Inventory turnover $\dfrac{507,400}{58,600}$		8.7	times
(e)	Inventory holding period $\dfrac{58,600}{507,400} \times 365$		42.1	days
(f)	Trade payables payment period $\dfrac{86,200}{507,400} \times 365$		62.0	days

Task 7.3

(a) Formulae

(i)	Return on capital employed	$\dfrac{\text{Profit from operations}}{\text{Total equity + non-current liabilities}} \times 100\%$
(ii)	Operating profit percentage	$\dfrac{\text{Profit from operations}}{\text{Revenue}} \times 100\%$
(iii)	Gross profit percentage	$\dfrac{\text{Gross profit}}{\text{Revenue}} \times 100\%$
(iv)	Asset turnover (net assets)	$\dfrac{\text{Revenue}}{\text{Total assets - current liabilities}}$
(v)	Gearing	$\dfrac{\text{Non-current liabilities}}{\text{Total equity + non-current liabilities}} \times 100\%$
(vi)	Interest cover	$\dfrac{\text{Profit from operations}}{\text{Finance costs}}$

(b) Calculations

(i)	Return on capital employed $\dfrac{2,189}{17,541} \times 100$	12.5	%
(ii)	Operating profit percentage $\dfrac{2,189}{8,420} \times 100$	26.0	%
(iii)	Gross profit percentage $\dfrac{4,884}{8,420} \times 100$	58.0	%
(iv)	Asset turnover (net assets) $\dfrac{8,420}{17,541}$	0.5	times
(v)	Gearing $\dfrac{5,000}{17,541} \times 100$	28.5	%
(vi)	Interest cover $\dfrac{2,189}{400}$	5.5	%

Task 7.4

(a) Formulae

(i)	Gross profit percentage	$\dfrac{\text{Gross profit}}{\text{Revenue}} \times 100\%$
(ii)	Operating profit percentage	$\dfrac{\text{Profit from operations}}{\text{Revenue}} \times 100\%$
(iii)	Current ratio	$\dfrac{\text{Current assets}}{\text{Current liabilities}}$
(iv)	Quick (acid test) ratio	$\dfrac{\text{Current assets } - \text{ inventories}}{\text{Current liabilities}}$
(v)	Inventory holding period	$\dfrac{\text{Inventories}}{\text{Cost of sales}} \times 365$
(vi)	Trade receivables collection period	$\dfrac{\text{Trade receivables}}{\text{Revenue}} \times 365$

(b) Calculations

(i)	Gross profit percentage $\dfrac{11,595}{21,473} \times 100$	54.0	%
(ii)	Operating profit percentage $\dfrac{4,080}{21,473} \times 100$	19.0	%
(iii)	Current ratio $\dfrac{4,875}{2,093}$	2.3	:1
(iv)	Quick (acid test) ratio $\dfrac{4,875 - 1,813}{2,093}$	1.5	:1
(v)	Inventory holding period $\dfrac{1,813}{9,878} \times 365$	67.0	days
(vi)	Trade receivables collection period $\dfrac{3,000}{21,473} \times 365$	51.0	days

Task 7.5

(a) Formulae

(i)	Return on total assets	$\dfrac{\text{Profit from operations}}{\text{Total assets}} \times 100\%$
(ii)	Operating expenses/revenue percentage	$\dfrac{\text{Dist. costs + Admin. expenses}}{\text{Revenue}} \times 100\%$
(iii)	Current ratio	$\dfrac{\text{Current assets}}{\text{Current liabilities}}$
(iv)	Quick (acid test) ratio	$\dfrac{\text{Current assets } - \text{ inventories}}{\text{Current liabilities}}$
(v)	Gearing ratio	$\dfrac{\text{Non-current liabilities}}{\text{Total equity + non-current liabilities}} \times 100\%$
(vi)	Interest cover	$\dfrac{\text{Profit from operations}}{\text{Finance costs}}$

(b) Calculations

(i)	Return on total assets $\dfrac{1,405}{30,319} \times 100$	4.6	%
(ii)	Operating expenses/revenue percentage $\dfrac{4,841+3,007}{20,562} \times 100$	38.2	%
(iii)	Current ratio $\dfrac{6,337}{2,906}$	2.2	:1
(iv)	Quick (acid test) ratio $\dfrac{2,325}{2,906}$	0.8	:1
(v)	Gearing ratio $\dfrac{14,000}{27,413}$	51.1	%
(vi)	Interest cover $\dfrac{1,405}{800}$	1.8	times

Task 7.6

(a) Formulae

(i) Return on capital employed	$\dfrac{\text{Profit from operations}}{\text{Total equity + non-current liabilities}} \times 100\%$
(ii) Return on equity	$\dfrac{\text{Profit after tax}}{\text{Total equity}} \times 100\%$
(iii) Inventory holding period	$\dfrac{\text{Inventories}}{\text{Cost of sales}} \times 365$
(iv) Trade receivables collection period	$\dfrac{\text{Trade receivables}}{\text{Revenue}} \times 365$
(v) Trade payables payment period	$\dfrac{\text{Trade payables}}{\text{Cost of sales}} \times 365$
(vi) Working capital cycle	Inventory days + Receivable days – Payable days
(vii) Asset turnover (total assets)	$\dfrac{\text{Revenue}}{\text{Total assets}}$

(b) Calculations

(i) Return on capital employed $\dfrac{588}{6,241+2,300} \times 100$	6.9	%
(ii) Return on equity $\dfrac{363}{6,241} \times 100$	5.8	%
(iii) Inventory holding period $\dfrac{649}{2,597} \times 365$	91.2	days
(iv) Trade receivables collection period $\dfrac{392}{4,900} \times 365$	29.2	days
(v) Trade payables payment period $\dfrac{286}{2,597} \times 365$	40.2	days
(vi) Working capital cycle 91.2 + 29.2 – 40.2	80.2	days
(vii) Asset turnover (total assets) $\dfrac{4,900}{9,082}$	0.5	times

Task 7.7

(a) Formulae

(i)	Gross profit percentage	$\dfrac{\text{Gross profit}}{\text{Revenue}} \times 100\%$
(ii)	Operating profit percentage	$\dfrac{\text{Profit from operations}}{\text{Revenue}} \times 100\%$
(iii)	Gearing	$\dfrac{\text{Non-current liabilities}}{\text{Total equity + non-current liabilities}} \times 100\%$
(iv)	Interest cover	$\dfrac{\text{Profit from operations}}{\text{Finance costs}}$
(v)	Current ratio	$\dfrac{\text{Current assets}}{\text{Current liabilities}}$
(vi)	Quick (acid test) ratio	$\dfrac{\text{Current assets} - \text{inventories}}{\text{Current liabilities}}$
(vii)	Trade receivables collection period	$\dfrac{\text{Trade receivables}}{\text{Revenue}} \times 365$
(viii)	Trade payables payment period	$\dfrac{\text{Trade payables}}{\text{Cost of sales}} \times 365$

(b) Calculations

(i)	Gross profit percentage $\dfrac{13{,}622}{27{,}800} \times 100$	49.0	%
(ii)	Operating profit percentage $\dfrac{2{,}780}{27{,}800} \times 100$	10.0	%
(iii)	Gearing $\dfrac{12{,}000}{13{,}537+12{,}000} \times 100$	47.0	%
(iv)	Interest cover $\dfrac{2{,}780}{840}$	3.3	times
(v)	Current ratio $\dfrac{5{,}207}{2{,}686}$	1.9	:1
(vi)	Quick (acid test) ratio $\dfrac{5{,}207-3{,}261}{2{,}686}$	0.7	:1
(vii)	Trade receivables collection period $\dfrac{1{,}946}{27{,}800} \times 365$	25.6	days
(viii)	Trade payables payment period $\dfrac{1{,}276}{14{,}178} \times 365$	32.8	days

Task 7.8

(a) **Formulae used to calculate the ratios**

(i)	Gross profit percentage	$\dfrac{\text{Gross profit}}{\text{Revenue}} \times 100\%$
(ii)	Operating profit percentage	$\dfrac{\text{Profit from operations}}{\text{Revenue}} \times 100\%$
(iii)	Return on equity	$\dfrac{\text{Profit after tax}}{\text{Total equity}} \times 100\%$
(iv)	Quick (acid test) ratio	$\dfrac{\text{Current assets - inventories}}{\text{Current liabilities}}$
(v)	Gearing	$\dfrac{\text{Non-current liabilities}}{\text{Total equity + non-current liabilities}} \times 100\%$
(vi)	Interest cover	$\dfrac{\text{Profit from operations}}{\text{Finance costs}}$
(vii)	Operating expenses/revenue percentage	$\dfrac{\text{Dist. costs + Admin. expenses}}{\text{Revenue}} \times 100\%$
(viii)	Asset turnover (total assets)	$\dfrac{\text{Revenue}}{\text{Total assets}}$

(b) **Calculation of the ratios**

(i)	Gross profit percentage $\dfrac{16,200}{36,000} \times 100$		45.0	%
(ii)	Operating profit percentage $\dfrac{3,240}{36,000} \times 100$		9.0	%
(iii)	Return on equity $\dfrac{866}{26,155} \times 100$		3.3	%
(iv)	Quick (acid test) ratio $\dfrac{7,123 - 2,376}{3,876}$		1.2	:1
(v)	Gearing $\dfrac{4,000}{26,155 + 4,000} \times 100$		13.3	%
(vi)	Interest cover $\dfrac{3,240}{280}$		11.6	times
(vii)	Operating expenses/revenue percentage $\dfrac{6,840 + 6,120}{36,000} \times 100$		36.0	%
(viii)	Asset turnover (total assets) $\dfrac{36,000}{34,031}$		1.1	times

Answers to interpreting financial statements

Note: based on the information available at the time this book was written, we anticipate that the tasks in this section would be human marked in the real assessment.

Task 8.1

(a) Rigby Ltd is operating on a high gross profit percentage, relatively high operating profit percentage but a fairly low asset turnover. This indicates a low volume, high margin type of business. The ROCE is the same as that of Rialto Ltd but Rialto Ltd has low gross and operating profit percentages but high asset turnover indicating a high volume, low margin business.

In terms of working capital Rialto Ltd has a reasonable current ratio but low quick ratio indicating fairly large inventory levels although with inventory turnover of 10.3 times this inventory is being turned over much more rapidly than in Rigby Ltd. Rialto Ltd has virtually no receivables and both companies take a reasonable amount of credit from suppliers.

Rialto Ltd is more highly geared than Rigby Ltd but with interest cover of 5 times this would not appear to be a major problem.

(b) From the ratios given it would appear that Rigby Ltd is the jeweller with relatively low revenue, high profit margins and slower inventory turnover. Rialto Ltd with higher, low margin revenue and almost no receivables would appear to be the supermarket.

Task 8.2

REPORT

To:	**Duncan Tweedy**
From:	**A Technician**
Date:	**October 20X3**
Subject:	**Comparison of profitability of Byrne Ltd and May Ltd**

The purpose of this report is to assess the relative profitability of the two companies, Byrne Ltd and May Ltd, in order to determine which company is likely to be the better investment. This will be done by using a number of key financial ratios in order to assess the performance of each company.

(a) **Comparative profitability**

May Ltd's return on capital is significantly higher than that of Byrne Ltd. The return on capital employed for May Ltd shows that the overall return for all the providers of capital (shareholders and long term lenders) is 32.1% compared to only 21.5% for the providers of capital in Byrne Ltd. Therefore from a potential shareholder's viewpoint May provides a better overall return.

May Ltd's gross profit percentage and operating profit percentage are both also significantly higher than those of Byrne Ltd. This indicates that both May's profit after cost of sales from trading activities and its overall profit after deducting other operating expenses are a higher proportion of it's sales revenue than those of Byrne Ltd. For each £1 of sales made during the reported period, May is generating more profit.

Finally May Ltd's earnings per share is almost twice that of Byrne Ltd. This tells a shareholder or potential shareholder that there are 82 pence of profits available for distribution for every share that is held. These profits will not all be distributed as a dividend as much of this will be retained in the business for future growth. However the higher earnings per share indicates how much more profit is available to each shareholder in May Ltd compared to profits available to individual shareholders in Byrne Ltd.

(b) **Conclusion**

The profitability ratios show us that May Ltd is using its capital base more efficiently and making more profit from each £1 of sales than Byrne Ltd. May Ltd is definitely the more profitable company (in relative terms).

Task 8.3

Notes for meeting

(a) **Comments on the changes in the ratios**

Current ratio

This seems to show that the company is in a very healthy position; the ratio has improved during the year. The company's current liabilities are covered almost three times by its current assets. Most people would regard this as more than adequate.

However, a very high current ratio can also mean that working capital is not being managed very efficiently and this is borne out by the other ratios.

Quick ratio

This has deteriorated from a satisfactory 1.1 to a slightly worrying 0.6 over the year. The fact that the fall has been so sharp is probably a cause for concern.

The fall in the quick ratio suggests that the improvement in the current ratio is mainly due to an increase in inventory levels. In addition, the high current ratio coupled with the relatively low quick ratio suggests that most of the company's current assets are in the form of inventory. These factors indicate that the company may be carrying too much inventory, which means that cash is being 'tied up' unnecessarily.

Trade receivables collection period

This has risen from 32 days to 48 days during the year, which means that customers are taking longer to pay. If sales have remained at a constant level during the year, this suggests that there may be credit control problems (customers being granted too much credit or staff failing to chase debts).

219

The ratio should be interpreted with caution. It is possible that this apparent increase in the collection period is due to increased sales towards the year end (as receivables at the year end would be high in relation to revenue for the year).

Trade payables payment period

This has fallen slightly during the year. If the ratio is considered in isolation there does not appear to be cause for concern (most suppliers grant a credit period of around 30 days and so 27 days appears reasonable).

However, note that at the end of the year the time taken to collect receivables is considerably longer than the time taken to pay suppliers (at the start of the year the payment period and the collection period were about the same). This may reflect poor management and could lead to cash flow problems.

Inventory holding period

This has risen significantly during the year. This increase appears to confirm what was suggested by the movements in the current ratio and quick ratio: inventory levels are very high and rising and the company is probably carrying too much inventory. Given that the quick ratio has fallen during the year, this situation may lead to cash flow problems.

The increase in inventory may not necessarily be a result of poor management. For example, the company may have received several big orders shortly before the year end and management may have deliberately purchased extra inventories in order to meet them.

(b) **Conclusion**

The overall picture given by these five ratios seems to suggest poor working capital management. The apparent increase in the level of inventory is a particular cause for concern and the company also appears to be having problems in collecting cash from customers.

Task 8.4

Sender's address

Ms Madge Keygone

Address

December 20X4

Dear Ms Keygone,

Asbee Ltd

As requested, I am writing to explain the significance of the ratios mentioned by the shareholder in your recent meeting.

(a) **Comparison with industry averages**

- The current ratio for Asbee Ltd is higher than the industry average, which suggests that the company has more current assets in relation to its current liabilities than is normal for the industry. On the face of it, this is a good sign as it indicates that Asbee Ltd has better liquidity than other companies in the same industry. On the other hand, the low quick ratio (see below) suggests that the company's current assets may largely consist of inventories and receivables, which are often difficult to convert into cash quickly. This could mean that Asbee Ltd may not be able to meet its current liabilities as they fall due and that therefore it is in a worse position than other similar companies.

- The quick ratio is slightly lower than the industry average. This suggests that Asbee Ltd has less cash and receivables in relation to its current liabilities than other companies in the industry. This means that the company's liquidity position appears to be worse than that of the rest of the industry. Asbee Ltd may have very little or no actual cash, with all or most of its quick assets made up of trade receivables.

- The inventory holding period is almost twice as long as the industry average and indicates that other companies in the industry sell inventory almost twice as quickly as Asbee Ltd. This is almost certainly one of the reasons why the current ratio is high compared to other companies. The current ratio and the inventories holding period taken together suggest that inventory levels are abnormally high. There are a number of possible reasons for this: a large number of old or obsolete items which should be written down to net realisable value; or lack of control over inventories.

- The trade receivables collection period is also longer than the industry average, suggesting that Asbee Ltd takes longer to collect amounts receivable from customers than other companies in the industry. This indicates that there are problems with the management of receivables. These may include poor credit control, failure to chase overdue amounts or an increase in the level of irrecoverable debts.

(b) Conclusion

The low quick ratio is probably the main reason why the shareholder is concerned. As stated above, Asbee Ltd's true liquidity could be rather worse than the quick ratio suggests. If the company has a bank overdraft rather than a positive cash balance, this would be worrying.

The shareholder is also probably concerned that too much cash has been absorbed by inventories. In addition he or she may believe that there are inventory control problems that are not being addressed.

In combination with the low quick ratio the receivables collection period suggests that the company has potential liquidity problems. Its liquidity appears to be worse than that of the rest of the industry and the shareholder will view this as a cause for concern.

I hope that this explanation has been helpful. Please do not hesitate to contact me if you have any further queries or if you require any further explanations.

Yours sincerely,

Task 8.5

REPORT

To: **Leopold Scratchy**

From: **Accounting Technician**

Subject: **Financial statements of Partridge Ltd and Carington Ltd**

Date: **June 20X5**

As requested, I have considered the risk and return of two potential investments. My analysis is based on the latest financial statements of the two companies. I have calculated four key ratios for each of the two companies.

(a) The relative risk and return of the two companies

Gross profit percentage

The two companies have approximately the same gross profit percentage and therefore equally profitable trading operations. A gross profit percentage of 59% appears to be reasonably healthy.

Return on equity

The return on the equity of Partridge Ltd is considerably higher than that of Carington Ltd. This shows that Partridge Ltd would provide a much higher return to an investor relative to its total equity (capital 'owned' by equity shareholders) than Carington Ltd.

Earnings per share

Earnings per share is also significantly higher for Partridge Ltd than for Carington Ltd. Partridge's profit available to pay dividends attributable to each ordinary share is higher than Carington's. Taken together with Partridge's higher return on equity, this suggests that Partridge Ltd is more profitable overall than Carington Ltd. As the two companies have the same gross profit percentage, it is probable that Carington Ltd has higher operating expenses relative to its sales (a lower operating profit percentage) than Partridge Ltd.

Gearing

Partridge Ltd has a high gearing ratio while Carington Ltd has a very low gearing ratio. This shows that Partridge Ltd is financed by loans (borrowings) as well as by equity capital (ordinary shares) and that loans make up quite a high percentage of its total capital employed. This contrasts with Carington Ltd, which has almost no loan finance. Partridge Ltd is a riskier investment than Carington Ltd. Interest on its loans must be paid regardless of the level of profit and this reduces the amount available for distribution to ordinary shareholders. This means that in a poor year, dividends to ordinary shareholders may be reduced or there may be no dividend at all.

(b) **Conclusion**

On the basis of the ratios calculated, an investment in Partridge Ltd would provide you with a much better return on the amount that you invest than an investment in Carington Ltd, assuming both companies maintain their current levels of profitability.

However, Partridge Ltd is much more highly geared than Carington Ltd and so Carington Ltd would be the safer investment of the two. Both companies are profitable, and while Carington Ltd appears to be less profitable overall, its return on equity and particularly its earnings per share still appear to be acceptable. You may need to decide on the level of risk that you are prepared to accept, relative to the return on your investment.

I hope that these comments are helpful. Please do not hesitate to contact me if you need any further assistance.

Task 8.6

REPORT

To: Peter Stewart

From: Accounting Technician

Subject: Review of financial statements of Hillhead Ltd

Date: DD/MM/YY

As requested, I have analysed the efficiency and effectiveness of the management of Hillhead Ltd, based on four key ratios.

(a) **The relative performance of the company for the past two years**

Gross profit percentage

The gross profit margin has fallen. This means that on average the business is making less gross profit for each sale made. There could be many reasons for this fall in gross profit margin, for example, raw material prices may have increased and Hillhead Ltd has been unable to pass on these price increases to customers. Alternatively, the increase in sales suggests that management may have cut prices to try and attract new customers.

Operating profit percentage

The operating profit percentage has improved. As sales have risen and the gross profit percentage has fallen, the increase in the operating profit percentage must be as a result of lower overhead costs. Hillhead Ltd has obviously had strong control of costs during the year.

Inventory holding period

Hillhead Ltd's inventory holding period has worsened significantly. The company is taking longer to convert its inventory into cash by selling it. This suggests that it has been less efficient in managing inventory in the current year.

Trade receivables collection period

The trade receivables collection period has also worsened significantly. It could be that management allowed more credit to its customers or it may be a sign of worsening credit control or the possibility of irrecoverable debts.

(b) **Suggestions for improvement of the ratios**

Gross profit percentage

The gross profit percentage could be improved if selling prices could be increased without a corresponding increase in costs. Alternatively, raw materials or goods for resale could be sourced for lower prices.

Operating profit percentage

This ratio will improve if cost savings can be made and revenue remains stable. If operating expenses have reduced in the current year, there may be little scope for reducing them any further.

Inventory holding period

The long inventory holding period may indicate old or obsolete inventory, so this may need to be written off. Management needs to improve inventory ordering and purchasing/manufacture so that high levels of inventory do not build up and 'tie up' cash.

Trade receivables collection period

As the trade receivables collection period has increased, management should assess the recoverability of receivables. Credit control procedures should be tightened so that cash can be collected on a timely basis.

Task 8.7

Sender's address

The Directors of Bateoven Ltd

Address

December 20X5

Dear Directors

Sources and uses of cash

As requested, I set out my comments on the way in which Bateoven Ltd has generated and used cash during the year ended 30 September 20X5.

Sources of cash

The company experienced a total operating cash inflow of £3,882,000. Approximately one-third of this inflow was absorbed by movements in working capital, leaving net cash generated from operations of £2,574,000.

The company raised additional cash of £5,000,000 from an issue of ordinary shares. It also increased its long-term loan by £4,100,000.

Uses of cash

The company spent cash of £9,138,000 on the purchase of new property, plant and equipment. This expenditure was largely covered by the additional cash of £9,100,000 raised from the share issue and the increase in long-term debt. This was presumably the reason for raising the additional finance.

There were also routine operating cash outflows of £560,000 in respect of interest on the long-term loan and £1,284,000 in respect of corporation tax. These were covered by cash generated from operations.

The company also paid a dividend of £2,000,000 on its ordinary shares. The remaining cash generated from operations was insufficient to cover the dividend payment. This appears to be the main reason why cash decreased by £1,308,000 during the year.

Further comments

Two areas give some cause for concern. The first is the extent to which cash from operations has been absorbed by changes in working capital. Inventories, trade receivables and trade payables have all increased significantly during the year and it is possible that cash has been tied up unnecessarily in this way.

The second is the payment of what appears to be a very large dividend in relation to profit from operations for the year. The company has to pay interest on the loan and must meet its tax liabilities, but it is not legally obliged to pay a dividend.

However, although the company now has a significant amount of long term debt, it still has a positive cash balance of £93,000, so it is unlikely to experience severe liquidity problems in the very short term.

I hope that this analysis has been helpful to you. Please do not hesitate to contact me should you require any further assistance.

Yours sincerely

Task 8.8

REPORT

To: The Directors of Knole Ltd

From: Accounting technician

Subject: The company's liquidity and cash flow

Date:

As requested, I have examined the company's financial statements for the years ended 31 October 20X7 and 20X8 and I set out my comments below.

(a) **The change in net cash from operating activities**

Profit from operations has increased by approximately 20% in the year. However, the net cash from operating activities has decreased from £7,110,000 in 20X7 to £5,973,000 in 20X8. This means that the company has generated less cash from its operations than in the previous year, despite the increase in profit.

During the year the company took out additional bank loans and this has resulted in an increase of £175,000 in interest paid. Tax paid has increased by £59,000, presumably as a result of the increase in operating profit. Both these increases are relatively modest.

The main reason for the decrease in cash is the movement in working capital in the year, which has reduced cash by £9,900,000. Inventories have increased by £4,840,000, compared with an increase of £3,606,000 in 20X7. If sales have increased, the increase in inventories is probably needed to meet customer demand. However, it could also have been caused by slow moving items or other problems. Trade receivables have increased by £2,640,000 in the period. Again, this could be because sales have increased towards the end of the year. An alternative explanation might be that customers are being allowed more credit or taking longer to pay. Trade payables have decreased by £2,420,000 in the year. This suggests that either the company is paying its suppliers too quickly or that the suppliers have changed their credit terms.

The changes in working capital mean that the cash generated by the company's operations is 'tied up' in inventories and trade receivables. This reduces the amount of cash available for paying interest on the bank loan and tax on profits. It also reduces the cash available for investing in property, plant and equipment and other non-current assets. It is almost certainly the reason why the company moved from a positive cash balance to a bank overdraft during the year. This is particularly surprising and worrying given the significant increase in profit from operations.

(b) **The liquidity and financial position of the company**

The current ratio and the quick (or acid test) ratio have both increased significantly during the year. The current ratio is very high and shows that in theory the company can comfortably meet its current liabilities. Similarly, the quick ratio shows that despite the cash outflow during the year, in theory the company should have no problems in meeting its day to day liabilities as they fall due. (The quick ratio is used as a measure of short term liquidity because it excludes inventories, which cannot be quickly converted into cash).

Most people would consider that a current ratio of 3.6 is far too high. The ratio confirms that the company almost certainly has too much inventory. This is one of the main reasons why the company has moved from a positive cash balance to an overdraft during the year. Again, the high quick ratio and the increase in the year show that the company is almost certainly not managing its trade receivables well. Like inventories, these need to be converted into cash much more quickly. Better working capital management would probably solve the company's cash flow problems.

The gearing ratio measures the extent to which the company is financed by debt rather than equity. The gearing ratio has increased during the year, which reflects the increase in bank loans. However, it is still very low. This suggests that the company should not have any problems in raising more finance in the longer term, should it need to. Knole Ltd is profitable and the low gearing means that investors will see it as a relatively safe investment.

If you have any questions, or require any further information, please do not hesitate to contact me.

AAT practice assessment 1
Pine Ltd
Time allowed: 2½ hours

Section 1

The following information is relevant to Task 1.1 and Task 1.2

You have been asked to help prepare the financial statements of Pine Ltd for the year ended 31 March 20X1. The company's trial balance as at 31 March 20X1 is shown below.

Pine Ltd

Trial balance as at 31 March 20X1

	Debit	Credit
	£'000	£'000
Share capital		50,000
Revaluation reserve at 1 April 20X0		12,000
Trade and other payables		5,342
Land & buildings – value/cost	81,778	
accumulated depreciation at 1 April 20X0		14,000
Plant and equipment – cost	24,000	
accumulated depreciation at 1 April 20X0		8,000
Trade and other receivables	9,886	
Accruals		517
4% bank loan repayable 20X8		16,000
Cash and cash equivalents	1,568	
Retained earnings		7,945
Interest paid	640	
Sales		80,908
Purchases	53,444	
Distribution costs	9,977	
Administrative expenses	6,755	
Inventories at 1 April 20X0	5,064	
Dividends paid	1,600	
	194,712	194,712

Further information:

- The inventories at the close of business on 31 March 20X1 cost £7,004,000.

- Land, which is not depreciated, is included in the trial balance at a value of £41,778,000. It is to be revalued at £51,000,000 and this revaluation is to be included in the financial statements for the year ended 31 March 20X1.

- Depreciation is to be provided for the year to 31 March 20X1 as follows:

  Buildings   5% per annum   Straight line basis

  Plant and equipment   25% per annum   Reducing balance basis

  Depreciation is apportioned as follows:

	%
Cost of sales	60
Distribution costs	30
Administrative expenses	10

- Trade receivables include a debt of £24,000 which is to be written off. Irrecoverable (bad) debts are to be classified as administrative expenses.

- Distribution costs of £160,000 owing at 31 March 20X1 are to be provided for.

- The corporation tax charge for the year has been calculated as £1,254,000.

- All of the operations are continuing operations.

Task 1.1

(a) **Draft the statement of comprehensive income for Pine Ltd for the year ended 31 March 20X1.**

(b) **Draft the statement of changes in equity for Pine Ltd for the year ended 31 March 20X1**

Pine Ltd

Statement of comprehensive income for the year ended 31 March 20X1

	£'000
Revenue	
Cost of sales	
Gross profit	
Distribution costs	
Administrative expenses	
Profit from operations	
Finance costs	

	£'000
Profit before tax	
Tax	
Profit for the period from continuing operations	
Other comprehensive income for the year	
Total comprehensive income for the year	

Workings

(Complete the left hand column by writing in the correct narrative from the list provided.)

Cost of sales		£'000
	▼	
	▼	
	▼	
	▼	

Picklist for narratives:

Accruals
Closing inventories
Depreciation
Opening inventories
Prepayments
Purchases

Distribution costs		£'000
	▼	
	▼	
	▼	

Picklist for narratives:

Accruals
Bad debt
Depreciation
Distribution costs
Prepayments

Administrative expenses		£'000
	▼	
	▼	
	▼	

Picklist for narratives:

Accruals
Administrative expenses
Bad debt
Depreciation
Prepayments

Pine Ltd

Statement of changes in equity for the year ended 31 March 20X1

	Share Capital £'000	Other Reserves £'000	Retained Earnings £'000	Total Equity £'000
Balance at 1 April 20X0				
Changes in equity for 20X1				
Total comprehensive income				
Dividends				
Issue of share capital				
Balance at 31 March 20X1				

Task 1.2

(a) **Draft the statement of financial position for Pine Ltd as at 31 March 20X1.**

Pine Ltd

Statement of financial position as at 31 March 20X1

(Complete the left hand column by writing in the correct line item from the list provided)

	£'000
Assets	
Non-current assets:	
▽	
Current assets:	
▽	
▽	
▽	
Total assets	
Equity and liabilities:	
Equity	
▽	
▽	
▽	
Total equity	
Non-current liabilities:	
▽	
Current liabilities:	
▽	
▽	
Total liabilities	
Total equity and liabilities	

Picklist for line items:

Bank loan
Cash and cash equivalents
Inventories
Property, plant and equipment
Retained earnings
Revaluation reserve
Share capital
Tax liability
Trade and other payables
Trade and other receivables

Workings

(Complete the left hand column by writing in the correct narrative from the list provided.)

Property, plant and equipment		£'000
	▼	
	▼	
	▼	
	▼	

Picklist for narratives:

Accumulated depreciation – land and buildings
Accumulated depreciation – plant and equipment
Land and buildings – value
Plant and equipment – cost

Trade and other receivables		£'000
	▼	
	▼	

Picklist for narratives:

Accruals: trial balance
Additional distribution costs accrual
Additional distribution costs prepaid
Bad debts
Prepayments
Trade and other payables
Trade and other receivables

Revaluation reserve		£'000
	▼	
	▼	

Picklist for narratives:

Dividends paid
Other comprehensive income for the year
Retained reserves at 1 April 20X0
Revaluation reserve at 1 April 20X0
Total comprehensive income for the year
Total profit for the year

Retained earnings		£'000
	▼	
	▼	
	▼	

Picklist for narratives:

Dividends paid
Other comprehensive income for the year
Retained earnings at 1 April 20X0
Revaluation reserve at 1 April 20X0
Total comprehensive income for the year
Total profit for the year

Trade and other payables		£'000
	▼	
	▼	
	▼	

Picklist for narratives:

Accruals: trial balance
Additional distribution costs accrued
Additional distribution costs prepaid
Bad debts
Dividends
Prepayments
Taxation liability
Trade and other payables
Trade and other receivables

Task 1.3

Elm plc will be undertaking some research and development activities in the near future. The directors of Elm plc understand that such activity may result in the recognition of an intangible asset.

Prepare brief notes for the directors of Elm plc to answer the following questions:

(a) **What is meant by an intangible asset according to IAS 38 *Intangible assets*?**

(b) **What would Elm plc have to demonstrate about an intangible asset arising from development activities before it can be recognised as an intangible asset in the financial statements?**

Task 1.4

(a) An increase in inventories will have a negative impact on cash flow in the calculation of net cash flows from operating activities.

Is this statement true or false?

True	
False	

(b) Bovey Ltd holds three distinct types of inventory in its warehouse at the end of its accounting year, which are valued as follows:

Product	FIFO (cost) £	LIFO (cost) £	NRV £
(i)	11,300	13,400	12,800
(ii)	7,600	4,200	5,900
(iii)	15,200	17,000	18,400
	34,100	34,600	37,100

At what value should inventories be stated in Bovey Ltd's financial statements according to IAS 2 *Inventories*?

£32,400	
£34,000	
£34,100	
£34,600	

(c) Teign Ltd prepares its financial statements to 30 September each year. The following events took place between 30 September and the date on which the financial statements were authorised for issue.

(i) The company made a major purchase of plant and machinery

(ii) A customer who owed the company money at 30 September was declared bankrupt

Which of the above is likely to be classified as an adjusting event according to IAS 10 *Events after the reporting period*?

(i) only	
(ii) only	
Both	
Neither of them	

(d) Fowey Ltd has four assets which the directors consider may have become impaired.

	Carrying amount £	Fair value less costs to sell £	Value in use £
(i)	10,000	12,000	14,000
(ii)	8,000	9,000	5,800
(iii)	7,000	3,800	7,200
(iv)	9,000	4,300	5,200

Which of the above assets will be impaired according to IAS 36 *Impairment of assets*?

(i) only	
(ii) only	
(iii) only	
(iv) only	

(e) Tamar Ltd is being sued by a supplier and will have to pay substantial damages if it loses the case. At its accounting year end lawyers advise the company that it is possible (i.e. less than a 50% likelihood of occurrence) that it may lose the case.

In accordance with IAS 37 *Provisions, contingent liabilities and contingent assets* the possible future outflow should be:

Recognised in the statement of financial position as a provision	
Recognised in the statement of financial position as a contingent liability	
Only disclosed as a note to the financial statements	
Neither recognised in the statement of financial position nor included in the notes	

(f) A lease that transfers substantially all of the risks and rewards of ownership to the lessee is known as:

A finance lease	
An operating lease	

Task 1.5

Lyd plc acquired 70% of the issued share capital of Wolf Ltd on 1 April 20X0 for £2,800,000. At that date Wolf Ltd had issued share capital of £2,000,000 and retained earnings of £280,000.

Extracts of the statements of financial position for the two companies one year later at 31 March 20X1 are as follows:

	Lyd plc £'000	Wolf Ltd £'000
ASSETS		
Investment in Wolf Ltd	2,800	
Property, plant and equipment	4,700	1,530
Current assets	2,400	2,090
Total assets	9,900	3,620
EQUITY AND LIABILITIES		
Equity		
Share capital	3,000	2,000
Retained earnings	5,200	540
Total equity	8,200	2,540
Non-current liabilities	600	480
Current liabilities	1,100	600
Total liabilities	1,700	1,080
Total equity and liabilities	9,900	3,620

Additional data

- Included within the current assets of Lyd plc and in the current liabilities of Wolf Ltd is an inter-company balance for £200,000.

- Lyd plc has decided non-controlling interest will be valued at their proportionate share of net assets.

(a) **Draft the consolidated statement of financial position for Lyd plc and its subsidiary undertaking as at 31 March 20X1.**

Lyd plc

Consolidated statement of financial position as at 31 March 20X1

	£'000
Assets	
Non-current assets:	
Intangible assets: goodwill	
Property, plant and equipment	
Current assets:	
Total assets	
Equity and liabilities	
Equity	
Share capital	
Retained earnings	
Non-controlling interest	
Total equity	
Non-current liabilities:	
Current liabilities:	
Total liabilities	
Total equity and liabilities	

Workings

(Complete the left hand column by writing in the correct narrative from the list provided.)

Goodwill		£'000
	▼	
	▼	
	▼	
Goodwill		

Picklist for narratives:

Price paid
Retained earnings – attributable to Lyd plc
Share capital – attributable to Lyd plc

Retained earnings		£'000
	▼	
	▼	

Picklist for narratives:

Lyd plc
Wolf Ltd – attributable to Lyd plc

Non-controlling interest (NCI)		£'000
	▼	
	▼	

Picklist for narratives:

Current assets – attributable to NCI
Non-current assets – attributable to NCI
Price paid
Retained earnings – attributable to NCI
Share capital – attributable to NCI

(b) Claw plc acquired 90% of the issued share capital and voting rights of Deer Ltd on 1 April 20X0.

Extracts from their statements of comprehensive income for the year ended 31 March 20X1 are shown below:

	Claw plc £'000	Deer Ltd £'000
Continuing operations		
Revenue	40,800	18,600
Cost of sales	(24,200)	(7,300)
Gross profit	16,600	11,300
Other income	1,800	–
Distribution costs & administrative expenses	(2,500)	(1,600)
Profit before tax	15,900	9,700

Additional data

- During the year Deer Ltd sold goods which had cost £100,000 to Claw plc for £480,000. Half of these goods still remain in inventory at the end of the year.

- Other income of Claw plc included a dividend received from Deer Ltd

- Deer Ltd had paid a dividend of £1,710,000 on 17 March 20X1.

Draft the consolidated statement of comprehensive income for Claw plc and its subsidiary undertaking up to and including the profit before tax line for the year ended 31 March 20X1.

Claw plc
Consolidated statement of comprehensive income for the year ended 31 March 20X1

	£'000
Continuing operations	
Revenue	
Cost of sales	
Gross profit	
Other income	
Operating expenses	
Profit before tax	

Workings

Revenue	£'000
Claw plc	
Deer Ltd	
Total inter-company adjustment	

Cost of sales	£'000
Claw plc	
Deer Ltd	
Total inter-company adjustment	

Section 2

Task 2.1

You have been asked to calculate ratios for Brook Ltd in respect of its financial statements for the year ending 31 March 20X1 to assist your manager in his analysis of the company.

Brook Ltd's statement of comprehensive income and statement of financial position are set out below.

Brook Ltd – Statement of comprehensive income for the year ended 31 March 20X1

	20X1 £'000
Continuing operations	
Revenue	24,800
Cost of sales	(12,772)
Gross profit	12,028
Distribution costs	(6,800)
Administrative expenses	(3,244)
Profit from operations	1,984
Finance costs	(372)
Profit before tax	1,612
Tax	(992)
Profit for the period from continuing operations	620

Brook Ltd – Statement of financial position as at 31 March 20X1

	20X1
	£'000
ASSETS	
Non-current assets	
Property, plant and equipment	18,200
Current assets	
Inventories	1,260
Trade receivables	2,320
Cash and cash equivalents	1,840
	5,420
Total assets	23,620
EQUITY AND LIABILITIES	
Equity	
Share capital	12,000
Retained earnings	7,212
Total equity	19,212
Non-current liabilities	
Bank loans	2,000
	2,000
Current liabilities	
Trade payables	1,416
Tax liabilities	992
	2,408
Total liabilities	4,408
Total equity and liabilities	23,620

(a) **State the formulae that are used to calculate each of the following ratios:**

(Write in the correct formula from the list provided)

(i) **Gross profit percentage**	▼

Formulae:

Gross profit/Total equity × 100

Gross profit/Revenue × 100

Gross profit/Total assets × 100

Gross profit/Total assets – current liabilities

(ii) **Operating profit percentage**	▼

Formulae:

Profit from operations/Revenue × 100

Profit from operations/Total assets × 100

Profit from operations/Total equity + Non-current liabilities × 100

Profit from operations/Finance costs × 100

(iii) **Return on capital employed**	▼

Formulae:

Profit after tax/Total equity × 100

Profit from operations/Total equity × 100

Profit after tax/Total equity + Non-current liabilities × 100

Profit from operations/Total equity + Non-current liabilities × 100

(iv) **Current ratio**	▼

Formulae:

Total assets/Total liabilities

Current assets – inventories/Current liabilities

Current assets/Current liabilities

Total assets – inventories/Total liabilities

(v)	Acid test ratio	▼

Formulae:

Current assets/Current liabilities

Total assets – Inventories/Total liabilities

Total assets/Total liabilities

Current assets – Inventories/Current liabilities

(vi)	Trade receivables collection period	▼

Formulae:

Trade payables/Cost of sales × 365

Trade receivables/Cost of sales × 365

Revenue/Trade receivables × 365

Trade receivables/Revenue × 365

(vii)	Inventory holding period (days)	▼

Formulae:

Inventories/Cost of sales × 365

Inventories/Revenue × 365

Cost of sales/Inventories × 365

Revenue/Inventories × 365

(viii)	Gearing ratio	▼

Formulae:

Current assets/Current liabilities

Revenue/Total assets – current liabilities

Non-current liabilities/Total equity + non-current liabilities x100

Profit after tax/Number of issued ordinary shares

(b) **Calculate the ratios to the nearest ONE DECIMAL PLACE.**

(i)	**Gross profit percentage**	%
(ii)	**Operating profit percentage**	%
(iii)	**Return on capital employed**	%
(iv)	**Current ratio**	:1
(v)	**Acid test ratio**	:1
(vi)	**Trade receivable collection period**	days
(vii)	**Inventory holding period (days)**	days
(viii)	**Gearing ratio**	%

Task 2.2

Nancy Charlton is considering buying shares in Limden Ltd and has asked you to assist her in determining the level of profitability and risk of the company. You have computed the following ratios in respect of Limden Ltd's financial statements for the last two years to assist you in your analysis.

	20X1	20X0
Gross profit percentage	46.0%	42.0%
Operating profit percentage	6.5%	8.0%
Return on equity	7.4%	10.8%
Gearing	35.2%	22.4%
Interest cover	2.9 times	7.5 times

Prepare a report to Nancy that includes:

(a) **A comment on the relative performance of the company for the two years based on the ratios calculated and what this tells you about the company.**

(b) **Advice, with reasons based on the ratios you have calculated, on whether or not Nancy should invest.**

Task 2.3

(a) (i) Which body is responsible for preparing and issuing International Financial Reporting Standards (IFRSs)?

    (ii) Briefly explain the purpose of IFRSs

    (iii) Which TWO documents are published for public comment during the process of setting an IFRS?

(b) Define the term 'liability' in accordance with the IASB *Conceptual Framework for Financial Reporting*.

AAT practice assessment 1
Pine Ltd
Answers

Section 1

Task 1.1

(a) **Pine Ltd**

Statement of comprehensive income for the year ended 31 March 20X1

	£'000
Revenue	80,908
Cost of sales (W)	(55,104)
Gross profit	25,804
Distribution costs (W)	(11,937)
Administrative expenses (W)	(7,379)
Profit from operations	6,488
Finance costs	(640)
Profit before tax	5,848
Tax	(1,254)
Profit for the period from continuing operations	4,594
Other comprehensive income for the year (Gain on revaluation of land (51,000 – 41,778))	9,222
Total comprehensive income for the year	13,816

Workings

Cost of sales	£'000
Opening inventories	5,064
Purchases	53,444
Depreciation (60% × 6,000)	3,600
Closing inventories	(7,004)
	55,104

Distribution costs	£'000
Distribution costs	9,977
Depreciation (30% × 6,000)	1,800
Accruals	160
	11,937

Administrative expenses	£'000
Administrative expenses	6,755
Depreciation (10% × 6,000)	600
Bad debt	24
	7,379

Depreciation
Buildings (5% × 81,778 − 41,778)   2,000
Plant and equipment (25% × (24,000 − 8,000))   4,000
    6,000

(b) **Pine Ltd**

Statement of changes in equity for the year ended 31 March 20X1

	Share Capital £'000	Other Reserves £'000	Retained Earnings £'000	Total Equity £'000
Balance at 1 April 20X0	50,000	12,000	7,945	69,945
Changes in equity for 20X1				
Total comprehensive income	0	9,222	4,594	13,816
Dividends	0	0	(1,600)	(1,600)
Issue of share capital	0	0	0	0
Balance at 31 March 20X1	50,000	21,222	10,939	82,161

Task 1.2

(a) **Pine Ltd**

Statement of financial position as at 31 March 20X1

	£'000
Assets	
Non-current assets:	
Property, plant and equipment (W)	87,000
Current assets:	
Inventories	7,004
Trade and other receivables (W)	9,862
Cash and cash equivalents	1,568
	18,434
Total assets	105,434
Equity and liabilities:	
Equity	
Share capital	50,000
Revaluation reserve (W)	21,222
Retained earnings (W)	10,939
Total equity	82,161
Non-current liabilities:	
Bank loan	16,000
Current liabilities:	
Trade and other payables (W)	6,019
Tax liability	1,254
	7,273
Total liabilities	23,273
Total equity and liabilities	105,434

Workings

Property, plant and equipment	£'000
Land and buildings – value (81,778 + 9,222)	91,000
Plant and equipment – Cost	24,000
Accumulated depreciation – land and buildings (14,000 + 2,000)	(16,000)
Accumulated depreciation – plant and equipment (8,000 + 4,000)	(12,000)
	87,000

Trade and other receivables	£'000
Trade and other receivables	9,886
Bad debts	(24)
	9,862

Revaluation reserve	£'000
Revaluation reserve at 1 April 20X0	12,000
Other comprehensive income for the year	9,222
	21,222

Retained earnings	£'000
Retained earnings at 1 April 20X0	7,945
Total profit for the year	4,594
Dividends paid	(1,600)
	10,939

Trade and other payables	£'000
Trade and other payables	5,342
Accruals: trial balance	517
Additional distribution costs accrual	160
	6,019

Task 1.3

Note: based on the information available at the time this book was written, we anticipate that this task would be human marked in the real assessment.

(a) IAS 38 *Intangible assets* defines an intangible asset as:

'an identifiable, non-monetary asset without physical substance'.

(b) IAS 38 states that an intangible asset arising from development can only be recognised if an entity can demonstrate all of the following:

- the technical feasibility of completing the intangible asset so that it will be available for use or sale

- its intention to complete the intangible asset and use or sell it

- its ability to use or sell the intangible asset

- how the intangible asset will generate probable future economic benefits

- the availability of adequate technical, financial and other resources to complete the development and to use or sell the intangible asset

- its ability to measure reliably the expenditure attributable to the intangible asset during its development.

Task 1.4

(a)

True	✓
False	

An increase in inventories means that more cash has been 'tied up' in working capital.

(b)

£32,400	✓
£34,000	
£34,100	
£34,600	

	£'000
Inventories	
Product I (Cost: FIFO)	11,300
Product II (NRV)	5,900
Product III (Cost: FIFO)	15,200
	32,400

Note that LIFO is not permitted as a valuation method by IAS 2 *Inventories*.

(c)

(i) only	
(ii) only	✓
Both	
Neither of them	

(d)

(i) only	
(ii) only	
(iii) only	
(iv) only	✓

IAS 36 states that an asset is impaired if its carrying amount exceeds its recoverable amount. Recoverable amount is the higher of fair value less costs to sell and value in use.

(e)

Recognised in the statement of financial position as a provision	
Recognised in the statement of financial position as a contingent liability	
Only disclosed as a note to the financial statements	✓
Neither recognised in the statement of financial position nor included in the notes	

This is a contingent liability because the outflow of economic benefit is only possible, rather than probable. Contingent liabilities are only disclosed and are not recognised in the statement of financial position.

(f)

A finance lease	✓
An operating lease	

Task 1.5

(a) **Lyd plc**

Consolidated statement of financial position as at 31 March 20X1

	£'000
Assets	
Non-current assets:	
Intangible assets: goodwill (W)	1,204
Property, plant and equipment	6,230
Current assets: (2,400 + 2,090 – 200)	4,290
Total assets	11,724
Equity and liabilities	
Equity	
Share capital	3,000
Retained earnings (W)	5,382
Non-controlling interest (W)	762
Total equity	9,144
Non-current liabilities:	1,080
Current liabilities: (1,100 + 600 – 200)	1,500
Total liabilities	2,580
Total equity and liabilities	11,724

Workings

Goodwill	£'000
Price paid	2,800
Share capital – attributable to Lyd plc (70% × 2,000)	(1,400)
Retained earnings – attributable to Lyd plc (70% × 280)	(196)
	1,204

Retained earnings	£'000
Lyd plc	5,200
Wolf Ltd – attributable to Lyd plc (70% × (540 – 280))	182
	5,382

Non-controlling interest (NCI)	£'000
Share capital – attributable to NCI (30% × 2,000)	600
Retained earnings – attributable to NCI (30% × 540)	162
	762

(b) **Claw plc**

Consolidated statement of comprehensive income for the year ended 31 March 20X1

	£'000
Continuing operations	
Revenue	58,920
Cost of sales	(31,210)
Gross profit	27,710
Other income	261
Operating expenses	(4,100)
Profit before tax	23,871

Workings

Revenue	£'000
Claw plc	40,800
Deer Ltd	18,600
Total inter-company adjustment	(480)
	58,920

Cost of sales	£'000
Claw plc	24,200
Deer Ltd	7,300
Total inter-company adjustment $(480 - (1/2 \times 380))$	(290)
	31,210

Section 2

Task 2.1

(a) **Formulae used to calculate the ratios**

(i) Gross profit percentage	$\dfrac{\text{Gross profit}}{\text{Revenue}} \times 100\%$
(ii) Operating profit percentage	$\dfrac{\text{Profit from operations}}{\text{Revenue}} \times 100\%$
(iii) Return on capital employed	$\dfrac{\text{Profit from operations}}{\text{Total equity + non-current liabilities}} \times 100\%$
(iv) Current ratio	$\dfrac{\text{Current assets}}{\text{Current liabilities}}$
(v) Acid test ratio	$\dfrac{\text{Current assets - inventories}}{\text{Current liabilities}}$
(vi) Trade receivable collection period	$\dfrac{\text{Trade receivables}}{\text{Revenue}} \times 365$
(vii) Inventory holding period (days)	$\dfrac{\text{Inventories}}{\text{Cost of sales}} \times 365$
(viii) Gearing ratio	$\dfrac{\text{Non-current liabilities}}{\text{Total equity + non-current liabilities}} \times 100\%$

(b) **Calculation of the ratios**

(i) **Gross profit percentage** $\dfrac{12,028}{24,800} \times 100$	48.5	%
(ii) **Operating profit percentage** $\dfrac{1,984}{24,800} \times 100$	8.0	%
(iii) **Return on capital employed** $\dfrac{1,984}{19,212 + 2,000} \times 100$	9.4	%
(iv) **Current ratio** $\dfrac{5,420}{2,408}$	2.3	:1
(v) **Acid test ratio** $\dfrac{5,420 - 1,260}{2,408}$	1.7	:1
(vi) **Trade receivable collection period** $\dfrac{2,320}{24,800} \times 365$	34.1	days
(vii) **Inventory holding period (days)** $\dfrac{1,260}{12,772} \times 365$	36.0	days
(viii) **Gearing ratio** $\dfrac{2,000}{19,212 + 2,000} \times 100$	9.4	%

....

Task 2.2

Note: based on the information available at the time this book was written, we anticipate that this task would be human marked in the real assessment.

REPORT

To: Nancy Charlton

From: Accounting Technician

Subject: Performance of Limden Ltd

Date: 18 June 20X1

As requested, I have analysed the financial performance of Limden Ltd, based on the ratios provided.

(a) **The relative performance of the company for the last two years**

Gross profit percentage

The gross profit percentage has improved over the two years. There are several possible reasons for this: the company may have increased its sales prices or been able to reduce its direct costs or both. Alternatively it may have changed the type of product that it sells (the sales mix), so that individual sales are more profitable than before.

Operating profit percentage

The operating profit percentage has fallen significantly. Because the gross profit percentage has improved, this suggests that selling and administrative expenses have increased during 20X1.

Return on equity

Return on equity has also fallen significantly. This is not surprising, given that operating profit percentage has also fallen. Less profit is being generated relative to the shareholders' investment in the company. This means that less profit will be available to pay dividends to shareholders.

Gearing

Gearing (the proportion of the company's finance obtained from borrowings) has increased. The company has probably taken out significant new loans during the year. The company has become a riskier investment as the increased interest payments will reduce profits available to shareholders still further.

Interest cover

Interest cover has fallen very sharply in 20X1. This is consistent with the increase in gearing and the fall in the operating profit percentage: the additional borrowings have increased finance costs and at the same time less profit is available to cover these costs. This fall in interest cover is another indication that the company has become a riskier investment.

(b) **Conclusion**

On the basis of the information provided, I advise you not to invest in this company. The company's trading operations appear to be profitable, but operating profit has decreased and the additional debt suggests that Limden Ltd would be a risky investment.

Task 2.3

Note: based on the information available at the time this book was written, we anticipate that this task would be human marked in the real assessment.

(a) (i) The International Accounting Standards Board (IASB) is responsible for preparing International Financial Reporting Standards (IFRSs)

(ii) The purpose of IFRSs is to require 'high quality, transparent and comparable information in financial statements and other financial reporting' to help investors, other participants in the world's capital markets and other users of financial information to make economic decisions'.

(iii) The IASB normally publishes a Discussion paper and then an Exposure draft during the process of developing a new IFRS.

(b) The *Conceptual Framework for Financial Reporting* defines a liability as 'a present obligation of an entity arising from past events, the settlement of which is expected to result in an outflow from the entity of resources embodying economic benefits'.

AAT practice assessment 2
Eigg Ltd
Time allowed: 2½ hours

Section 1

The following information is relevant to Task 1.1 and Task 1.2

You have been asked to prepare the statement of cash flows and statement of changes in equity for Eigg Ltd for the year ended 31 March 20X1.

The most recent statement of comprehensive income and statement of financial position (with comparatives for the previous year) of Eigg Ltd are set out below.

Eigg Ltd – Statement of comprehensive income for the year ended 31 March 20X1

Continuing operations	£'000
Revenue	44,800
Cost of sales	(24,640)
Gross profit	20,160
Dividends received	120
Gain on disposal of property, plant and equipment	448
Distribution costs	(9,408)
Administrative expenses	(4,480)
Profit from operations	6,840
Finance costs	(105)
Profit before tax	6,735
Tax	(2,884)
Profit for the period from continuing operations	3,851

Eigg Ltd – Statement of financial position as at 31 March 20X1

	20X1	20X0
	£'000	£'000
ASSETS		
Non-current assets		
Property, plant and equipment	27,890	21,340
Current assets		
Inventories	5,914	4,928
Trade receivables	4,480	5,376
Cash and cash equivalents	280	0
	10,674	10,304
Total assets	38,564	31,644
EQUITY AND LIABILITIES		
Equity		
Share capital	4,500	3,000
Share premium	3,000	2,000
Retained earnings	24,216	20,642
Total equity	31,716	25,642
Non-current liabilities		
Bank loans	1,500	500
	1,500	500
Current liabilities		
Trade payables	2,464	4,435
Tax liabilities	2,884	887
Bank overdraft	0	180
	5,348	5,502
Total liabilities	6,848	6,002
Total equity and liabilities	38,564	31,644

Further information:

- The total depreciation charge for the year was £4,458,000.
- Property, plant and equipment costing £878,000 with accumulated depreciation of £334,000 was sold in the year.

- All sales and purchases were on credit. Other expenses were paid for in cash.
- A dividend of £277,000 was paid during the year.

Task 1.1

(a) **Prepare a reconciliation of profit from operations to net cash from operating activities for Eigg Ltd for the year ended 31 March 20X1.**

(Complete the left hand column by writing in the correct line item from the list provided.)

Reconciliation of profit from operations to net cash from operating activities

		£'000
	▼	
Adjustments for:		
	▼	
	▼	
	▼	
	▼	
	▼	
	▼	
Cash generated by operations		
	▼	
	▼	
Net cash from operating activities		

Line items:

Adjustment in respect of inventories
Adjustment in respect of trade payables
Adjustment in respect of trade receivables
Depreciation
Dividends received
Gain on disposal of property, plant and equipment
Interest paid
New bank loans
Proceeds on disposal of property, plant and equipment
Profit after tax
Profit before tax
Profit from operations
Purchases of property, plant and equipment
Tax paid

(b) **Prepare the statement of cash flows for Eigg Ltd for the year ended 31 March 20X1.**

(Complete the left hand column by writing in the correct line item from the list provided.)

Eigg Ltd

Statement of cash flows for the year ended 31 March 20X1

	£'000
Net cash from operating activities	
Investing activities	
▼	
▼	
▼	
Net cash used in investing activities	
Financing activities	
▼	
▼	
▼	
Net cash from financing activities	
Net increase/(decrease) in cash and cash equivalents	
Cash and cash equivalents at the beginning of the year	
Cash and cash equivalents at the end of the year	

Line items:

Adjustment in respect of inventories
Adjustment in respect of trade payables
Adjustment in respect of trade receivables
Dividends paid
Dividends received
New bank loans
Proceeds of share issue
Proceeds on disposal of property, plant and equipment
Purchases of property, plant and equipment

Workings

(Complete the left hand column by writing in the correct narrative from the list provided.)

Proceeds on disposal of property, plant and equipment (PPE)	£'000
▼	
▼	

Narratives:

Carrying amount of PPE sold
Depreciation charge
Gain on disposal
PPE at end of year
PPE at start of year

Purchases of property, plant and equipment (PPE)	£'000
PPE at start of year	
▼	
▼	
▼	
Total PPE additions	

Narratives:

Carrying amount of PPE sold
Depreciation charge
Gain on disposal of PPE
PPE at end of year

Task 1.2

(a) **Draft the statement of changes in equity for Eigg Ltd for the year ended 31 March 20X1.**

(Complete the left hand column by writing in the correct line item from the list provided)

Eigg Ltd

Statement of changes in equity for the year ended 31 March 20X1

	Share Capital £'000	Other Reserves £'000	Retained Earnings £'000	Total Equity £'000
Balance at 1 April 20X0				
Changes in equity for 20X1				
Profit for the year				
Dividends				
Issue of share capital				
Balance at 31 March 20X1				

Task 1.3

(a) **Define the terms 'finance lease' and operating lease' in accordance with IAS 17 *Leases*.**

(b) (i) **Explain how operating leases are accounted for in the financial statements of the lessee.**

   (ii) **Explain how finance leases are accounted for in the financial statements of the lessee at the commencement of the lease term only.**

Task 1.4

(a) **Salmon Ltd has incurred a substantial bad debt amounting to 15% of its profit before tax. In accordance with IAS 1 *Presentation of financial statements*, how should this item be presented in Salmon Ltd's statement of comprehensive income and/or notes to the financial statements?**

Not disclosed separately and treated as a distribution cost	
Disclosed as an extraordinary item	
Not disclosed separately and treated as an administrative expense	
Its nature and amount disclosed separately	

(b) The following expenditures and receipts relate to a new item of manufacturing equipment:

	£
Invoiced price of the equipment	26,454
Delivery costs	1,200
Direct costs of testing that the equipment is operating in the manner intended by management	3,160
Proceeds from the sale of samples produced when testing equipment	(1,600)
Costs of advertising and promotional activities in relation to a new product to be produced by the equipment	1,825
Net costs	31,039

The costs to be included in property, plant and equipment will be:

£31,039	
£29,214	
£30,814	
£32,639	

(c) **Which of the following is the correct definition of investment property in accordance with IAS 40 *Investment property*?**

Property held for use in the production or supply of goods or services	
Property held for sale in the ordinary course of business	
Property held to earn rentals or for capital appreciation or both	
Property held for administrative purposes	

(d) IFRS 3 *Business combinations* identifies key requirements of the acquisition method.

   (i)   identifying the acquirer

   (ii) determining the acquisition date

   (iii) recognising and measuring the identifiable assets acquired, liabilities assumed and any non-controlling interest in the acquiree

   (iv) recognising and measuring goodwill or a gain from a bargain purchase

   Which of the above statements are key requirements of the acquisition method?

Elements (i), (ii) and (iii) only	
Elements (ii), (iii) and (iv) only	
Elements (i), (ii) and (iv) only	
All of the above	

(e) Alton Ltd purchased an item of plant for £440,000 on 1 January 20X5. The useful life was anticipated as being 8 years and the residual value was estimated as £120,000. Alton Ltd depreciates plant on a straight line basis.

   The residual value was still considered to be £120,000 at 1 January 20X9 but the remaining useful life was reassessed to be 5 years.

   What is the depreciation charge for the item of plant for the current year to 31 December 20X9?

£32,000	
£40,000	
£55,000	
£64,000	

(f) IAS 27 *Consolidated and separate financial statements* states that control is presumed to exist when the parent owns, directly or indirectly through subsidiaries, more than half of the shares in an entity unless, in exceptional circumstances, it can be clearly demonstrated that such ownership does not constitute control.

   Is this statement true or false?

True	
False	

Task 1.5

Fenway plc acquired 80% of the issued share capital and voting rights of Boston Ltd on 1 January 20X0 for £5,930,000. At that date Boston Ltd had issued share capital of £3,200,000, share premium of £1,200,000 and retained earnings of £240,000.

Extracts of the statements of financial position for the two companies one year later at 31 December 20X0 are as follows:

	Fenway plc £'000	Boston Ltd £'000
ASSETS		
Non-current assets		
Investment in Boston Ltd	6,230	
Property, plant and equipment	3,145	4,230
	9,375	4,230
Current assets	2,070	1,238
Total assets	11,445	5,468
EQUITY AND LIABILITIES		
Equity		
Share capital	4,000	3,200
Share premium	2,300	1,200
Retained earnings	3,520	340
Total equity	9,820	4,740
Non-current liabilities	900	540
Current liabilities	725	188
Total liabilities	1,625	728
Total equity and liabilities	11,445	5,468

Additional data:

- At 1 January 20X0 the fair value of the non-current assets of Boston Ltd was £800,000 more than the book value. This revaluation has not been recorded in the books of Boston Ltd (ignore any effect on the depreciation for the year).

- On 1 November 20X0, Fenway plc made an interest free long term loan of £300,000 to Boston Ltd, and classified it as part of its investment in Boston Ltd. Boston Ltd has classified the loan as a non-current liability in its financial statements. No loan repayment has yet been made.

- The directors of Fenway plc have concluded that goodwill has been impaired by £200,000 during the year.

- Fenway plc has decided non-controlling interest will be valued at their proportionate share of net assets.

Draft the consolidated statement of financial position for Fenway plc and its subsidiary undertaking as at 31 December 20X0.

Fenway plc

Consolidated statement of financial position as at 31 December 20X0

	£'000
Assets	
Non-current assets:	
Goodwill	
Property, plant and equipment	
Current assets:	
Total assets	
Equity and liabilities	
Equity	
Share capital	
Share premium	
Retained earnings	
Non-controlling interest	
Total equity	
Non-current liabilities	
Current liabilities	
Total liabilities	
Total equity and liabilities	

Workings

(Complete the left hand column by writing in the correct narrative from the list provided.)

Goodwill		£'000
	▼	
	▼	
	▼	
	▼	
	▼	
	▼	
Goodwill		

Narratives:

Impairment
Price paid
Retained earnings – attributable to Fenway plc
Revaluation reserve – attributable to Fenway plc
Share capital – attributable to Fenway plc
Share premium – attributable to Fenway plc

Non-controlling interest (NCI)		£'000
	▼	
	▼	
	▼	
	▼	

Narratives:

Current assets – attributable to NCI
Impairment
Non-current assets – attributable to NCI
Price paid
Retained earnings – attributable to NCI
Revaluation reserve – attributable to NCI
Share capital – attributable to NCI
Share premium – attributable to NCI

Retained earnings		£'000
	▼	
	▼	
	▼	

Narratives:

Boston Ltd – attributable to Fenway plc
Fenway plc
Impairment
Revaluation

Section 2

Task 2.1

You have been given the financial statements of Elgin Ltd for the year ending 31 December 20X0. You are now required to prepare financial ratios to assist your manager in her analysis of the company.

Elgin Ltd's statement of comprehensive income and statement of financial position are set out below.

Elgin Ltd – Statement of comprehensive income for the year ended 31 December 20X0

	£'000
Continuing operations	
Revenue	74,300
Cost of sales	(46,429)
Gross profit	27,871
Distribution costs	(9,960)
Administrative expenses	(8,140)
Profit from operations	9,771
Finance costs	(1,656)
Profit before tax	8,115
Tax	(1,742)
Profit for the period from continuing operations	6,373

Elgin Ltd – Statement of financial position as at 31 December 20X0

	20X1
	£'000
ASSETS	
Non-current assets	
Property, plant and equipment	64,300
Current assets	
Inventories	14,260
Trade receivables	12,542
Cash and cash equivalents	2,146
	28,948
Total assets	93,248
EQUITY AND LIABILITIES	
Equity	
Ordinary share capital (£1 shares)	40,000
Retained earnings	18,650
Total equity	58,650
Non-current liabilities	
Bank loans	20,400
	20,400
Current liabilities	
Trade payables	12,456
Tax liabilities	1,742
	14,198
Total liabilities	34,598
Total equity and liabilities	93,248

(a) **State the formulae that are used to calculate each of the following ratios:**

(Write in the correct formula from the list provided)

(i) Earnings per share	▼

Formulae:

Profit after tax/Total equity

Profit after tax/Number of issued ordinary shares

Profit from operations/Number of issued ordinary shares

Profit from operations/Total equity

(ii) Operating profit percentage	▼

Formulae:

Profit from operations/Total equity + Non-current liabilities × 100

Profit from operations/Total assets × 100

Profit from operations/Revenue × 100

Profit from operations/Finance costs × 100

(iii) Return on total assets	▼

Formulae:

Profit after tax/Total assets × 100

Profit from operations/Total equity + Non-current liabilities × 100

Profit from operations/Total assets × 100

Profit after tax/Total equity + non-current liabilities × 100

(iv) Acid test ratio	▼

Formulae:

Current assets – inventories/Current liabilities

Total assets/Total liabilities

Total assets – inventories/Total liabilities

Current assets/Current liabilities

(v) **Trade payables payment period**	▼

Formulae:

Trade payables/Revenue × 365

Total liabilities/Cost of sales × 365

Trade payables/Cost of sales × 365

Trade receivables/Revenue × 365

(vi) **Inventory holding period (days)**	▼

Formulae:

Inventories/Revenue × 365

Inventories/Cost of sales × 365

Revenue/Inventories × 365

Cost of sales/Inventories × 365

(vii) **Asset turnover (net assets)**	▼

Formulae:

Revenue/Total assets

Revenue/Current assets

Revenue/Total assets – current liabilities

Net assets/Operating profit

(viii) **Interest cover**	▼

Formulae:

Profit before tax/Finance costs

Profit from operations/Finance costs

Profit after tax/Finance costs

Revenue/Finance costs

(b) **Calculate the ratios to the nearest ONE DECIMAL PLACE.**

(i)	**Earnings per share** (there have been no share issues during the year)		pence
(ii)	**Operating profit percentage**		%
(iii)	**Return on total assets**		%
(iv)	**Acid test ratio**		:1
(v)	**Trade payables payment period**		days
(vi)	**Inventory holding period (days)**		days
(vii)	**Asset turnover (net assets)**		times
(viii)	**Interest cover**		times

Task 2.2

Mike Rivers, the managing director of Humber Ltd, is concerned that his company is not managing its working capital efficiently. He has sent you an e-mail asking for your assistance in identifying any problem area(s) and for your suggestions as to how these can be remedied.

You have calculated the following ratios in respect of Humber Ltd's latest financial statements and have also obtained the industry average for each of these for comparative purposes.

	Humber Ltd	Industry average
Current ratio	9.3:1	2.8:1
Inventory holding period	38 days	30 days
Trade receivables collection period	72 days	54 days
Trade payables payment period	57 days	63 days

Prepare an e-mail reply to Mike that includes:

(a) **Comments on whether Humber Ltd has performed better or worse, in respect of the calculated ratios, as compared to the industry averages.**

(b) **THREE suggestions as to how the working capital of Humber Ltd could be more effectively managed.**

Task 2.3

(a) **What is the objective of general purpose financial reporting according to the IASB *Conceptual Framework for Financial Reporting*?**

(b) **Give THREE reasons why users might be interested in the information contained in financial statements.**

AAT practice assessment 2
Eigg Ltd
Answers

Section 1

Task 1.1

(a) **Eigg Ltd**

Reconciliation of profit from operations to net cash from operating activities

	£'000
Profit from operations	6,840
Adjustments for:	
Depreciation	4,458
Dividends received	(120)
Gain on disposal of property, plant and equipment	(448)
Adjustment in respect of inventories (5,914 – 4,928)	(986)
Adjustment in respect of trade receivables (5,376 – 4,480)	896
Adjustment in respect of trade payables (4,435 – 2,464)	(1,971)
Cash generated by operations	8,669
Tax paid	(887)
Interest paid	(105)
Net cash from operating activities	7,677

(b) **Eigg Ltd**

Statement of cash flows for the year ended 31 March 20X1

	£'000
Net cash from operating activities	7,677
Investing activities	
Purchases of property, plant and equipment (W)	(11,552)
Proceeds on disposal of property, plant and equipment (W)	992
Dividends received	120
Net cash used in investing activities	(10,440)

	£'000
Financing activities	
Proceeds of share issue (7,500 – 5,000)	2,500
New bank loans (1,500 – 500)	1,000
Dividends paid	(277)
Net cash from financing activities	3,223
Net increase/(decrease) in cash and cash equivalents	460
Cash and cash equivalents at the beginning of the year	(180)
Cash and cash equivalents at the end of the year	280

Workings

Proceeds on disposal of property, plant and equipment (PPE)	£'000
Carrying amount of PPE sold	544
Gain on disposal	448
	992

Purchases of property, plant and equipment (PPE)	£'000
PPE at start of year	21,340
Depreciation charge	(4,458)
Carrying amount of PPE sold	(544)
PPE at end of year	(27,890)
Total PPE additions	(11,552)

Task 1.2

(a) **Eigg Ltd**

Statement of changes in equity for the year ended 31 March 20X1

	Share Capital £'000	Other Reserves £'000	Retained Earnings £'000	Total Equity £'000
Balance at 1 April 20X0	3,000	2,000	20,642	25,642
Changes in equity for 20X1				
Profit for the year	0	0	3,851	3,851
Dividends	0	0	(277)	(277)
Issue of share capital	1,500	1,000	0	2,500
Balance at 31 March 20X1	4,500	3,000	24,216	31,716

Task 1.3

Note: based on the information available at the time this book was written, we anticipate that this task would be human marked in the real assessment.

(a) A finance lease is a lease that transfers substantially all the risks and rewards incidental to ownership of an asset to the lessee.

An operating lease is a lease other than a finance lease (that is, a lease that does not transfer the risks and rewards of ownership of an asset to the lessee).

(b) (i) If an entity leases an asset under an operating lease, the lease payments are charged to profit or loss on a straight line basis unless another systematic basis is more appropriate. The leased asset is not recognised in the statement of financial position.

(ii) If an entity leases an asset under a finance lease, it recognises the lease as an asset in the statement of financial position. It also recognises a liability for the outstanding lease payments. The asset and the liability are measured at the fair value of the leased asset, or the present value of the minimum lease payments (if this is lower).

BPP
LEARNING MEDIA

Task 1.4

(a)

Not disclosed separately and treated as a distribution cost	
Disclosed as an extraordinary item	
Not disclosed separately and treated as an administrative expense	
Its nature and amount disclosed separately	✓

(b)

£31,039	
£29,214	✓
£30,814	
£32,639	

	£
Invoiced price of the equipment	26,454
Delivery costs	1,200
Direct costs of testing that the equipment is operating in the manner intended by management	3,160
Proceeds from the sale of samples produced when testing equipment	(1,600)
Net costs	29,214

Only costs that are directly attributable to bringing the asset to the location and condition necessary for it to be capable of operating in the manner intended by management may be included.

(c)

Property held for use in the production or supply of goods or services	
Property held for sale in the ordinary course of business	
Property held to earn rentals or for capital appreciation or both	✓
Property held for administrative purposes	

(d)

Elements (i), (ii) and (iii) only	
Elements (ii), (iii) and (iv) only	
Elements (i), (ii) and (iv) only	
All of the above	✓

(e)

£32,000	✓
£40,000	
£55,000	
£64,000	

Net carrying amount at 1 January 20X9:

	£
Cost	440,000
Depreciation ((440,000 – 120,000) ÷ 8 × 4)	(160,000)
	280,000
Charge for 20X9 (280,000 – 120,000 ÷ 5)	32,000

(f)

True	
False	✓

IAS 27 states that control is presumed to exist when the parent owns, directly or indirectly through subsidiaries, more than half of the **voting power** in an entity unless, in exceptional circumstances, it can be clearly demonstrated that such ownership does not constitute control. Not all shares carry votes. Sometimes there is more than one class of equity (voting) shares with different voting rights.

Task 1.5

Fenway plc

Consolidated statement of financial position as at 31 December 20X0

	£'000
Assets	
Non-current assets:	
Goodwill (W)	1,378
Property, plant and equipment (3,145 + 4,230 + 800)	8,175
	9,553
Current assets:	3,308
Total assets	12,861
Equity and liabilities	
Equity	
Share capital	4,000
Share premium	2,300
Retained earnings (W)	3,400
Non-controlling interest (W)	1,108
Total equity	10,808
Non-current liabilities (900 + 540 – 300)	1,140
Current liabilities	913
Total liabilities	2,053
Total equity and liabilities	12,861

Workings

Goodwill	£'000
Price paid (6,230 – 300)	5,930
Share capital – attributable to Fenway plc (80% x 3,200)	(2,560)
Share premium – attributable to Fenway plc (80% × 1,200)	(960)
Revaluation reserve – attributable to Fenway plc (80% × 800)	(640)
Retained earnings – attributable to Fenway plc (80% × 240)	(192)
Impairment	(200)
Goodwill	1,378

Non-controlling interest (NCI)	£'000
Share capital – attributable to NCI (20% x 3,200)	640
Share premium – attributable to NCI (20% × 1,200)	240
Revaluation reserve – attributable to NCI (20% × 800)	160
Retained earnings – attributable to NCI (20% × 340)	68
	1,108

Retained earnings	£'000
Fenway plc	3,520
Boston Ltd – attributable to Fenway plc (80% × (340 – 240))	80
Impairment	(200)
	3,400

Section 2

Task 2.1

(a) **Formulae used to calculate the ratios**

(i) Earnings per share	$\dfrac{\text{Profit after tax}}{\text{Number of issued ordinary shares}}$
(ii) Operating profit percentage	$\dfrac{\text{Profit from operations}}{\text{Revenue}} \times 100\%$
(iii) Return on total assets	$\dfrac{\text{Profit from operations}}{\text{Total assets}} \times 100\%$
(iv) Acid test ratio	$\dfrac{\text{Current assets - inventories}}{\text{Current liabilities}}$
(v) Trade payables payment period	$\dfrac{\text{Trade payables}}{\text{Cost of sales}} \times 365$
(vi) Inventory holding period (days)	$\dfrac{\text{Inventories}}{\text{Cost of sales}} \times 365$
(vii) Asset turnover (net assets)	$\dfrac{\text{Revenue}}{\text{Total assets} - \text{current liabilities}}$
(viii) Interest cover	$\dfrac{\text{Profit from operations}}{\text{Finance costs}}$

(b) Calculation of the ratios

(i)	**Earnings per share** $\dfrac{6,373}{40,000}$		15.9	pence
(ii)	**Operating profit percentage** $\dfrac{9,771}{74,300} \times 100$		13.2	%
(iii)	**Return on total assets** $\dfrac{9,771}{93,248} \times 100$		10.5	%
(iv)	**Acid test ratio** $\dfrac{28,948 - 14,260}{14,198}$		1.0	:1
(v)	**Trade payables payment period** $\dfrac{12,456}{46,429} \times 365$		97.9	days
(vi)	**Inventory holding period (days)** $\dfrac{14,260}{46,429} \times 365$		112.1	days
(vii)	**Asset turnover (net assets)** $\dfrac{74,300}{93,248 - 14,198}$		0.9	times
(viii)	**Interest cover** $\dfrac{9,771}{1,656}$		5.9	times

Task 2.2

Note: based on the information available at the time this book was written, we anticipate that this task would be human marked in the real assessment.

From: aatstudent@dfsexam

To: mikerivers@isp.com

Date: 1 September 20X1

Subject: Working capital of Humber Ltd

As requested, I have compared the accounting ratios computed from the financial statements of Humber Ltd with the industry averages. I set out my comments and suggestions below.

(a) Current ratio

Humber Ltd has a much 'better' current ratio than the industry average. This means that it has significantly more current assets with which to meet its current liabilities as they fall due than other businesses in the same industry. However, a current ratio of 9.3:1 is extremely high. Taken together with the other ratios, it suggests that current assets may consist mainly of inventories and trade receivables rather than cash. This normally indicates inefficient management of working capital.

Inventory holding period

The inventory holding period is worse than the industry average. Humber Ltd holds its inventories for a longer period than other businesses in the industry. Possible reasons for this include falling sales and/or poor inventory control. Alternatively, Hunter Ltd's inventories may include a high proportion of slow moving or obsolete items.

Trade receivables collection period

This is significantly worse than the industry average. On average, Humber Ltd's customers take 18 days longer to pay their debts than those of similar businesses and this may lead to cash flow problems. Again, there are several possible reasons for the long collection period. Management may be deliberately offering generous credit terms or trade receivables could include a high proportion of bad debts. The problem may simply be caused by poor credit control.

Trade payables payment period

On average, Humber Ltd pays its suppliers sooner than other businesses in the industry. This may be as a result of pressure from particular suppliers or alternatively management may be taking advantage of settlement discounts. Prompt payment may lead to better relationships and can be viewed as a good sign in that the company appears to have the cash available. However, when taken together with the other ratios the short payment period is another indication of poor working capital management which may lead to cash flow problems.

(b) **How working capital management might be improved**

Inventory levels could be reduced by reducing selling prices to get rid of slow moving items and/or improving inventory control and purchasing so that large levels of inventories are not allowed to build up.

Trade receivables could be reduced by better credit control. For example, management could reduce credit periods for certain customers or introduce/improve procedures for collecting outstanding amounts.

Management could also increase the length of time taken to pay suppliers by taking advantage of the full credit period available and/or negotiating longer credit periods.

Task 2.3

Note: based on the information available at the time this book was written, we anticipate that this task would be human marked in the real assessment.

(a) The objective of general purpose financial reporting is to provide financial information about the reporting entity that is useful to existing and potential investors, lenders and other creditors in making decisions about providing resources to the entity.

(b) The introduction to the *Conceptual Framework* lists the following decisions that users may need to make, based on the information in general purpose financial statements prepared for external users:

- to decide when to buy, hold or sell an equity investment.
- to assess the stewardship or accountability of management.
- to assess the ability of the entity to pay and provide other benefits to its employees.
- to assess the security for amounts lent to the entity.
- to determine taxation policies.
- to determine distributable profits and dividends.
- to prepare and use national income statistics.
- to regulate the activities of entities.

Tutorial note: Candidates only needed to give THREE of the above.

BPP practice assessment 1
Ricschtein Ltd
Time allowed: 2½ hours

Section 1

The following information is relevant to Task 1.1 and Task 1.2

You have been asked to help prepare the financial statements of Ricschtein Ltd for the year ended 31 March 20X7. The company's trial balance as at 31 March 20X7 is shown below.

Ricschtein Ltd

Trial balance as at 31 March 20X7

	Debit £'000	Credit £'000
Share capital		7,000
Trade payables		2,236
Property, plant and equipment – cost	39,371	
Property, plant and equipment – accumulated depreciation		13,892
Trade receivables	4,590	
Accruals		207
7% bank loan repayable 20Y2		14,000
Cash at bank	423	
Retained earnings		9,552
Interest	490	
Sales		36,724
Purchases	21,749	
Distribution costs	5,517	
Administrative expenses	3,904	
Loss on business disposed of during the year	347	
Inventories as at 1 April 20X6	6,120	
Dividends paid	1,100	
	83,611	83,611

Further information:

- The share capital of the company consists of ordinary shares with a nominal value of £1.

- At the beginning of the year the issued share capital was 7,000,000 ordinary shares. At the end of the year another 3,000,000 ordinary shares were issued at a price of £3.00 per share. Due to a misunderstanding about the date of the share issue, this has not been accounted for in the ledger accounts in the trial balance.

- The inventories at the close of business on 31 March 20X7 cost £7,304,000.

- Administrative expenses of £87,000 relating to February 20X7 have not been included in the trial balance.

- The company paid £36,000 insurance costs in June 20X6, which covered the period from 1 July 20X6 to 30 June 20X7. This was included in the administrative expenses in the trial balance.

- Interest on the bank loan for the last six months of the year has not been included in the accounts in the trial balance.

- The corporation tax charge for the year has been calculated as £1,170,000.

- The loss on a business disposed of during the year relates to a retail operation sold in the year. All of the other operations are continuing operations.

Task 1.1

(a) **Draft the statement of comprehensive income for Ricschtein Ltd for the year ended 31 March 20X7.**

Ricschtein Ltd

Statement of comprehensive income for the year ended 31 March 20X7

	£'000
Continuing operations	
Revenue	
Cost of sales	
Gross profit	
Distribution costs	
Administrative expenses	
Profit/(loss) from operations	
Finance costs	
Profit/(loss) before tax	
Tax	
Profit/(loss) for the period from continuing operations	
Discontinued operations	
Profit/(loss) for the period from discontinued operations	
Profit for the period	

Workings

(Complete the left hand column by writing in the correct narrative from the list provided.)

302

Cost of sales		£'000
	▼	
	▼	
	▼	

Picklist for narratives:

Accruals
Closing inventories
Opening inventories
Prepayments
Purchases

Administrative expenses		£'000
	▼	
	▼	
	▼	

Picklist for narratives:

Accruals
Administrative expenses
Prepayments

(b) **Draft the statement of changes in equity for Ricschtein Ltd for the year ended 31 March 20X7.**

Ricschtein Ltd

Statement of changes in equity for the year ended 31 March 20X7

	Share Capital £'000	Other Reserves £'000	Retained Earnings £'000	Total Equity £'000
Balance at 1 April 20X6				
Changes in equity for 20X7				
Total comprehensive income				
Dividends				
Issue of share capital				
Balance at 31 March 20X7				

Task 1.2

(a) **Draft the statement of financial position for Ricschtein Ltd as at 31 March 20X7.**

(Complete the left hand column by writing in the correct line item from the list)

Ricschtein Ltd
Statement of financial position as at 31 March 20X7

	£'000
Assets	
Non-current assets:	
▼	
Current assets:	
▼	
▼	
▼	
Total assets	
Equity and liabilities:	
Equity	
▼	
▼	
▼	
Total equity	
Non-current liabilities:	
▼	
Current liabilities:	
▼	
▼	
Total liabilities	
Total equity and liabilities	

Picklist for line items:
Bank loan
Cash and cash equivalents
Inventories
Property, plant and equipment
Retained earnings
Share capital
Share premium
Tax payable
Trade and other payables
Trade and other receivables

Workings

(Complete the left hand column by writing in the correct narrative from the list provided.)

Trade and other receivables		£'000
	▼	
	▼	

Picklist for narratives:

Accruals: trial balance
Additional administrative expenses accrual
Additional administrative expenses prepaid
Additional finance costs accrual
Additional finance costs prepaid
Trade and other payables
Trade and other receivables

Retained earnings		£'000
	▼	
	▼	
	▼	

Picklist for narratives:

Dividends paid
Premium paid on share issue
Profit/(loss) for the period from continuing operations
Retained earnings at 1 April 20X6
Total profit for the year

Trade and other payables		£'000
	▼	
	▼	
	▼	
	▼	

Picklist for narratives:

Accruals: trial balance
Additional administrative expenses accrual
Additional administrative expenses prepaid
Additional finance costs accrual
Additional finance costs prepaid
Dividends
Tax payable
Trade and other payables
Trade and other receivables

Task 1.3

Ricschtein Ltd purchases goods for resale. The directors of the company would like you to clarify the accounting treatment of inventories and when to recognise revenue arising from the sale of goods. Answer the following queries of the directors.

(a) **What are inventories according to IAS 2 *Inventories*? How are inventories measured? What is included in the cost of inventories?**

(b) **What is revenue according to IAS 18 *Revenue*? How should it be measured? When should revenue be recognised?**

Task 1.4

(a) According to IAS 8 *Accounting policies, changes in accounting estimates and errors* a change in depreciation method is:

A change in an accounting policy	
A change in an accounting estimate	

(b) At the beginning of the year, Broad Ltd had the following balance:

Accrued interest payable   £12,000 credit

During the year, Broad Ltd charged interest payable of £41,000 to profit or loss. The closing balance on accrued interest payable account at the end of the year was £15,000 credit.

How much interest paid should Broad Ltd show in its statement of cash flows for the year?

£38,000	
£41,000	
£44,000	
£53,000	

(c) **Which of the following statements are correct, according to IAS 36 *Impairment of assets*?**

(i)   All non-current assets must be reviewed for impairment annually.

(ii) An impairment loss must be recognised immediately in profit or loss, except that all or part of a loss on a revalued asset should be charged against any related revaluation surplus.

(iii) If individual assets cannot be tested for impairment, it may be necessary to test a group of assets as a unit.

1 and 2 only	
1 and 3 only	
2 and 3 only	
1, 2 and 3	

(d) A company leases some plant on 1 January 20X4. The fair value of the plant is £9,000, and the company leases it for four years, paying four annual instalments of £3,000 beginning on 31 December 20X4.

The company uses the sum of the digits method to allocate interest.

What is the interest charge for the year ended 31 December 20X5?

£600	
£750	
£900	
£1,000	

(e) **Which of the following events after the reporting period would normally be classified as a *non-adjusting event*, according to IAS 10 *Events after the reporting period*?**

(i) The company announced a plan to discontinue an operation

(ii) A customer was discovered to be insolvent

1 only	
2 only	
Both 1 and 2	
Neither 1 nor 2	

(f) Deep Ltd owns an office building which is surplus to requirements and is currently vacant. The directors intend to refurbish the building and then sell it.

The building is an investment property.

Is this statement true or false?

True	
False	

Task 1.5

The Managing Director of Harris plc has asked you to prepare the statement of financial position for the group. Harris plc has one subsidiary, Skye Ltd. The statements of financial position of the two companies as at 31 March 20X8 are set out below.

Statements of financial position as at 31 March 20X8

	Harris plc £'000	Skye Ltd £'000
Non-current assets		
Property, plant and equipment	47,875	31,913
Investment in Skye Ltd	32,000	
	79,875	31,913
Current assets		
Inventories	25,954	4,555
Trade and other receivables	14,343	3,656
Cash and cash equivalents	1,956	47
	42,253	8,258
Total assets	122,128	40,171
Equity and liabilities		
Equity		
Share capital	57,000	15,000
Retained earnings	26,160	14,340
Total equity	83,160	29,340
Non-current liabilities		
Long-term loans	20,000	7,000
Current liabilities		
Trade and other payables	14,454	3,685
Tax liabilities	4,514	146
	18,968	3,831
Total liabilities	38,968	10,831
Total equity and liabilities	122,128	40,171

Further information:

- The share capital of Skye Ltd consists of ordinary shares of £1 each. Ownership of these shares carries voting rights in Skye Ltd.
- Harris plc acquired 9,000,000 shares in Skye Ltd on 1 April 20X7.
- At 1 April 20X7 the balance of retained earnings of Skye Ltd was £11,260,000.
- The directors of Harris plc have concluded that goodwill has been impaired by £4,000,000 during the year.
- Non-controlling interest is measured as the proportionate share of the fair value of Skye Ltd's net assets.

Draft a consolidated statement of financial position for Harris plc and its subsidiary as at 31 March 20X8.

Harris plc

Consolidated statement of financial position as at 31 March 20X8

	£'000
Assets	
Non-current assets:	
Intangible assets: goodwill	
Property, plant and equipment	
Current assets:	
Inventories	
Trade and other receivables	
Cash and cash equivalents	
Total assets	
Equity and liabilities	
Equity attributable to owners of the parent	
Share capital	
Retained earnings	
Non-controlling interest	
Total equity	
Non-current liabilities:	
Long-term loans	
Current liabilities:	
Trade and other payables	
Tax liabilities	
Total liabilities	
Total equity and liabilities	

Workings

(Complete the left hand column by writing in the correct narrative from the list provided.)

Goodwill		£'000
	▾	
	▾	
	▾	
	▾	

Picklist for narratives:

Impairment
Price paid
Retained earnings – attributable to Harris plc
Share capital – attributable to Harris plc

Retained earnings		£'000
	▾	
	▾	
	▾	

Picklist for narratives:

Harris plc
Impairment
Skye Ltd – attributable to Harris plc

Non-controlling interest (NCI)		£'000
	▾	
	▾	

Picklist for narratives:

Current assets – attributable to NCI
Impairment
Non-current assets – attributable to NCI
Price paid
Retained earnings – attributable to NCI
Share capital – attributable to NCI

Section 2

Task 2.1

David Alexander is a shareholder in Cairngorm Ltd. He has asked you to assist him by calculating ratios in respect of the financial statements for the year ended 31 March 20X9. The financial statements of Cairngorm Ltd are set out below:

Cairngorm Ltd

Statement of comprehensive income for the year ended 31 March 20X9

	£'000
Continuing operations	
Revenue	14,800
Cost of sales	(7,770)
Gross profit	7,030
Distribution costs	(3,700)
Administrative expenses	(2,072)
Profit from operations	1,258
Finance costs	(630)
Profit before tax	628
Tax	(294)
Profit for the period from continuing operations	334

Cairngorm Ltd

Statement of financial position as at 31 March 20X9

	£'000
Non-current assets	
Property, plant and equipment	18,916
Current assets	
Inventories	1,632
Trade and other receivables	1,776
Cash and cash equivalents	0
	3,408
Total assets	22,324
Equity and liabilities	
Equity	
Share capital	6,500
Retained earnings	5,138
Total equity	11,638
Non-current liabilities	
Bank loans	9,000
Current liabilities	
Trade payables	855
Tax liabilities	294
Bank overdraft	537
	1,686
Total liabilities	10,686
Total equity and liabilities	22,324

(a) **State the formulae that are used to calculate the following ratios:**

(Write in the correct formula from the list provided)

(i) **Gross profit percentage**	▼

Formulae:

Gross profit/Total equity × 100

Gross profit/Revenue × 100

Gross profit/Total assets × 100

Gross profit/Total assets – current liabilities

(ii) **Return on total assets**	▼

Formulae:

Profit after tax/Total assets × 100

Profit from operations/Total assets × 100

Profit from operations/Total equity × 100

Profit from operations/Total equity + Non-current liabilities × 100

(iii) **Inventory holding period**	▼

Formulae:

Inventories/cost of sales × 365

Inventories/revenue × 365

Cost of sales/inventories × 365

Revenue/inventories × 365

(iv) **Trade receivables collection period**	▼

Formulae:

Trade payables/Cost of sales × 365

Trade receivables/Cost of sales × 365

Revenue/Trade receivables × 365

Trade receivables/Revenue × 365

(v) **Trade payables payment period**	▼

Formulae:

Trade payables/Revenue × 365

Trade payables/Cost of sales × 365

Revenue/Trade payables × 365

Cost of sales/Trade payables × 365

(vi) **Working capital cycle**	▼

Formulae:

Current assets/Current liabilities

Current assets – inventories/Current liabilities

Inventory days + Receivables days – Payables days

Inventory days + Receivables days + Payables days

(vii) **Gearing**	▼

Formulae:

Current assets/Current liabilities

Revenue/Total assets – current liabilities

Non-current liabilities/Total equity + non-current liabilities

Profit after tax/Number of issued ordinary shares

(viii) **Interest cover**	▼

Formulae:

Finance costs/profit from operations

Finance costs/revenue

Profit from operations/finance costs

Revenue/finance costs

(b) Calculate the following ratios to the nearest ONE DECIMAL PLACE.

(i)	Gross profit percentage	%
(ii)	Return on total assets	%
(iii)	Inventory holding period (days)	days
(iv)	Trade receivables collection period	days
(v)	Trade payables payment period	days
(vi)	Working capital cycle	days
(vii)	Gearing ratio	%
(viii)	Interest cover	times

Task 2.2

John Brams is a shareholder of Ma Leer Ltd. He has obtained some ratios that are based on the financial statements of the company for the last two years. He is interested in how the directors have managed the business in the past year and in the company's financial performance. You have been asked to analyse the financial performance of the company using the ratios computed. The ratios John has obtained are set out below. Sales revenue has remained relatively stable throughout 20X4 and 20X5.

Ratio	20X5	20X4
Return on capital employed	15%	19%
Gross profit percentage	46%	42%
Operating profit percentage	20%	22%
Expense/revenue percentage	26%	24%
Asset turnover (based on net assets)	0.75	0.86

Prepare a report for John Brams that includes the following.

(a) **Your comments on the financial performance of Ma Leer Ltd for the two years based on your analysis of the ratios and what this tells you about the company**

(b) **Your opinion, with reasons based on your analysis of the ratios above, as to how well the company has been managed during the year.**

Task 2.3

(a) **Set out the accounting equation and define the elements in the equation.**

(b) **Briefly explain how the profit for the year affects the elements in the accounting equation.**

BPP practice assessment 1
Ricschtein Ltd
Answers

Section 1

Task 1.1

(a) **Ricschtein Ltd**

Statement of comprehensive income for the year ended 31 March 20X7

	£'000
Continuing operations	
Revenue	36,724
Cost of sales (W)	(20,565)
Gross profit	16,159
Distribution costs	(5,517)
Administrative expenses (W)	(3,982)
Profit/(loss) from operations	6,660
Finance costs (490 + 490)	(980)
Profit/(loss) before tax	5,680
Tax	(1,170)
Profit/(loss) for the period from continuing operations	4,510
Discontinued operations	
Profit/(loss) for the period from discontinued operations	(347)
Profit for the period	4,163

Workings

Cost of sales	£'000
Opening inventories	6,120
Purchases	21,749
Closing inventories	(7,304)
	20,565

Administrative expenses	£'000
Administrative expenses	3,904
Accruals	87
Prepayments (36 × 3/12)	(9)
	3,982

(b) **Ricschtein Ltd**

Statement of changes in equity for the year ended 31 March 20X7

	Share Capital £'000	Other Reserves £'000	Retained Earnings £'000	Total Equity £'000
Balance at 1 April 20X6	7,000	0	9,552	16,552
Changes in equity for 20X7				
Total comprehensive income	0	0	4,163	4,163
Dividends	0	0	(1,100)	(1,100)
Issue of share capital	3,000	6,000	0	9,000
Balance at 31 March 20X7	10,000	6,000	12,615	28,615

Task 1.2

(a) **Ricschtein Ltd**

Statement of financial position as at 31 March 20X7

	£'000
Assets	
Non-current assets:	
Property, plant and equipment (39,371 – 13,892)	25,479
Current assets:	
Inventories	7,304
Trade and other receivables (W)	4,599
Cash and cash equivalents (423 + 9,000)	9,423
	21,326
Total assets	46,805
Equity and liabilities:	
Equity	
Share capital (7,000 + 3,000)	10,000
Share premium	6,000
Retained earnings (W)	12,615
Total equity	28,615
Non-current liabilities:	
Bank loan	14,000
Current liabilities:	
Trade and other payables (W)	3,020
Tax payable	1,170
	4,190
Total liabilities	18,190
Total equity and liabilities	46,805

Workings

Trade and other receivables	£'000
Trade and other receivables	4,590
Additional administrative expenses prepaid	9
	4,599

Retained earnings	£'000
Retained earnings at 1 April 20X6	9,552
Total profit for the year	4,163
Dividends paid	(1,100)
	12,615

Trade and other payables	£'000
Trade and other payables	2,236
Accruals: trial balance	207
Additional administrative expenses accrual	87
Additional finance costs accrual	490
	3,020

Task 1.3

Note: based on the information available at the time this book was written, we anticipate that this task would be human marked in the real assessment.

(a) Inventories are assets held by an entity that are for sale in the ordinary course of business.

IAS 2 *Inventories* requires inventories to be recognised in the financial statements at the lower of cost and net realisable value.

The cost of inventories should include the purchase price, import duties and other taxes, and transport, handling and other costs directly attributable to the acquisition of the finished goods. Essentially, all costs incurred in bringing the inventories to their present location and condition can be included.

(b) IAS 18 *Revenue* defines revenue as the 'gross inflows of economic benefits received and receivable by the entity on its own account'.

IAS 18 states that revenue should be measured at the 'fair value of the consideration received or receivable'.

Revenue from the sale of goods should be recognised when the following conditions have been satisfied:

(i) The entity has transferred to the buyer the significant risks and rewards of ownership of the goods

(ii) The entity retains neither continuing managerial involvement nor effective control over the goods sold

(iii) The amount of revenue can be measured reliably

(iv) It is probable that economic benefits associated with the transaction will flow to the entity and

(v) The costs incurred or to be incurred in respect of the transaction can be measured reliably.

Task 1.4

(a)

A change in an accounting policy	
A change in an accounting estimate	✓

(b)

£38,000	✓
£41,000	
£44,000	
£53,000	

	£
Opening balance	12,000
Profit or loss	41,000
Closing balance	(15,000)
	38,000

(c)

1 and 2 only	
1 and 3 only	
2 and 3 only	✓
1, 2 and 3	

Statement 1 is incorrect. In most cases, an impairment review need only be carried out if there is some indication that impairment has incurred. Only goodwill and intangible assets with an indefinite useful life must be reviewed annually.

(d)

£600	
£750	
£900	✓
£1,000	

The interest charge is 3/10 × £3,000

(e)

1 only	✓
2 only	
Both 1 and 2	
Neither 1 nor 2	

(f)

True	
False	✓

A property held for sale in the ordinary course of business is not an investment property.

Task 1.5

Harris plc

Consolidated statement of financial position as at 31 March 20X8

	£'000
Assets	
Non-current assets:	
Intangible assets: goodwill (W)	12,244
Property, plant and equipment	79,788
	92,032
Current assets:	
Inventories	30,509
Trade and other receivables	17,999
Cash and cash equivalents	2,003
	50,511
Total assets	142,543
Equity and liabilities	
Equity attributable to owners of the parent	
Share capital	57,000
Retained earnings (W)	24,008
	81,008
Non-controlling interest (W)	11,736
Total equity	92,744
Non-current liabilities:	
Long-term loans	27,000
Current liabilities:	
Trade and other payables	18,139
Tax liabilities	4,660
	22,799
Total liabilities	49,799
Total equity and liabilities	142,543

Workings

Note: **Group structure**

Harris plc owns 60% of Skye Ltd (9,000,000/15,000,000)

Goodwill	£'000
Price paid	32,000
Share capital – attributable to Harris plc (60% × 15,000)	(9,000)
Retained earnings – attributable to Harris plc (60% × 11,260)	(6,756)
Impairment	(4,000)
	12,244

Retained earnings	£'000
Harris plc	26,160
Skye Ltd – attributable to Harris plc (60% × (14,340 – 11,260))	1,848
Impairment	(4,000)
	24,008

Non-controlling interest (NCI)	£'000
Share capital – attributable to NCI (40% × 15,000)	6,000
Retained earnings – attributable to NCI (40% × 14,340)	5,736
	11,736

Section 2

Task 2.1

(a) **Formulae used to calculate the ratios**

(i)	Gross profit percentage	$\dfrac{\text{Gross profit}}{\text{Revenue}} \times 100\%$
(ii)	Return on total assets	$\dfrac{\text{Profit from operations}}{\text{Total assets}} \times 100\%$
(iii)	Inventory holding period	$\dfrac{\text{Inventories}}{\text{Cost of sales}} \times 365$
(iv)	Trade receivables collection period	$\dfrac{\text{Trade receivables}}{\text{Revenue}} \times 365$
(v)	Trade payables payment period	$\dfrac{\text{Trade payables}}{\text{Cost of sales}} \times 365$
(vi)	Working capital cycle	Inventory days + Receivables days – Payables days
(vii)	Gearing ratio	$\dfrac{\text{Non-current liabilities}}{\text{Total equity + non-current liabilities}} \times 100\%$
(viii)	Interest cover	$\dfrac{\text{Profit from operations}}{\text{Finance costs}}$

(b) Calculation of the ratios

(i)	Gross profit percentage $\dfrac{7,030}{14,800} \times 100$	47.5	%
(ii)	Return on total assets $\dfrac{1,258}{22,324} \times 100$	5.6	%
(iii)	Inventory holding period (days) $\dfrac{1,632}{7,770} \times 365$	76.7	days
(iv)	Trade receivables collection period $\dfrac{1,776}{14,800} \times 365$	43.8	days
(v)	Trade payables payment period $\dfrac{855}{7,770} \times 365$	40.2	days
(vi)	Working capital cycle 76.7 + 43.8 − 40.2	80.3	days
(vii)	Gearing ratio $\dfrac{9,000}{11,638 + 9,000} \times 100$	43.6	%
(viii)	Interest cover $\dfrac{1,258}{630}$	2.0	times

Task 2.2

Note: based on the information available at the time this book was written, we anticipate that this task would be human marked in the real assessment.

REPORT

To: John Brams

From: Accounting Technician

Subject: Financial performance of Ma Leer Ltd

Date:

As requested, I have analysed the financial performance of Ma Leer Ltd, based on the ratios provided.

(a) The financial performance of the company

Return on capital employed

Return on capital employed has deteriorated significantly during the year. This suggests that investors are not obtaining as a good a return on the capital that they have invested as in previous years. There are two reasons for this. The company is slightly less profitable in 20X5 than it was in 20X4. In addition the company is not generating as much profit (or return) from its capital (assets) as in the previous year.

Gross profit percentage

This has improved significantly during the year. There could be several reasons for this. One reason is costs of sales may have fallen. Alternatively the company may have changed its 'sales mix', so that, although the overall sales revenue has remained stable, it has sold a greater proportion of products with a higher gross margin.

Operating profit percentage and expense/revenue percentage

There has been a slight fall in the company's operating profit percentage. This has occurred despite the improvement in the gross profit percentage during the year. There must have been a significant rise in operating expenses (such as administrative expenses). This is confirmed by the expenses/revenue percentage, which has risen slightly. This suggests that 'non-trading' expenses have risen fairly sharply compared with sales. Alternatively there may have been a large unusual expense of some kind during the year.

Asset turnover

Asset turnover has fallen during the year. The company appears to be operating less efficiently than in the previous year and is therefore generating less sales revenue relative to the capital invested in the business (represented by its net assets). There are a number of possible reasons for this, including investment in new assets towards the end of the year. However, the other ratios suggest that the most likely reason for the fall is either that sales have been disappointing following increased investment (an expected rise in sales has not materialised) or that the company now has a higher proportion of assets that are not being used to generate sales.

(b) **How well the company has been managed**

The overall picture is of a company which is probably not being managed as well as in previous years. Operating expenses seem to be disproportionately high compared with sales, suggesting poor control, and the company appears to be operating less efficiently than before, failing to turn increased investment in assets into additional profit. The fact that the company's gross profit percentage has increased despite this indicates that there is nothing fundamentally wrong with the business and that with better management there could be considerable scope for improvement in return on capital employed and overall performance.

Task 2.3

(a) The accounting equation is:

Assets – Liabilities = Equity

The elements in the accounting equation are defined in the IASB *Conceptual Framework for Financial Reporting*:

'An asset is a resource controlled by an entity as a result of past events and from which future economic benefits are expected to flow to the entity.'

'A liability is a present obligation arising from past events, the settlement of which is expected to result in the outflow from the entity of resources embodying economic benefits.'

'Equity is the residual interest in the assets of the entity after deducting all its liabilities.'

(b) A profit arises when income exceeds expenses in the accounting period. If a profit has been made then the net assets of the entity will increase. The same profit also increases the equity of the entity as it accrues to the owners of the entity.

BPP practice assessment 2
Kenadie Ltd
Time allowed: 2½ hours

Section 1

The following information is relevant to Task 1.1 and Task 1.2

You have been asked to prepare a statement of cash flows and a statement of changes in equity for Kenadie Ltd for the year ended 30 September 20X6. The statement of comprehensive income and statement of financial position (with comparatives for the previous year) of Kenadie Ltd are set out below.

Kenadie Ltd

Statement of comprehensive income for the year ended 30 September 20X6

	£'000
Continuing operations	
Revenue	31,461
Cost of sales	(16,304)
Gross profit	15,157
Loss on disposal of property, plant and equipment	(183)
Distribution costs	(5,663)
Administrative expenses	(3,681)
Profit from operations	5,630
Finance costs – interest on loan	(800)
Profit before tax	4,830
Tax	(919)
Profit for the period from continuing operations	3,911

Kenadie Ltd

Statement of financial position as at 30 September

	20X6	20X5
ASSETS	£'000	£'000
Non-current assets		
Property, plant and equipment	29,882	19,100
Current assets		
Inventories	4,837	4,502
Trade receivables	5,244	4,978
Cash and cash equivalents	64	587
	10,145	10,067

Kenadie Ltd

Statement of financial position as at 30 September

Total assets	40,027	29,167
EQUITY AND LIABILITIES		
Equity		
Share capital	8,000	5,000
Share premium account	2,500	1,000
Retained earnings	15,570	12,359
Total equity	26,070	18,359
Non-current liabilities		
Bank loan	10,000	7,000
Current liabilities		
Trade payables	3,038	2,954
Tax liabilities	919	854
	3,957	3,808
Total liabilities	13,957	10,808
Total equity plus liabilities	40,027	29,167

Further information:

- The total depreciation charge for the year was £2,172,000.

- Property, plant and equipment costing £1,103,000, with accumulated depreciation of £411,000, was sold in the year.

- All sales and purchases were on credit. Other expenses were paid for in cash.

- A dividend of £700,000 was paid during the year.

Task 1.1

(a) **Prepare a reconciliation of profit from operations to net cash from operating activities for Kenadie Ltd for the year ended 30 September 20X6.**

(Complete the left hand column by writing in the correct line item from the list provided.)

Reconciliation of profit from operations to net cash from operating activities

		£'000
	▽	
Adjustments for:		
	▽	
	▽	
	▽	
	▽	
	▽	
Cash generated by operations		
	▽	
	▽	
Net cash from operating activities		

Picklist for line items:

Adjustment in respect of inventories
Adjustment in respect of trade payables
Adjustment in respect of trade receivables
Depreciation
Loss on disposal of property, plant and equipment
Interest paid
New bank loans
Proceeds on disposal of property, plant and equipment
Profit after tax
Profit before tax
Profit from operations
Purchases of property, plant and equipment
Tax paid

(b) **Prepare the statement of cash flows for Kenadie Ltd for the year ended 30 September 20X6.**

(Complete the left hand column by writing in the correct line item from the list provided.)

Kenadie Ltd

Statement of cash flows for the year ended 30 September 20X6

	£'000	£'000
Net cash from operating activities		
Investing activities		
▼		
▼		
Net cash used in investing activities		
Financing activities		
▼		
▼		
▼		
Net cash from financing activities		
Net increase/(decrease) in cash and cash equivalents		
Cash and cash equivalents at the beginning of the year		
Cash and cash equivalents at the end of the year		

Picklist for line items:

Adjustment in respect of inventories
Adjustment in respect of trade payables
Adjustment in respect of trade receivables
Dividends paid
New bank loans
Proceeds of share issue
Proceeds on disposal of property, plant and equipment
Purchases of property, plant and equipment

Workings

(Complete the left hand column by writing in the correct narrative from the list provided.)

Proceeds on disposal of property, plant and equipment (PPE)	£'000
▼	
▼	

Picklist for narratives:

Carrying amount of PPE sold
Depreciation charge
Loss on disposal
PPE at end of year
PPE at start of year

Purchases of property, plant and equipment (PPE)	£'000
PPE at start of year	
▼	
▼	
▼	
Total PPE additions	

Picklist for narratives:

Carrying amount of PPE sold
Depreciation charge
Loss on disposal of PPE
PPE at end of year

Task 1.2

(a) **Draft the statement of changes in equity for Kenadie Ltd for the year ended 30 September 20X6.**

(Complete the left hand column by writing in the correct line item from the list provided.)

Kenadie Ltd

Statement of changes in equity for the year ended 30 September 20X6

	Share Capital	Other Reserves	Retained Earnings	Total Equity
	£'000	£'000	£'000	£'000
Balance at 1 October 20X5				
Changes in equity for 20X6				
Profit for the year				
Dividends				
Issue of share capital				
Balance at 30 September 20X6				

Task 1.3

Otto Line is the managing director of Morel Ltd. He would like you to advise him on the accounting treatment of some matters that have arisen during the financial year as follows.

• During the year the board of Morel Ltd decided to close down a division of the company and developed a detailed plan for implementing the decision. Morel Ltd wrote to customers warning them to seek an alternative source of supply. Redundancy notices were sent to the staff of the division. The board has a reliable estimate that the cost of closing the division would be £1,854,000.

• During the year three people were seriously injured as a result of food poisoning. It was claimed that the food poisoning came from products sold by Morel Ltd. Legal proceedings have started seeking damages from the company of £2,000,000. Lawyers working for Morel Ltd have advised that it is probable that the company will not be found liable.

Prepare notes for a meeting with the directors to answer the following questions.

(a) **What is meant by a 'provision', according to IAS 37 *Provisions, contingent liabilities and contingent assets.*?**

(b) **When should a provision be recognised?**

(c) **How should Morel Ltd should treat the two matters set out in the data above in its financial statements?**

Task 1.4

This task consists of 6 true/false / multiple choice type questions.

(a) The following measures relate to a non-current asset:

  (i)   Carrying amount £20,000
  (ii) Fair value less costs to sell £18,000
  (iii) Value in use £22,000
  (iv) Replacement cost £50,000

What is the recoverable amount of the asset, according to IAS 36 *Impairment of assets*?

£18,000	
£20,000	
£22,000	
£50,000	

(b) A company purchased a machine at a cost of £24,000. Delivery costs totalled £1,000, the cost of installing the machine was £2,000 and there were also general administrative expenses of £3,500 in connection with the purchase.

What amount should be recognised as the cost of the machine, according to IAS 16 *Property, plant and equipment*?

£24,000	
£25,000	
£27,000	
£30,500	

(c) At the year-end, Chabrol Ltd has the following liabilities:

  (i)   Loan notes issued five years ago, due for repayment within one year

  (ii) Trade payables due for settlement more than twelve months after the year-end, within the normal course of the operating cycle

  (iii) Trade payables due for settlement within twelve months after the year end, within the normal course of the operating cycle

  (iv) Bank overdrafts

According to IAS 1 *Presentation of financial statements,* which of these liabilities is a current liability?

All four items	
(i), (iii) and (iv) only	
(i) and (ii) only	
(ii), (iii) and (iv) only	

(d) Goodwill arising on a business combination is never amortised.

Is this statement true or false?

True	
False	

(e) A business sells three products and at the year-end details of the inventories of these products are:

	Cost £	Selling price £	Selling costs £
Basic	14,300	15,700	2,400
Standard	21,600	21,300	1,000
Premium	17,500	28,600	1,800

At what value should closing inventories be recognised in the statement of financial position?

£51,100	
£53,100	
£53,400	
£65,600	

(f) Godard Ltd prepares its financial statements to 31 March each year. On 15 April there was a fire at the company's premises and its entire inventories were destroyed. The financial statements had not yet been authorised for issue.

According to IAS 10 *Events after the reporting period*, this is:

An adjusting event	
A non-adjusting event	

Task 1.5

The Managing Director of Wraymand plc has asked you to prepare the statement of comprehensive income. The company has one subsidiary, Blonk Ltd. The statements of comprehensive income of the two companies for the year ended 31 March 20X7 are set out below.

Statements of comprehensive income for the year ended 31 March 20X7

	Wraymand plc £'000	Blonk Ltd £'000
Continuing operations		
Revenue	38,462	12,544
Cost of sales	(22,693)	(5,268)
Gross profit	15,769	7,276
Other income – dividend from Blonk Ltd	580	–
Distribution costs	(6,403)	(2,851)
Administrative expenses	(3,987)	(2,466)
Profit from operations	5,959	1,959
Finance costs	(562)	(180)
Profit before tax	5,397	1,779
Tax	(1,511)	(623)
Profit for the period from continuing operations	3,886	1,156

Further information:

- Wraymand plc acquired 75% of the ordinary share capital of Blonk Ltd on 1 April 20X6.

- During the year Wraymand plc sold goods which had cost £1,100,000 to Blonk Ltd for £1,600,000. Three quarters of the goods had been sold by Blonk Ltd by the end of the year.

Draft a consolidated statement of comprehensive income for Wraymand plc and its subsidiary for the year ended 31 March 20X7.

Wraymand plc

Consolidated statement of comprehensive income for the year ended 31 March 20X7

	£'000
Continuing operations	
Revenue	
Cost of sales	
Gross profit	
Other income	
Distribution costs	
Administrative expenses	
Profit from operations	
Finance costs	
Profit before tax	
Tax	
Profit for the period from continuing operations	
Attributable to:	
Equity holders of the parent	
Non-controlling interest	

Workings

Revenue	£'000
Wraymand plc	
Blonk Ltd	
Total inter-company adjustment	

Cost of sales	£'000
Wraymand plc	
Blonk Ltd	
Total inter-company adjustment	

Section 2

Task 2.1

You have been asked to assist a shareholder in Forth Ltd. She has asked you to calculate ratios in respect of the financial statements of the company for the year ending 31 October 20X7. The financial statements of Forth Ltd are set out below:

Forth Ltd

Statement of comprehensive income for the year ended 31 October 20X7

	£'000
Continuing operations	
Revenue	2,400
Cost of sales	(1,392)
Gross profit	1,008
Distribution costs	(540)
Administrative expenses	(240)
Profit from operations	228
Finance costs	(91)
Profit before tax	137
Tax	(44)
Profit for the period from continuing operations	93

Forth Ltd

Statement of financial position as at 31 October 20X7

Assets	£'000
Non-current assets	
Property, plant and equipment	4,750
Current assets	
Inventories	320
Trade receivables	360
Cash and cash equivalents	0
	680
Total assets	5,430
Equity and liabilities	
Equity	
Share capital	2,500
Retained earnings	1,239
Total equity	3,739
Non-current liabilities	
Bank loans	1,300
Current liabilities	
Trade payables	195
Tax liabilities	44
Bank overdraft	152
	391
Total liabilities	1,691
Total equity and liabilities	5,430

(a) **State the formulae that are used to calculate each of the following ratios:**

(Write in the correct formula from the list provided)

(i) Gross profit percentage	▼

Formulae:

Gross profit/Total equity × 100

Gross profit/Revenue × 100

Gross profit/Total assets × 100

Gross profit/Total assets – current liabilities

(ii) Operating profit percentage	▼

Formulae:

Profit from operations/Revenue × 100

Profit from operations/Total assets × 100

Profit from operations/Total equity + Non-current liabilities × 100

Profit from operations/Finance costs × 100

(iii) Return on total assets	▼

Formulae:

Profit after tax/Total assets × 100

Profit from operations/Total assets × 100

Profit from operations/Total equity × 100

Profit from operations/Total equity + Non-current liabilities × 100

(iv) Administrative expenses/revenue percentage	▼

Formulae:

Administrative expenses/Revenue × 100

Distribution costs + administrative expenses/Revenue × 100

Administrative expenses/Cost of sales × 100

Revenue/Administrative expenses × 100

(v) Current ratio	

Formulae:

Total assets/Total liabilities

Current assets – inventories/Current liabilities

Current assets/Current liabilities

Total assets – inventories/Total liabilities

(vi) Inventory holding period	

Formulae:

Inventories/cost of sales × 365

Inventories/revenue × 365

Cost of sales/inventories × 365

Revenue/inventories × 365

(vii) Trade receivables collection period	

Formulae:

Trade payables/Cost of sales × 365

Trade receivables/Cost of sales × 365

Revenue/Trade receivables × 365

Trade receivables/Revenue × 365

(viii) Asset turnover (based on total assets)	

Formulae:

Revenue/Total assets

Revenue/Total assets – current liabilities

Revenue/Total assets – total liabilities

Total assets – total liabilities/Revenue

(b) **Calculate the ratios to the nearest ONE DECIMAL PLACE.**

(i)	Gross profit percentage		%
(ii)	Operating profit percentage		%
(iii)	Return on total assets		%
(iv)	Administrative expenses/revenue percentage		%
(v)	Current ratio		:1
(vi)	Inventory holding period		days
(vii)	Trade receivables collection period		days
(viii)	Asset turnover (based on total assets)		times

Task 2.2

You have been asked by the Managing Director of Gariroads Ltd to advise the company on the feasibility of raising a loan to finance the expansion of its activities.

A meeting has already been held with the bank and they have been sent a copy of the financial statements of the company for the past two years. The Managing Director wants you to comment on the likelihood of the bank lending the company money on the basis of the financial position revealed in the financial statements alone.

You have calculated the following ratios in respect of Gariroads Ltd's financial statements for the last two years to assist you in your analysis.

		20X7	*20X6*
(i)	Current ratio	2.2	2.1
(ii)	Quick ratio	0.8	1.3
(iii)	Gearing ratio	51.1%	31.2%
(iv)	Interest cover	1.8 times	4.5 times

Prepare a letter for the Managing Director of Gariroads that includes the following:

(a) **Comments on how the liquidity and financial position of Gariroads Ltd has changed over the two years based solely on the ratios calculated, suggesting possible reasons for the changes.**

(b) **A conclusion, with reasons, as to whether it is likely that the bank will lend the company money based solely on the ratios calculated and their analysis.**

Task 2.3

(a) **What is the objective of general purpose financial reporting according to the IASB *Conceptual Framework for Financial Reporting?***

(b) **Give ONE example of a PRIMARY user of general purpose financial reports (financial statements) and explain their need for the information in financial statements.**

(c) **Briefly explain ONE limitation of general purpose financial reports.**

BPP practice assessment 2
Kenadie Ltd
Answers

Section 1

Task 1.1

(a) Reconciliation of profit from operations to net cash from operating activities

	£'000
Profit from operations	5,630
Adjustments for:	
Depreciation	2,172
Loss on disposal of property, plant and equipment	183
Adjustment in respect of inventories (4,837 – 4,502)	(335)
Adjustment in respect of trade receivables (5,244 – 4,978)	(266)
Adjustment in respect of trade payables (3,038 – 2,954)	84
Cash generated by operations	7,468
Tax paid	(854)
Interest paid	(800)
Net cash from operating activities	5,814

(b) Kenadie Ltd

Statement of cash flows for the year ended 30 September 20X6

	£'000	£'000
Net cash from operating activities		5,814
Investing activities		
Purchases of property, plant and equipment (W)	(13,646)	
Proceeds on disposal of property, plant and equipment (W)	509	
Net cash used in investing activities		(13,137)
Financing activities		
Proceeds of share issue (10,500 – 6,000)	4,500	
New bank loans (10,000 – 7,000)	3,000	
Dividends paid	(700)	
Net cash from financing activities		6,800
Net increase/(decrease) in cash and cash equivalents		(523)
Cash and cash equivalents at the beginning of the year		587
Cash and cash equivalents at the end of the year		64

Workings

Proceeds on disposal of property, plant and equipment (PPE)	£'000
Carrying amount of PPE sold	692
Loss on disposal	(183)
	509

Purchases of property, plant and equipment (PPE)	£'000
PPE at start of year	19,100
Depreciation charge	(2,172)
Carrying amount of PPE sold	(692)
PPE at end of year	(29,882)
Total PPE additions	(13,646)

Task 1.2

(a) **Kenadie Ltd**

Statement of changes in equity for the year ended 30 September 20X6

	Share Capital	Other Reserves	Retained Earnings	Total Equity
	£'000	£'000	£'000	£'000
Balance at 1 October 20X5	5,000	1,000	12,359	18,359
Changes in equity for 20X6				
Profit for the year	0	0	3,911	3,911
Dividends	0	0	(700)	(700)
Issue of share capital	3,000	1,500	0	4,500
Balance at 30 September 20X6	8,000	2,500	15,570	26,070

Task 1.3

Note: based on the information available at the time this book was written, we anticipate that this task would be human marked in the real assessment.

(a) IAS 37 *Provisions, contingent liabilities and contingent assets* defines a provision as a liability of uncertain timing or amount. A liability is a present obligation of the entity arising from past events, the settlement of which is expected to result in an outflow of economic benefits.

(b) A provision should be recognised when:

- An entity has a present obligation as a result of a past event. The obligation can be either legal or constructive; and

- It is probable that an outflow of resources embodying economic benefits will be required to settle the obligation; and

- A reliable estimate can be made of the amount of the obligation.

(c) **Accounting treatment of matters arising during the financial year**

(i) **Closure of a division**

Morel Ltd has a constructive obligation to carry out the closure because it has communicated the decision to the people who will be affected: its customers and its employees. This communication appears to have taken place before the year end. It is probable that there will be an outflow of resources embodying economic benefits: the company will incur costs as a result of closing the division. A reliable estimate has been made of the costs. Therefore the company should recognise a provision of £1,854,000 at its year end.

(ii) **Legal proceedings**

Because the company will probably not be liable it is unlikely that there is a present obligation or that there will be an outflow of resources embodying economic benefits. Therefore no provision should be made. However, the company does have a contingent liability (unless the chances of its being found liable for damages are remote). Details of the claim should be disclosed in the notes to the financial statements.

Task 1.4

(a)

£18,000	
£20,000	
£22,000	✓
£50,000	

Recoverable amount is the higher of value in use and fair value less costs to sell.

(b)

£24,000	
£25,000	
£27,000	✓
£30,500	

The cost of property, plant and equipment is the cost of bringing it into working condition for its intended use. Therefore the cost includes delivery and installation costs but does not include the administrative expenses.

	£
Cost	
Purchase price	24,000
Delivery costs	1,000
Installation costs	2,000
	27,000

(c)

All four items	✓
(i), (iii) and (iv) only	
(i) and (ii) only	
(ii), (iii) and (iv) only	

IAS 1 states that a liability is current if an entity expects to settle it within its normal operating cycle. Even though item 2 is due more than twelve months after the year end it is a current liability. Note: this situation is extremely rare.

(d)

True	✓
False	

Goodwill arising on a business combination is recognised at cost in the statement of financial position and reviewed for impairment each year.

(e)

£51,100	✓
£53,100	
£53,400	
£65,600	

	Inventory value
	£
Basic – NRV (15,700 – 2,400)	13,300
Standard – NRV (21,300 – 1,000)	20,300
Premium – cost	17,500
	51,100

(f)

An adjusting event	
A non-adjusting event	✓

Task 1.5

Wraymand plc

Consolidated statement of comprehensive income for the year ended 31 March 20X7

	£'000
Continuing operations	
Revenue (W)	49,406
Cost of sales (W)	(26,486)
Gross profit	22,920
Other income	–
Distribution costs (6,403 + 2,851)	(9,254)
Administrative expenses (3,987 + 2,466)	(6,453)
Profit from operations	7,213
Finance costs (562 + 180)	(742)
Profit before tax	6,471
Tax (1,511 + 623)	(2,134)
Profit for the period from continuing operations	4,337
Attributable to:	
Equity holders of the parent	4,048
Non-controlling interest (25% × 1,156)	289
	4,337

Workings

Revenue	£'000
Wraymand plc	38,462
Blonk Ltd	12,544
Total inter-company adjustment	(1,600)
	49,406

Cost of sales	£'000
Wraymand plc	22,693
Blonk Ltd	5,268
Total inter-company adjustment (1,600 − (1/4 × 500))	(1,475)
	26,486

Section 2

Task 2.1

(a) Formulae used to calculate the ratios

(i) Gross profit percentage	$\dfrac{\text{Gross profit}}{\text{Revenue}} \times 100\%$
(ii) Operating profit percentage	$\dfrac{\text{Profit from operations}}{\text{Revenue}} \times 100\%$
(iii) Return on total assets	$\dfrac{\text{Profit from operations}}{\text{Total assets}} \times 100\%$
(iv) Administrative expenses/revenue percentage	$\dfrac{\text{Administrative expenses}}{\text{Revenue}}$
(v) Current ratio	$\dfrac{\text{Current assets}}{\text{Current liabilities}}$
(vi) Inventory holding period	$\dfrac{\text{Inventories}}{\text{Cost of sales}} \times 365$
(vii) Trade receivables collection period	$\dfrac{\text{Trade receivables}}{\text{Revenue}} \times 365$
(viii) Asset turnover (based on total assets)	$\dfrac{\text{Revenue}}{\text{Total assets}}$

(b) Calculation of ratios

(i)	Gross profit percentage $\dfrac{1{,}008}{2{,}400} \times 100$	42.0	%
(ii)	Operating profit percentage $\dfrac{228}{2{,}400} \times 100$	9.5	%
(iii)	Return on total assets $\dfrac{228}{5{,}430} \times 100$	4.2	%
(iv)	Administrative expenses/revenue percentage $\dfrac{240}{2{,}400} \times 100$	10.0	%
(v)	Current ratio $\dfrac{680}{391}$	1.7	:1
(vi)	Inventory holding period $\dfrac{320}{1{,}392} \times 365$	83.9	days
(vii)	Trade receivables collection period $\dfrac{360}{2{,}400} \times 365$	54.8	days
(viii)	Asset turnover (based on total assets) $\dfrac{2{,}400}{5{,}430}$	0.44	times

Task 2.2

Note: based on the information available at the time this book was written, we anticipate that this task would be human marked in the real assessment.

Accounting Technician

20 High Street

Anytown

20 June 20X7

Dear Sir,

As requested, I have reviewed the key ratios calculated from the financial statements of Gariroads Ltd to establish whether further finance could be obtained for expansion.

(a) *Commentary on liquidity and financial position*

There has been a slight increase in the current ratio in the year which is positive and the overall ratio is at a comfortable level above 2. The company's current assets have increased relative to its current liabilities.

However, the quick ratio shows a worsening position as it has fallen from 1.3 to 0.8 showing that Gariroads may struggle to meet its obligations from assets that are quickly convertible into cash. The fact that the current ratio has risen while the quick ratio has fallen suggests that it is the level of inventories that has risen, rather than trade receivables or cash. It is quite likely that the level of cash has fallen during the year, possibly even that a positive cash balance has become an overdraft.

The gearing ratio has increased in the year from a relatively safe 31% to a high 51%. New loans have been taken out during the year and the company is likely to be seen as risky by future lenders. The sharp increase in the gearing ratio suggests that total borrowings may have more than doubled compared with the previous year.

Interest cover has decreased from 4.5 times to 1.8 times which again would be seen as a risk factor by lenders. The most obvious reason for the worrying fall in interest cover is the sharp increase in the amount that the company has borrowed. Other reasons for this could include a fall in profit from operations and/or higher interest rates on the additional loan. Because there are less profits available to cover the interest payments, future lenders would be very cautious about lending money to Gariroads Ltd.

(b) *Conclusion*

Overall, Gariroads has a worsening liquidity position and increased gearing in 20X7 compared to 20X6. While the company is still able to meet its interest payments, the ability to do so has decreased. If the fall in interest cover is partly the result of falling profits, this is a very worrying sign.

Gariroads is already very highly geared. A potential lender would view the company as a risky and unattractive prospect. On the basis of these four ratios, it is unlikely that the bank would lend further cash to the business at the moment, unless there is a very strong possibility of increased profits and much better interest cover in the near future.

Yours faithfully

Accounting Technician

Task 2.3

Note: based on the information available at the time this book was written, we anticipate that this task would be human marked in the real assessment.

(a) The IASB *Conceptual Framework for Financial Reporting* states that the objective of general purpose financial reporting is to provide financial information about the reporting entity that is useful to existing and potential investors, lenders and other creditors in making decisions about providing resources to the entity.

(b) Examples of primary users of financial information and their information needs:

Existing and potential investors

Investors and potential investors need information to help them determine whether they should buy, hold or sell their investment. They need information which helps them to assess the ability of the entity to pay dividends and to assess the potential changes in the market price of their investment.

Existing and potential lenders and other creditors

Lenders need information that helps them to make decisions about providing or settling loans. They need information which helps them to assess whether their loans and the interest attaching to them will be paid when due.

Tutorial note: Candidates only needed to write about ONE example of a PRIMARY user. According to the IASB *Conceptual Framework*, the primary users are the providers of capital (ie, those given in the answer to part (a) above). Although there may be other users of financial statements, eg, employees, the government, the public, general purpose financial statements are not primarily prepared for them.

(c) Limitations of general purpose financial reports (according to the IASB *Conceptual Framework*):

- **They are not designed to show the value of a reporting entity** (the market value of the company's shares). However, they provide information that may help users to estimate its value.

- **They may not meet the needs of every individual user**. Individual investors, lenders and other creditors (primary users) may have different information needs, which may conflict.

- **They are prepared primarily for existing and potential investors, lenders and other creditors**. Other groups of people, such as regulators and members of the public, may be interested in financial information about an entity. These groups may find general purpose financial reports useful, but they are **not primarily directed towards these other groups**.

- **They are based on estimates, judgements and models rather than exact depictions**. The *Conceptual Framework* establishes the concepts that underlie those estimates, judgements and models.

Tutorial note: Candidates only needed to write about ONE example.

BPP practice assessment 3
Nevis Ltd
Time allowed: 2½ hours

Section 1

The following information is relevant to Task 1.1 and Task 1.2

You have been asked to help prepare the financial statements of Nevis Ltd for the year ended 31 March 20X9. The company's trial balance as at 31 March 20X9 is shown below.

Nevis Ltd

Trial balance as at 31 March 20X9

	Debit £'000	Credit £'000
Share capital		14,000
Trade and other payables		2,642
Motor vehicles – cost	21,840	
Motor vehicles – acc depreciation at 1 April 20X8		4,675
Plant and equipment – cost	32,800	
Plant and equipment – acc depreciation at 1 April 20X8		16,000
Trade and other receivables	4,567	
Accruals		239
6% bank loan repayable 20Y6		12,000
Cash at bank	3,519	
Retained earnings		6,590
Interest	360	
Sales		65,113
Purchases	44,000	
Distribution costs	2,905	
Administrative expenses	4,098	
Inventories as at 1 April 20X8	5,640	
Dividends paid	1,530	
	121,259	121,259

Further information:

- The inventories at the close of business on 31 March 20X9 were valued at £6,806,000.

- The company hired some temporary office space for the period 1 March to 31 May 20X9. The contract price for the three months was £144,000 and this was paid in full on 8 March. Office rental is included in administrative expenses.

- Depreciation is to be provided for the year to 31 March 20X9 as follows:

| Motor vehicles | 25% per annum | Straight line basis |
| Plant and equipment | 20% per annum | Reducing balance basis |

  Depreciation is apportioned as follows:

	%
Cost of sales	50
Distribution costs	20
Administrative expenses	30

- Interest on the bank loan for the last six months of the year has not been included in the accounts in the trial balance.

- The corporation tax charge for the year has been calculated as £2,540,000.

- All of the operations are continuing operations.

Task 1.1

(a) **Draft the statement of comprehensive income for Nevis Ltd for the year ended 31 March 20X9.**

Nevis Ltd

Statement of comprehensive income for the year ended 31 March 20X9

	£'000
Continuing operations	
Revenue	
Cost of sales	____
Gross profit	
Distribution costs	
Administrative expenses	____
Profit/(loss) from operations	
Finance costs	____
Profit/(loss) before tax	
Tax	____
Profit/(loss) for the period from continuing operations	____

Workings

(Complete the left hand column by writing in the correct narrative from the list provided.)

Cost of sales	£'000
▼	
▼	
▼	
▼	

Picklist for narratives:

Accruals
Closing inventories
Depreciation
Opening inventories
Prepayments
Purchases

Distribution costs	£'000
▼	
▼	

Picklist for narratives:

Accruals
Depreciation
Distribution costs
Prepayments

Administrative expenses	£'000
▼	
▼	
▼	

Picklist for narratives:

Accruals
Administrative expenses
Depreciation
Prepayment

Task 1.2

(a) **Draft the statement of financial position for Nevis Ltd as at 31 March 20X9.**

Nevis Ltd

(Complete the left hand column by writing in the correct line item from the list provided)

Statement of financial position as at 31 March 20X9

	£'000
Assets	
Non-current assets	
▼	____
Current assets	
▼	
▼	
▼	____
	____
Total assets	====
Equity and liabilities	
Equity	
▼	
▼	____
Total equity	____
Non-current liabilities	
▼	____
Current liabilities	
▼	
▼	____
	____
Total liabilities	____
Total equity and liabilities	====

Picklist for line items:

Bank loan
Cash and cash equivalents
Inventories
Property, plant and equipment
Retained earnings
Share capital
Tax liabilities
Trade and other payables
Trade and other receivables

Workings

(Complete the left hand column by writing in the correct narrative from the list provided.)

Property, plant and equipment		£'000
	▼	
	▼	
	▼	
	▼	

Picklist for narratives:

Accumulated depreciation – motor vehicles
Accumulated depreciation – plant and equipment
Motor vehicles – Cost
Plant and equipment – Cost

Trade and other receivables		£'000
	▼	
	▼	

Picklist for narratives:

Accruals: trial balance
Additional administrative expenses accrual
Additional administrative expenses prepaid
Additional finance costs accrued
Additional finance costs prepaid
Prepayments
Trade and other payables
Trade and other receivables

Retained earnings		£'000
	▼	
	▼	
	▼	

Picklist for narratives:

Dividends paid
Other comprehensive income for the year
Retained earnings at 1 April 20X8
Total comprehensive income for the year
Total profit for the year

Trade and other payables		£'000
	▼	
	▼	
	▼	

Picklist for narratives:

Accruals: trial balance
Additional administrative expenses accrual
Additional administrative expenses prepaid
Additional finance costs accrual
Additional finance costs prepaid
Dividends
Prepayments
Tax liabilities
Trade and other payables
Trade and other receivables

Task 1.3

The directors of Munro Ltd are planning to purchase an intangible asset in the near future. They believe that this asset will have an indefinite life and are aware that this means that it will be necessary to carry out an impairment review each year.

Prepare brief notes to answer the following points for the directors:

(a) **State how, according to IAS 36** *Impairment of assets*, **an impairment loss is calculated and which two figures are needed.**

(b) **Explain what is meant by each of these figures.**

(c) **State how an impairment loss is to be treated in the financial statements.**

Task 1.4

(a) According to IAS 8 *Accounting policies, changes in accounting estimates and errors*, a company can only change an accounting policy if the change is required by a standard.

Is this statement true or false?

True	
False	

(b) Webb Ltd has a possible obligation as a result of a claim against it by a customer. The company's solicitors have advised the directors that there is a 30% chance that the claim will be successful.

In the financial statements for the period, Webb Ltd should:

Disclose a contingent liability	
Recognise a provision	

(c) **Guidance on the application and interpretation of International Financial Reporting Standards is provided by:**

The International Accounting Standards Board	
The IFRS Foundation	
The IFRS Interpretations Committee	
The IFRS Advisory Council	

(d) A company sold some plant which had cost £100,000 for £20,000. At the time of sale the carrying amount of the plant was £18,000.

Which of the following correctly states the treatment of the transaction in the company's statement of cash flows for the period?

Proceeds of sale	Profit on sale	
Cash inflow under financing activities	Deducted from profit in calculating net cash from operating activities	
Cash inflow under investing activities	Added to profit in calculating net cash from operating activities.	
Cash inflow under financing activities	Added to profit in calculating net cash from operating activities	
Cash inflow under investing activities	Deducted from profit in calculating net cash from operating activities	

(e) Harvey Ltd has a non-current asset that has been classified as 'held for sale'. On 1 October 20X1 (the date on which the decision was taken to sell the asset) its carrying amount was £750,000. It was being depreciated at 25% on a reducing balance basis. Harvey Ltd has been advised that the fair value of the asset is £740,000 and expects to incur costs of £10,000 in making the sale.

At what amount should the asset be shown in the financial statements of Harvey Ltd for the year ended 31 December 20X1?

£703,125	
£730,000	
£740,000	
£750,000	

(f) **According to IAS 38 *Intangible assets*, which of the following statements are true?**

(i) Internally generated brands should never be capitalised

(ii) Intangible assets can be revalued upwards

(i) only	
(ii) only	
Both (i) and (ii)	
Neither (i) nor (ii)	

Task 1.5

Data

Teal plc acquired 80% of the issued share capital of Amber Ltd on 1 January 20X9 for £4,600,000. At that date Amber Ltd had issued share capital of £3,000,000 and retained earnings of £840,000.

The summarised statements of financial position for the two companies one year later at 31 December 20X9 are as follows:

	Teal plc £'000	Amber Ltd £'000
ASSETS		
Investment in Amber Ltd	4,600	
Non-current assets	7,500	4,590
Current assets	3,800	1,570
Total assets	15,900	6,160
EQUITY AND LIABILITIES		
Equity		
Share capital	5,000	3,000
Retained earnings	7,800	1,510
Total equity	12,800	4,510
Non-current liabilities	1,000	750
Current liabilities	2,100	900
Total liabilities	3,100	1,650
Total equity and liabilities	15,900	6,160

Additional data

- The fair value of the non-current assets of Amber Ltd at 1 January 20X9 was £4,200,000. The book value of the non-current assets at 1 January 20X9 was £3,900,000. The revaluation has not been recorded in the books of Amber Ltd (ignore any effect on the depreciation for the year).

- The directors of Teal plc have decided that non-controlling interest will be valued at the proportionate share of Amber Ltd's net assets.

(a) **Draft the consolidated statement of financial position for Teal plc and its subsidiary as at 31 December 20X9.**

Teal plc

Consolidated statement of financial position as at 31 December 20X9

	£'000
Assets	
Non-current assets:	
Intangible assets: goodwill	
Property, plant and equipment	
Current assets	
Total assets	
Equity and liabilities	
Equity attributable to owners of the parent	
Share capital	
Retained earnings	
Non-controlling interest	
Total equity	
Non-current liabilities	
Current liabilities	
Total liabilities	
Total equity and liabilities	

Workings

(Complete the left hand column by writing in the correct narrative from the list provided.)

Goodwill		£'000
	▼	
	▼	
	▼	
	▼	

Picklist for narratives:

Price paid
Retained earnings – attributable to Teal plc
Revaluation reserve – attributable to Teal plc
Share capital – attributable to Teal plc

Retained earnings		£'000
	▼	
	▼	

Picklist for narratives:

Amber Ltd – attributable to Teal plc
Revaluation
Teal plc

Non-controlling interest (NCI)		£'000
	▼	
	▼	
	▼	

Picklist for narratives:

Current assets – attributable to NCI
Non-current assets – attributable to NCI
Price paid
Retained earnings – attributable to NCI
Revaluation reserve – attributable to NCI
Share capital – attributable to NCI

Data

Blue plc acquired 75% of the issued share capital of Brown Ltd on 1 January 20X9.

Summarised statements of comprehensive income for the year ended 31 December 20X9 are shown below:

	Blue plc £'000	Brown Ltd £'000
Continuing operations		
Revenue	61,200	22,300
Cost of sales	(29,100)	(8,600)
Gross profit	32,100	13,700
Other income – dividend from Brown Ltd	2,500	–
Operating expenses	(3,750)	(1,900)
Profit from operations	30,850	11,800

Additional data

- During the year Blue plc sold goods which had cost £600,000 to Brown Ltd for £1,000,000. None of these goods remain in inventory at the end of the year.

- Goodwill of £900,000 arose on the acquisition. The directors of Blue plc have concluded that goodwill has been impaired by 10% during the year.

(b) **Draft the consolidated statement of comprehensive income for Blue plc and its subsidiary up to and including the profit from operations line for the year ended 31 December 20X9.**

Blue plc

Consolidated statement of comprehensive income for the year ended 31 December 20X9

	£'000
Continuing operations	
Revenue	
Cost of sales	
Gross profit	
Other income	
Operating expenses	
Profit from operations	

Workings

Revenue	£'000
Blue plc	
Brown Ltd	
Total inter-company adjustment	

Cost of sales	£'000
Blue plc	
Brown Ltd	
Total inter-company adjustment	

Section 2

Task 2.1

Lucy Carmichael is considering buying shares in Tweed Ltd. She wishes to assess the level of profitability and risk of the company. She has asked you to assist her by calculating ratios in respect of the financial statements of the company for the year ended 31 March 20X8. The financial statements of Tweed Ltd are set out below.

Tweed Ltd

Statement of comprehensive income the year ended 31 March 20X8

	£'000
Continuing operations	
Revenue	16,000
Cost of sales	(8,640)
Gross profit	7,360
Distribution costs	(3,600)
Administrative expenses	(2,880)
Profit from operations	880
Finance costs	(308)
Profit before tax	572
Tax	(117)
Profit for the period from continuing operations	455

Tweed Ltd

Statement of financial position as at 31 March 20X8

	£'000
Assets	
Non-current assets	
Property, plant and equipment	9,800
Current assets	
Inventories	1,728
Trade receivables	1,600
Cash and cash equivalents	0
	3,328
Total assets	13,128
Equity and liabilities	
Share capital	3,000
Retained earnings	4,372
Total equity	7,372
Non-current liabilities	
Bank loans	4,400
Current liabilities	
Trade payables	1,210
Tax liabilities	117
Bank overdraft	29
	1,356
Total liabilities	5,756
Total equity and liabilities	13,128

(a) **State the formulae that are used to calculate each of the following ratios:**

(Write in the correct formula from the list provided)

(i) Return on capital employed	▼

Formulae:

Profit after tax/Total equity × 100

Profit from operations/Total equity × 100

Profit after tax/Total equity + Non-current liabilities × 100

Profit from operations/Total equity + Non-current liabilities × 100

(ii) Return on equity	▼

Formulae:

Profit after tax/Total equity × 100

Profit before tax/Total equity × 100

Profit from operations/Total equity × 100

Profit from operations/Total equity + Non-current liabilities × 100

(iii) Operating profit percentage	▼

Formulae:

Profit from operations/Revenue × 100

Profit from operations/Total assets × 100

Profit from operations/Total equity + Non-current liabilities × 100

Profit from operations/Finance costs × 100

(iv) Gross profit percentage	▼

Formulae:

Gross profit/Total equity × 100

Gross profit/Revenue × 100

Gross profit/Total assets × 100

Gross profit/Total assets – current liabilities

(v) Quick (acid test) ratio	▼

Formulae:

Current assets/Current liabilities

Total assets – inventories/Total liabilities

Total assets/Total liabilities

Current assets – inventories/Current liabilities

(vi) Asset turnover (net assets)	▼

Formulae:

Revenue/Total assets – current liabilities

Revenue/Total assets – total liabilities

Total assets – current liabilities/Revenue

Total assets – total liabilities/Revenue

(vii) Trade payables payment period	▼

Formulae:

Trade payables/Revenue × 365

Trade payables/Cost of sales × 365

Revenue/Trade payables × 365

Cost of sales/Trade payables × 365

(viii) Interest cover	▼

Formulae:

Finance costs/profit from operations

Finance costs/revenue

Profit from operations/finance costs

Revenue/finance costs

(b) **Calculate the following ratios to the nearest ONE DECIMAL PLACE.**

(i)	Return on capital employed		%
(ii)	Return on equity		%
(iii)	Operating profit percentage		%
(iv)	Gross profit percentage		%
(v)	Quick (acid test) ratio		:1
(vi)	Asset turnover (net assets)		times
(vii)	Trade payables payment period		days
(viii)	Interest cover		times

Task 2.2

The directors of Goramsee Ltd have asked you to comment on the change in net cash from operating activities between the year ended 31 March 20X6 and the year ended 31 March 20X7. A note on net cash from operating activities for the period that reconciles it with profit from operations has been prepared.

Goramsee Ltd

Reconciliation of operating profit to net cash inflow from operating activities

	20X7	20X6
	£'000	£'000
Profit from operations	6,938	5,721
Adjustments for:		
Depreciation	4,217	2,843
Gain on disposal of property, plant and equipment	(434)	(86)
Increase in inventories	(1,176)	(102)
Increase in trade receivables	(873)	(85)
Increase/(Decrease) in trade payables	(118)	113
Cash generated by operations	8,554	8,404
Income taxes paid	(1,314)	(1,276)
Interest paid	(560)	(420)
Net cash from operating activities	6,680	6,708

Prepare a report for the Directors of Goramsee Ltd to explain the change in net cash from operating activities between 20X6 and 20X7.

Task 2.3

You have a friend who is a shareholder in a small private company. She has been looking at the company's latest financial statements and is slightly confused by some of the terms used in the statement of financial position, in particular by the terms labelled 'current'. On checking the internet she has found out that these terms are defined in something called IAS 1, but she has been unable to find any further information.

Write short notes to explain how IAS 1 *Presentation of financial statements* defines the following terms:

(a) **Current assets.**
(b) **Current liabilities.**

....

BPP practice assessment 3
Nevis Ltd

Answers

Section 1

Task 1.1

(a) **Nevis Ltd**

Statement of comprehensive income for the year ended 31 March 20X9

	£'000
Continuing operations	
Revenue	65,113
Cost of sales (W)	(47,244)
Gross profit	17,869
Distribution costs (W)	(4,669)
Administrative expenses (W)	(6,648)
Profit/(loss) from operations	6,552
Finance costs (6% × 12,000)	(720)
Profit/(loss) before tax	5,832
Tax	(2,540)
Profit/(loss) for the period from continuing operations	3,292

Workings

Cost of sales	£'000
Opening inventories	5,640
Purchases	44,000
Depreciation (50% × 8,820)	4,410
Closing inventories	(6,806)
	47,244

Distribution costs	£'000
Distribution costs	2,905
Depreciation (20% × 8,820)	1,764
	4,669

Administrative expenses	£'000
Administrative expenses	4,098
Depreciation (30% × 8,820)	2,646
Prepayment (144 × 2/3)	(96)
	6,648

	£'000
Depreciation	
Motor vehicles (25% × 21,840)	5,460
Plant and equipment (20% × 32,800 – 16,000)	3,360
	8,820

Task 1.2

(a) **Nevis Ltd**

Statement of financial position as at 31 March 20X9

	£'000
Assets	
Non-current assets	
Property, plant and equipment (W)	25,145
Current assets	
Inventories	6,806
Trade and other receivables (W)	4,663
Cash and cash equivalents	3,519
	14,988
Total assets	40,133
Equity and liabilities	
Equity	
Share capital	14,000
Retained earnings (W)	8,352
Total equity	22,352

	£'000
Non-current liabilities	
Bank loan	12,000
Current liabilities	
Trade and other payables (W)	3,241
Tax liabilities	2,540
	5,781
Total liabilities	17,781
Total equity and liabilities	40,133

Workings

Property, plant and equipment	£'000
Motor vehicles – Cost	21,840
Plant and equipment – Cost	32,800
Accumulated depreciation – motor vehicles (4,675 + 5,460)	(10,135)
Accumulated depreciation – plant and equipment (16,000 + 3,360)	(19,360)
	25,145

Trade and other receivables	£'000
Trade and other receivables	4,567
Additional administrative expenses prepaid	96
	4,663

Retained earnings	£'000
Retained earnings at 1 April 20X8	6,590
Total profit for the year	3,292
Dividends paid	(1,530)
	8,352

Trade and other payables	£'000
Trade and other payables	2,642
Accruals: trial balance	239
Additional finance costs accrual	360
	3,241

Task 1.3

Note: based on the information available at the time this book was written, we anticipate that this task would be human marked in the real assessment.

(a) IAS 36 *Impairment of assets* states that if an asset's carrying amount is greater than its recoverable amount, the asset is impaired. The impairment loss is the difference between an asset's carrying amount and its recoverable amount.

(b) The carrying amount of an asset is the amount at which it is recognised in the statement of financial position after deducting accumulated depreciation or amortisation and accumulated impairment losses.

An asset's recoverable amount is the higher of its fair value less costs to sell and its value in use. IAS 36 defines value in use as the present value of the future cash flows expected to be derived from an asset, including any cash flows arising on its disposal.

(c) An impairment loss is normally recognised as an expense in profit or loss. However, if the asset has previously been revalued upwards the loss is recognised in other comprehensive income as a revaluation decrease and set against the revaluation surplus. If the loss is greater than the revaluation surplus, the excess is recognised in profit or loss.

Task 1.4

(a)

True	
False	✓

A company can also change an accounting policy if the new policy results in the financial statements providing more relevant and more reliable information.

(b)

Disclose a contingent liability	✓
Recognise a provision	

(c)

The International Accounting Standards Board	
The IFRS Foundation	
The IFRS Interpretations Committee	✓
The IFRS Advisory Council	

(d)

Proceeds of sale	Profit on sale	
Cash inflow under financing activities	Deducted from profit in calculating net cash from operating activities	
Cash inflow under investing activities	Added to profit in calculating net cash from operating activities.	
Cash inflow under financing activities	Added to profit in calculating net cash from operating activities	
Cash inflow under investing activities	Deducted from profit in calculating net cash from operating activities	✓

The company has made a profit on disposal, so this amount is deducted in calculating net cash from operating activities.

(e)

£703,125	
£730,000	✓
£740,000	
£750,000	

Fair value less costs to sell (£740,000 – £10,000) is lower than carrying amount (£750,000). Non-current assets held for sale are not depreciated.

(f)

(i) only	
(ii) only	
Both (i) and (ii)	✓
Neither (i) nor (ii)	

Although it is rare for an intangible asset to be revalued, IAS 38 allows a choice between the cost model and the revaluation model.

Task 1.5

(a) **Teal plc**

Consolidated statement of financial position as at 31 December 20X9

	£'000
Assets	
Non-current assets:	
Intangible assets: goodwill (W)	1,288
Property, plant and equipment (7,500 + 4,590 + 300)	12,390
Current assets	5,370
Total assets	19,048
Equity and liabilities	
Equity attributable to owners of the parent	
Share capital	5,000
Retained earnings (W)	8,336
Non-controlling interest (W)	962
Total equity	14,298
Non-current liabilities	1,750
Current liabilities	3,000
Total liabilities	4,750
Total equity and liabilities	19,048

Workings

Goodwill	£'000
Price paid	4,600
Share capital – attributable to Teal plc (80% × 3,000)	(2,400)
Retained earnings – attributable to Teal plc (80% × 840)	(672)
Revaluation reserve – attributable to Teal plc (80% × 300)	(240)
	1,288

Retained earnings	£'000
Teal plc	7,800
Amber Ltd – attributable to Teal plc (80% × (1,510 – 840))	536
	8,336

Non-controlling interest (NCI)	£'000
Share capital – attributable to NCI (20% × 3,000)	600
Retained earnings – attributable to NCI (20% × 1,510)	302
Revaluation reserve – attributable to NCI (20% × 300)	60
	962

(b) **Blue plc**

Consolidated statement of comprehensive income for the year ended 31 December 20X9

	£'000
Continuing operations	
Revenue (W)	82,500
Cost of sales (W)	(36,700)
Gross profit	45,800
Other income	0
Operating expenses (3,750 + 1,900 + 90)	(5,740)
Profit from operations	40,060

Workings

	£'000
Blue plc	61,200
Brown Ltd	22,300
Total inter-company adjustment	(1,000)
	82,500

	£'000
Blue plc	29,100
Brown Ltd	8,600
Total inter-company adjustment	(1,000)
	36,700

Section 2

Task 2.1

(a) Formulae used to calculate the ratios

(i) Return on capital employed	$\dfrac{\text{Profit from operations}}{\text{Total equity + non-current liabilities}} \times 100\%$
(ii) Return on equity	$\dfrac{\text{Profit after tax}}{\text{Total equity}} \times 100\%$
(iii) Operating profit percentage	$\dfrac{\text{Profit from operations}}{\text{Revenue}} \times 100\%$
(iv) Gross profit percentage	$\dfrac{\text{Gross profit}}{\text{Revenue}} \times 100\%$
(v) Quick (acid test) ratio	$\dfrac{\text{Current assets - inventories}}{\text{Current liabilities}}$
(vi) Asset turnover (net assets)	$\dfrac{\text{Revenue}}{\text{Total assets - current liabilities}}$
(vii) Trade payables payment period	$\dfrac{\text{Trade payables}}{\text{Cost of sales}} \times 365$
(viii) Interest cover	$\dfrac{\text{Profit from operations}}{\text{Finance costs}}$

(b) **Calculation of the ratios**

(i) Return on capital employed $\dfrac{880}{7,372+4,400} \times 100$	7.5	%
(ii) Return on equity $\dfrac{455}{7,372} \times 100$	6.2	%
(iii) Operating profit percentage $\dfrac{880}{16,000} \times 100$	5.5	%
(iv) Gross profit percentage $\dfrac{7,360}{16,000} \times 100$	46.0	%
(v) Quick (acid test) ratio $\dfrac{1,600}{1,356}$	1.2	:1
(vi) Asset turnover (net assets) $\dfrac{16,000}{13,128-1,356}$	1.4	times
(vii) Trade payables payment period $\dfrac{1,210}{8,640} \times 365$	51.1	days
(viii) Interest cover $\dfrac{880}{308}$	2.9	times

Task 2.2

Note: based on the information available at the time this book was written, we anticipate that this task would be human marked in the real assessment.

REPORT

To: Directors of Goramsee Ltd

From: Accountant

Date: June 20X7

Subject: Comments on operating cashflow of Goramsee Ltd

The reconciliation note shows an increase in profit from operations in 20X7, although this increase does not continue into cash from operations, which has fallen slightly in the year. There are a number of reasons why the cash from operations has fallen.

- There has been a significant cash outflow relating to inventories. The inventory balance in the statement of financial position has increased suggesting that control over inventory levels has weakened in the year. It may be a deliberate policy by management to ensure that there is sufficient inventory available, but it could also indicate slow moving or obsolete inventory.

- Trade receivables have also increased in the year which suggests that credit control policies have worsened. It is important that customers pay on time to avoid any irrecoverable debts occurring. Both the negative movement in receivables and inventory have reduced operating cash flow by £2 million.

- Trade payables have decreased slightly which suggests that suppliers have been paid too quickly. It would appear that Goramsee Ltd is paying suppliers before receiving cash from customers. It would improve cash flow if the company could delay payments to suppliers.

- There has been a slight increase in interest and tax paid during the year but this has not had a significant effect on cash flow.

    The key reason for the reduction in operating cash flow is the poor control of working capital. This needs addressing urgently as it has already caused a positive cash balance to become an overdraft and the company needs to halt any further deterioration of its cash position.

....

Task 2.3

Note: based on the information available at the time this book was written, we anticipate that this task would be human marked in the real assessment.

(a)   An asset is a current asset if:

- It is cash or a cash equivalent (a short term investment or deposit that can be easily converted into cash); or

- The entity expects to collect, sell or consume it within its normal operating cycle; or

- It is held primarily for trading and is expected to be realised (received) within twelve months after the reporting period

(b)   A liability is a current liability if:

- The entity expects to settle it in its normal operating cycle; or

- It is held primarily for trading and is due to be settled (paid) within twelve months after the reporting period

BPP practice assessment 4
Martin Ltd
Time allowed: 2½ hours

Section 1

The following information is relevant to Task 1.1 and Task 1.2

You have been asked to help prepare the financial statements of Martin Ltd for the year ended 31 October 20X9. The company's trial balance as at 31 October 20X9 is shown below.

Martin Ltd

Trial balance as at 31 October 20X9

	Debit	Credit
	£'000	£'000
Share capital		9,000
Trade and other payables		1,347
Property, plant and equipment – cost	39,880	
Property, plant and equipment – accumulated depreciation		21,780
Trade and other receivables	2,234	
Accruals		146
8% bank loan repayable 20Y6		14,000
Cash at bank	9,654	
Retained earnings		3,465
Interest	560	
Sales		46,433
Purchases	32,553	
Distribution costs	2,450	
Administrative expenses	3,444	
Inventories as at 1 November 20X8	4,466	
Dividends paid	930	
	96,171	96,171

Additional data:

- The inventories at the close of business on 31 October 20X9 were valued at £4,987,000. On 4 November 20X9, goods included in this total at a value of £550,000 were found to be damaged and were sold for £300,000.

- Land, which is non-depreciable, is included in the trial balance at a value of £8,000,000. It is to be revalued at £12,000,000 and this revaluation is to be included in the financial statements for the year ended 31 October 20X9.

- The company paid £512,000 for one year's insurance on 1 February 20X9, this is due to expire on 31 January 20Y0. Insurance is included in administrative expenses.

- Distribution costs of £66,000 owing at 31 October 20X9 are to be accrued.

- Interest on the bank loan for the last six months of the year has not been included in the accounts in the trial balance.

- The corporation tax charge for the year has been calculated as £980,000.

- All of the operations are continuing operations.

Task 1.1

(a) **Draft the statement of comprehensive income for Martin Ltd for the year ended 31 October 20X9.**

Martin Ltd

Statement of comprehensive Income for the year ended 31 October 20X9

	£'000
Continuing operations	
Revenue	
Cost of sales	_____
Gross profit	
Distribution costs	
Administrative expenses	_____
Profit/(loss) from operations	
Finance costs	
Profit/(loss) before tax	
Tax	_____
Profit/(loss) for the period from continuing operations	
Other comprehensive income	
Gain on revaluation	_____
Total comprehensive income for the year	_____

Workings

(Complete the left hand column by writing in the correct narrative from the list provided.)

Cost of sales	£'000
▽	
▽	
▽	

Picklist for narratives:

Accruals
Closing inventories
Opening inventories
Prepayments
Purchases

Distribution costs	£'000
▽	
▽	

Picklist for narratives:

Accruals
Distribution costs
Prepayments

Administrative expenses	£'000
▽	
▽	

Picklist for narratives:

Accruals
Administrative expenses
Prepayment

Task 1.2

(a) **Draft the statement of financial position for Martin Ltd as at 31 October 20X9.**

Martin Ltd

(Complete the left hand column by writing in the correct line item from the list provided)

Statement of financial position as at 31 October 20X9

	£'000
Assets	
Non-current assets	
▼	_____
Current assets:	
▼	
▼	
▼	_____
	_____
Total assets	_____
Equity and liabilities	
Equity	
▼	
▼	
▼	_____
Total equity	_____
Non-current liabilities:	
▼	_____
Current liabilities:	
▼	
▼	_____
	_____
Total liabilities	_____
Total equity and liabilities	_____

Picklist for line items:

Bank loan
Cash and cash equivalents
Inventories
Property, plant and equipment
Retained earnings
Revaluation reserve
Share capital
Tax liabilities
Trade and other payables
Trade and other receivables

Workings

(Complete the left hand column by writing in the correct narrative from the list provided.)

Property, plant and equipment		£'000
	▼	
	▼	
	▼	

Picklist for narratives:

Property, plant and equipment – Cost
Property, plant and equipment -Accumulated depreciation
Revaluation

Trade and other receivables		£'000
	▼	
	▼	

Picklist for narratives:

Accruals: trial balance
Additional distribution costs accrual
Additional distribution costs prepaid
Additional finance costs accrual
Additional finance costs prepaid
Administrative expenses accrual
Administrative expenses prepaid
Trade and other payables
Trade and other receivables

Retained earnings		£'000
	▼	
	▼	
	▼	

Picklist for narratives:

Dividends paid
Other comprehensive income for the year
Retained earnings at 1 November 20X8
Revaluation reserve
Total comprehensive income for the year
Total profit for the year

Trade and other payables		£'000
	▼	
	▼	
	▼	
	▼	

Picklist for narratives:

Accruals: trial balance
Additional distribution costs accrual
Additional distribution costs prepaid
Additional finance costs accrual
Additional finance costs prepaid
Administrative expenses accrual
Administrative expenses prepaid
Dividends
Tax payable
Trade and other payables
Trade and other receivables

Task 1.3

The objective of IAS 16 *Property, plant and equipment* is to prescribe the accounting treatment for property, plant and equipment.

(a) **When should items of property, plant and equipment be recognised as assets?**

(b) **Which costs should be included on initial recognition of property, plant and equipment?**

Task 1.4

(a) **Which, if any, of the following two statements are correct, according to IAS 1 *Presentation of financial statements*?**

    (i)   Financial statements should be prepared at least annually.

    (ii)   A complete set of financial statements must include notes.

(i) only	
(ii) only	
Both (i) and (ii)	
Neither (i) nor (ii)	

(b) **Which of the following items would not appear as a line item** in a company's statement of changes in equity, according to IAS 1 *Presentation of financial statements?*

Dividends paid	
Gain on revaluation of properties	
Issue of share capital	
Total comprehensive income for the year	

(c) Waveney Ltd uses the direct method to prepare its statement of cash flows. Cost of sales for the year is £1,250,000. Inventories increased by £80,000 during the year and trade payables increased by £190,000 during the year.

What amount should appear in the statement of cash flows for cash paid to suppliers?

£1,060,000	
£1,140,000	
£1,330,000	
£1,360,000	

(d) According to IFRS 8 *Operating segments*, all companies must disclose information about their operating segments.

Is this statement true or false?

True	
False	

(e) On 15 March 20X7, Yare Ltd received an order for goods with a sales value of £900,000. The customer paid a deposit of £90,000.

At 31 March 20X7 the goods had not yet been despatched.

According to IAS 18 *Revenue*, how should Yare Ltd report this transaction in its financial statements for the year ended 31 March 20X7?

Revenue £900,000; trade receivable £810,000	
Revenue £90,000; trade receivable £nil	
Revenue £nil; trade payable £90,000	
Revenue £90,000; trade payable £90,000; trade receivable £90,000	

(f) Ouse plc owns 45% of the voting rights of Avon Ltd and has power to appoint all the members of the board of directors.

In relation to Ouse plc, Avon Ltd is:.

An associate	
A subsidiary	

Task 1.5

The Managing Director of Wells plc has asked you to prepare the statement of financial position for the group.

Wells plc has one subsidiary, Wilkie Ltd.

The statements of financial position of the two companies as at 31 October 20X9 are set out below.

Statements of financial position as at 31 October 20X9

	Wells plc £'000	Wilkie Ltd £'000
Non-current assets		
Property, plant and equipment	44,352	19,884
Investment in Wilkie Ltd	19,000	
	63,352	19,884
Current assets		
Inventories	14,670	3,432
Trade and other receivables	6,756	2,249
Cash and cash equivalents	1,245	342
	22,671	6,023
Total assets	86,023	25,907
Equity and liabilities		
Equity		
Share capital	35,000	12,000
Retained earnings	26,036	8,332
Total equity	61,036	20,332
Non-current liabilities		
Long-term loans	14,000	4,000
Current liabilities		
Trade and other payables	8,877	1,445
Tax liabilities	2,110	130
	10,987	1,575
Total liabilities	24,987	5,575
Total equity and liabilities	86,023	25,907

Additional data

- The share capital of Wilkie Ltd consists of ordinary shares of £1 each. Ownership of these shares carries voting rights in Wilkie Ltd.

- Wells plc acquired 9,000,000 shares in Wilkie Ltd on 1 November 20X8.

- At 1 November 20X8 the balance of retained earnings of Wilkie Ltd was £5,344,000.

- Included in trade and other receivables for Wells plc and in trade and other payables for Wilkie Ltd is an inter-company transaction for £1,250,000 that took place in early October 20X9.

- The directors of Wells plc have concluded that goodwill has been impaired by £1,500,000 during the year.

- Wells plc has decided non-controlling interests will be valued at their proportionate share of net assets.

Draft a consolidated statement of financial position for Wells plc and its subsidiary as at 31 October 20X9.

Wells plc

Consolidated statement of financial position as at 31 October 20X9

	£'000
Assets	
Non-current assets:	
Intangible assets: goodwill	
Property, plant and equipment	
Current assets:	
Inventories	
Trade and other receivables	
Cash and cash equivalents	
Total assets	
Equity and liabilities	
Equity attributable to owners of the parent	
Share capital	
Retained earnings	
Non-controlling interest	
Total equity	

	£'000
Non-current liabilities:	
Long-term loans	
Current liabilities:	
Trade and other payables	
Tax liabilities	
Total liabilities	
Total equity and liabilities	

Workings

(Complete the left hand column by writing in the correct narrative from the list provided.)

Goodwill		£'000
	▼	
	▼	
	▼	
	▼	

Picklist for narratives:

Impairment
Price paid
Retained earnings – attributable to Wells plc
Share capital – attributable to Wells plc

Retained earnings		£'000
	▼	
	▼	
	▼	

Picklist for narratives:

Impairment

Wells plc

Wilkie Ltd – attributable to Wells plc

Non-controlling interest (NCI)		£'000
	▼	
	▼	

Picklist for narratives:

Current assets – attributable to NCI
Impairment
Non-current assets – attributable to NCI
Price paid
Retained earnings – attributable to NCI
Share capital – attributable to NCI

Section 2

Task 2.1

You have been asked to calculate ratios for Sienna Ltd in respect of its financial statements for the year ending 31 October 20X9 to assist your manager in his analysis of the company.

Sienna Ltd's statement of comprehensive income and statement of financial position are set out below.

Sienna Ltd

Statement of comprehensive income for the year ended 31 October 20X9

	£'000
Continuing Operations	
Revenue	37,384
Cost of sales	(21,458)
Gross profit	15,926
Distribution costs	(6,142)
Administrative expenses	(6,158)
Profit from operations	3,626
Finance costs	(639)
Profit before tax	2,987
Tax	(687)
Profit for the period from continuing operations	2,300

Sienna Ltd

Statement of financial position as at 31 October 20X9

ASSETS	£'000
Non-current assets	
Property, plant and equipment	23,366
Current assets	
Inventories	4,461
Trade receivables	3,115
Cash and cash equivalents	213
	7,789
Total assets	31,155
EQUITY AND LIABILITIES	
Equity	
Share capital	3,000
Retained earnings	16,679
Total equity	19,679
Non-current liabilities	
Bank loans	8,000
Current liabilities	
Trade and other payables	2,789
Tax liabilities	687
	3,476
Total liabilities	11,476
Total equity plus liabilities	31,155

(a) **State the formulae that are used to calculate each of the following ratios:**

(Write in the correct formula from the list provided)

(i) Return on capital employed	▼

Formulae:

Profit after tax/Total equity × 100

Profit from operations/Total equity × 100

Profit after tax/Total equity + Non-current liabilities × 100

Profit from operations/Total equity + Non-current liabilities × 100

(ii) Operating profit percentage	▼

Formulae:

Profit from operations/Revenue × 100

Profit from operations/Total assets × 100

Profit from operations/Total equity + Non-current liabilities × 100

Profit from operations/Finance costs × 100

(iii) Gross profit percentage	▼

Formulae:

Gross profit/Total equity × 100

Gross profit/Revenue × 100

Gross profit/Total assets × 100

Gross profit/Total assets – current liabilities

(iv) Asset turnover (net assets)	▼

Formulae:

Revenue/Total assets – current liabilities

Revenue/Total assets – total liabilities

Total assets – current liabilities/Revenue

Total assets – total liabilities/Revenue

(v) Return on equity	▼

Formulae:

Profit after tax/Total equity × 100

Profit before tax/Total equity × 100

Profit from operations/Total equity × 100

Profit from operations/Total equity + Non-current liabilities × 100

(vi) Quick (acid test) ratio	▼

Formulae:

Current assets/Current liabilities

Total assets – inventories/Total liabilities

Total assets/Total liabilities

Current assets – inventories/Current liabilities

(vii) Inventory turnover	▼

Formulae:

Cost of sales/Inventories

Inventories/Cost of sales

Inventories/Revenue

Revenue/Inventories

(viii) Interest cover	▼

Formulae:

Finance costs/profit from operations

Finance costs/revenue

Profit from operations/finance costs

Revenue/finance costs

(b) **Calculate the ratios to the nearest ONE DECIMAL PLACE.**

(i) Return on capital employed	%
(ii) Operating profit percentage	%
(iii) Gross profit percentage	%
(iv) Asset turnover (net assets)	times
(v) Return on equity	%
(vi) Quick (acid test) ratio	:1
(vii) Inventory turnover	times
(viii) Interest cover	times

Task 2.2

Louise Michaels is a shareholder in Hoy Ltd. She wishes to assess the effectiveness of the management in using its resources. She has asked you to assist her by analysing the financial statements of the company, which are set out below.

Louise has obtained a report from the internet that gives the industry ratio averages for the sector in which Hoy Ltd operates.

She has emailed you and asked you to explain some of the points she is unsure about. A copy of the email is shown below

From: lm1000@warmmail.com

To: aatstudent@dfsexam

Date: 27 November 20X9

Subject: Accounting ratios

Hi

I found these sector ratios on the internet. This is the same sector as the company I have invested in. The profit figures are straightforward but I'm a bit lost about the rest. Can you help?

Many thanks

Louise

417

	Industry averages	Hoy Ltd
Gearing	65.00%	88.65%
Current ratio	1.6:1	1.9:1
Acid test ratio	0.9:1	0.7:1
Trade receivables collection period	33 days	25.6 days
Trade payables payment period	36 days	32.9 days

Prepare an email reply for Louise that includes:

(a) **Comments on whether the company has performed better or worse, based on the ratios calculated compared to the industry averages and what this tells you about the company.**

(b) **Advice, with reasons, to Louise as to whether or not to continue with her investment.**

Task 2.3

(a) **List the elements that appear in financial statements according to the *Conceptual Framework for Financial Reporting*.**

(b) **Define the elements that appear in the statement of financial position of a company in accordance with the definitions in the *Conceptual Framework for Financial Reporting*.**

BPP practice assessment 4
Martin Ltd

Answers

Section 1

Task 1.1

(a) **Martin Ltd**

Statement of comprehensive income for the year ended 31 October 20X9

	£'000
Continuing operations	
Revenue	46,433
Cost of sales (W)	(32,282)
Gross profit	14,151
Distribution costs (W)	(2,516)
Administrative expenses (W)	(3,316)
Profit/(loss) from operations	8,319
Finance costs (8% × 14,000)	(1,120)
Profit/(loss) before tax	7,199
Tax	(980)
Profit/(loss) for the period from continuing operations	6,219
Other comprehensive income	
Gain on revaluation (12,000 – 8,000)	4,000
Total comprehensive income for the year	10,219

Workings

Cost of sales	£'000
Opening inventories	4,466
Purchases	32,553
Closing inventories (4,987 – 250)	(4,737)
	32,282

Distribution costs	£'000
Distribution costs	2,450
Accruals	66
	2,516

Administrative expenses	£'000
Administrative expenses	3,444
Prepayment (512 × 3/12)	(128)
	3,316

Task 1.2

(a) **Martin Ltd**

Statement of financial position as at 31 October 20X9

	£'000
Assets	
Non-current assets	
Property, plant and equipment (W)	22,100
Current assets	
Inventories (4,987 – 250)	4,737
Trade and other receivables (W)	2,362
Cash and cash equivalents	9,654
	16,753
Total assets	38,853
Equity and liabilities	
Equity	
Share capital	9,000
Revaluation reserve	4,000
Retained earnings (W)	8,754
Total equity	21,754
Non-current liabilities	

BPP LEARNING MEDIA

	£'000
Bank loan	14,000
Current liabilities	
Trade and other payables (W)	2,119
Tax liabilities	980
	3,099
Total liabilities	17,099
Total equity and liabilities	38,853

Workings

Property, plant and equipment	£'000
Property, plant and equipment – Cost	39,880
Property, plant and equipment – Accumulated depreciation	(21,780)
Revaluation	4,000
	22,100

Trade and other receivables	£'000
Trade and other receivables	2,234
Administrative expenses prepaid	128
	2,362

Retained earnings	£'000
Retained earnings at 1 November 20X8	3,465
Total profit for the year	6,219
Dividends paid	(930)
	8,754

Trade and other payables	£'000
Trade and other payables	1,347
Accruals: trial balance	146
Additional distribution costs accrual	66
Additional finance costs accrual	560
	2,119

Task 1.3

Note: based on the information available at the time this book was written, we anticipate that this task would be human marked in the real assessment.

(a) IAS 16 states that items of property, plant, and equipment should be recognised as assets when two conditions are met:

- It is probable that future economic benefits associated with the item will flow to the entity; and

- The cost of the asset can be measured reliably.

(b) The cost of an item of property, plant and equipment is:

- Its purchase price, including import duties and after deducting trade discounts and rebates; and

- Any costs directly attributable to bringing the item to the location and condition necessary for it to be capable of operating in the manner intended by management.

Task 1.4

(a)

(i) only	
(ii) only	
Both (i) and (ii)	✓
Neither (i) nor (ii)	

(b)

Dividends paid	
Gain on revaluation of properties	✓
Issue of share capital	
Total comprehensive income for the year	

A gain on revaluation of properties is reported as a line item in other comprehensive income, but in the statement of changes in equity it forms part of total comprehensive income for the year.

(c)

£1,060,000	
£1,140,000	✓
£1,330,000	
£1,360,000	

	£'000
Cost of sales	1,250
Increase in inventories	80
Increase in trade payables	(190)
	1,140

(d)

True	
False	✓

IFRS 8 applies to public companies; companies in the process of becoming public companies; and any other companies that choose to disclose segment information

(e)

Revenue £900,000; trade receivable £810,000	
Revenue £90,000; trade receivable £nil	
Revenue £nil; trade payable £90,000	✓
Revenue £90,000; trade payable £90,000; trade receivable £90,000	

No revenue should be recognised, because Yare Ltd has not yet transferred the significant risks and rewards of ownership to the buyer.

(f)

An associate	
A subsidiary	✓

Although Ouse plc owns less than 50% of the voting rights, it controls Avon Ltd.

Task 1.5

Wells plc

Consolidated statement of financial position as at 31 October 20X9

	£'000
Assets	
Non-current assets:	
Intangible assets: goodwill (W)	4,492
Property, plant and equipment	64,236
	68,728
Current assets:	
Inventories	18,102
Trade and other receivables (6,756 + 2,249 – 1,250)	7,755
Cash and cash equivalents	1,587
	27,444
Total assets	96,172
Equity and liabilities	
Equity attributable to owners of the parent	
Share capital	35,000
Retained earnings (W)	26,777
	61,777
Non-controlling interest (W)	5,083
Total equity	66,860
Non-current liabilities:	
Long-term loans	18,000
Current liabilities:	
Trade and other payables (8,877 + 1,445 – 1,250)	9,072
Tax liabilities	2,240
	11,312
Total liabilities	29,312
Total equity and liabilities	96,172

Workings

Note: **Group structure**

Wells plc owns 75% of Wilkie Ltd (9,000,000/12,000,000)

Goodwill	£'000
Price paid	19,000
Share capital – attributable to Wells plc (75% × 12,000)	(9,000)
Retained earnings – attributable to Wells plc (75% × 5,344)	(4,008)
Impairment	(1,500)
	4,492

Retained earnings	£'000
Wells plc	26,036
Wilkie Ltd – attributable to Wells plc (75% × (8,332 – 5,344))	2,241
Impairment	(1,500)
	26,777

Non-controlling interest (NCI)	£'000
Share capital – attributable to NCI (25% × 12,000)	3,000
Retained earnings – attributable to NCI (25% × 8,332)	2,083
	5,083

Section 2

Task 2.1

(a) Formulae used to calculate the ratios

(i)	Return on capital employed	$\dfrac{\text{Profit from operations}}{\text{Total equity + non-current liabilities}} \times 100\%$
(ii)	Operating profit percentage	$\dfrac{\text{Profit from operations}}{\text{Revenue}} \times 100\%$
(iii)	Gross profit percentage	$\dfrac{\text{Gross profit}}{\text{Revenue}} \times 100\%$
(iv)	Asset turnover (net assets)	$\dfrac{\text{Revenue}}{\text{Total assets} - \text{current liabilities}}$
(v)	Return on equity	$\dfrac{\text{Profit after tax}}{\text{Total equity}} \times 100\%$
(vi)	Quick (acid test) ratio	$\dfrac{\text{Current assets} - \text{inventories}}{\text{Current liabilities}}$
(vii)	Inventory turnover	$\dfrac{\text{Cost of sales}}{\text{Inventories}}$
(viii)	Interest cover	$\dfrac{\text{Profit from operations}}{\text{Finance costs}}$

(b) **Calculation of the ratios**

(i)	Return on capital employed $\dfrac{3,626}{27,679} \times 100$		13.1	%
(ii)	Operating profit percentage $\dfrac{3,626}{37,384} \times 100$		9.7	%
(iii)	Gross profit percentage $\dfrac{15,926}{37,384} \times 100$		42.6	%
(iv)	Asset turnover (net assets) $\dfrac{37,384}{27,679}$		1.35	times
(v)	Return on equity $\dfrac{2,300}{19,679} \times 100$		11.7	%
(vi)	Quick (acid test) ratio $\dfrac{7,789 - 4,461}{3,476}$		0.96	:1
(vii)	Inventory turnover $\dfrac{21,458}{4,461}$		4.8	times
(viii)	Interest cover $\dfrac{3,626}{639}$		5.7	times

Task 2.2

Note: based on the information available at the time this book was written, we anticipate that this task would be human marked in the real assessment.

From: aatstudent@dfsexam

To: lm1000@warmmail.com

Date: 2 December 20X9

Subject: Comparison of accounting ratios of Hoy Ltd with industry averages

As requested, I have compared the accounting ratios computed from the financial statements of Hoy Ltd with the industry averages. I set out my comments below.

(a) Gearing

At 88.5%, Hoy Ltd's gearing ratio is considerably higher than the industry average. This shows that Hoy Ltd has a relatively high level of long-term borrowings or debt, which means that it is a riskier investment than most other companies in the industry.

Current ratio

The current ratio is better than the industry average. Hoy Ltd's current liabilities are covered almost twice by its current assets.

Acid test (quick) ratio

This is lower than the industry average; Hoy Ltd's current liabilities are greater than its trade receivables plus its cash. This means that Hoy Ltd is less likely to be able to meet its liabilities in the short term than most other companies in the industry sector. Because the current ratio is relatively high, Hoy Ltd must have a high level of inventories.

Trade receivables collection period

At 25.6 days, this is considerably better than the industry average and suggests that Hoy Ltd is more efficient at collecting its debts than most other companies in the industry. This means that more cash will be available to pay suppliers and lenders.

Trade payables payment period

Again, this is slightly lower than the industry average. This suggests that Hoy Ltd pays its suppliers relatively quickly, possibly more quickly than is necessary. This may be one of the reasons that the company has relatively few 'quick' assets.

(b) Conclusion

On the basis of these ratios, you should not continue to invest in this company. The low acid test ratio, together with the low trade payables payment period, suggest that the company is not managing its liquid resources particularly well. The high gearing ratio is a worrying sign. The company appears to be a risky investment and probably suffers a high level of interest. This means that fewer profits will be available for shareholders.

Task 2.3

Note: based on the information available at the time this book was written, we anticipate that this task would be human marked in the real assessment.

(a) The elements that appear in financial statements are:

- Assets
- Liabilities
- Equity
- Income
- Expenses

(b) Assets, liabilities and equity appear in the statement of financial position of a company. The *Conceptual Framework for Financial Reporting* defines them as follows:

Assets are resources controlled by an entity as a result of past events and from which future economic benefits are expected to flow to the entity.

Liabilities are present obligations of an entity arising from past events, the settlement of which is expected to result in an outflow from the entity of resources embodying economic benefits.

Equity is the residual interest in the assets of an entity after deducting all its liabilities.

BPP practice assessment 5
Phantom Ltd
Time allowed: 2½ hours

Section 1

The following information is relevant to Task 1.1 and Task 1.2

You have been asked to prepare the statement of cash flows and statement of changes in equity for Phantom Ltd for the year ended 31 October 20X1.

The most recent statement of comprehensive income and statement of financial position (with comparatives for the previous year) of Phantom Ltd are set out below.

Phantom Ltd – Statement of comprehensive income for the year ended 31 October 20X1.

Continuing operations	£'000
Revenue	85,000
Cost of sales	(50,400)
Gross profit	34,600
Dividends received	200
Gain on disposal of property, plant and equipment	756
Distribution costs	(18,480)
Administrative expenses	(15,120)
Profit from operations	1,956
Finance costs	(420)
Profit before tax	1,536
Tax	(705)
Profit for the period from continuing operations	831

Phantom Ltd – Statement of financial position as at 31 October 20X1

	20X1 £'000	20X0 £'000
ASSETS		
Non-current assets		
Property, plant and equipment	35,783	26,890
Current assets		
Inventories	6,552	5,544
Trade receivables	6,720	5,880
Cash and cash equivalents	0	476
	13,272	11,900
Total assets	49,055	38,790
EQUITY AND LIABILITIES		
Equity		
Share capital	9,000	6,000
Share premium	3,000	2,000
Retained earnings	24,863	24,198
Total equity	36,863	32,198
Non-current liabilities		
Bank loans	6,000	800
	6,000	800
Current liabilities		
Trade payables	5,040	4,536
Tax liabilities	705	1,256
Bank overdraft	447	0
	6,192	5,792
Total liabilities	12,192	6,592
Total equity and liabilities	49,055	38,790

Further information:

- The total depreciation charge for the year was £2,898,000.

- Property, plant and equipment costing £998,000 with accumulated depreciation of £256,000 was sold in the year.

- All sales and purchases were on credit. Other expenses were paid for in cash.
- A dividend of £166,000 was paid during the year.

Task 1.1

(a) **Prepare a reconciliation of profit from operations to net cash from operating activities for Phantom Ltd for the year ended 31 October 20X1.**

(Complete the left hand column by writing in the correct line item from the list provided.)

Reconciliation of profit from operations to net cash from operating activities

	£'000
▼	
Adjustments for:	
▼	
▼	
▼	
▼	
▼	
▼	
Cash generated by operations	
▼	
▼	
Net cash from operating activities	

Picklist for line items:
Adjustment in respect of inventories
Adjustment in respect of trade payables
Adjustment in respect of trade receivables
Depreciation
Dividends received
Gain on disposal of property, plant and equipment
Interest paid
New bank loans
Proceeds on disposal of property, plant and equipment
Profit after tax
Profit before tax
Profit from operations
Purchases of property, plant and equipment
Tax paid

(b) **Prepare the statement of cash flows for Phantom Ltd for the year ended 31 October 20X1.**

(Complete the left hand column by writing in the correct line item from the list provided.)

Phantom Ltd

Statement of cash flows for the year ended 31 October 20X1

	£'000	£'000
Net cash from operating activities		
Investing activities		
▼		
▼		
▼		
Net cash used in investing activities		
Financing activities		
▼		
▼		
▼		
Net cash from financing activities		
Net increase/(decrease) in cash and cash equivalents		
Cash and cash equivalents at the beginning of the year		
Cash and cash equivalents at the end of the year		

Picklist for line items:

Adjustment in respect of inventories
Adjustment in respect of trade payables
Adjustment in respect of trade receivables
Dividends paid
Dividends received
New bank loans
Proceeds of share issue
Proceeds on disposal of property, plant and equipment
Purchases of property, plant and equipment

Workings

(Complete the left hand column by writing in the correct narrative from the list provided.)

Proceeds on disposal of property, plant and equipment (PPE)		£'000
	▼	
	▼	

Picklist for narratives:

Carrying amount of PPE sold
Depreciation charge
Gain on disposal
PPE at end of year
PPE at start of year

Purchases of property, plant and equipment (PPE)		£'000
PPE at start of year		
	▼	
	▼	
	▼	
Total PPE additions		

Picklist for narratives:

Carrying amount of PPE sold
Depreciation charge
Gain on disposal of PPE
PPE at end of year

Task 1.2

(a) Draft the statement of changes in equity for Phantom Ltd for the year ended 31 October 20X1.

Phantom Ltd

Statement of changes in equity for the year ended 31 October 20X1

	Share Capital £'000	Other Reserves £'000	Retained Earnings £'000	Total Equity £'000
Balance at 1 November 20X0				
Changes in equity for 20X1				
Profit for the year				
Dividends				
Issue of share capital				
Balance at 31 October 20X1				

Task 1.3

Birch plc has recently purchased a property which the directors intend to treat as an investment property. The directors understand that investment property can be measured at cost less accumulated depreciation in the same way as an ordinary item of property, plant and equipment. They also understand that they have the option of an alternative accounting treatment that may provide more useful information to users of the company's financial statements.

(a) (i) Define the term 'investment property' in accordance with IAS 40 *Investment property.*

    (ii) Give an example of investment property that meets this definition.

(b) Explain how investment property would be accounted for in the financial statements of Birch plc after its initial recognition if the directors decide to adopt the alternative accounting treatment set out in IAS 40 *Investment property.*

Task 1.4

(a) According to IAS 36 *Impairment of assets*, the recoverable amount of an asset is the lower of fair value less costs to sell and value in use.

Is this statement true or false?

True	
False	

(b) Glasbury Ltd prepares its financial statements to 31 October each year. The following events took place between 31 October and the date on which the financial statements were authorised for issue.

(i) A customer claimed to have been injured by a faulty product and has started legal proceedings to claim damages from the company. The faulty product was purchased on 10 December.

(ii) The company made a 1 for 6 bonus issue of £1 ordinary shares.

Which of the above is likely to be classified as a non-adjusting event according to IAS 10 *Events after the reporting period*?

(i) only	
(ii) only	
Both	
Neither of them	

(c) Vowchurch Ltd purchased a building for £600,000 on 1 November 20X0. The building was depreciated over 20 years on a straight line basis.

On 1 November 20X4 the building was valued at £700,000 and its remaining useful life was estimated at 20 years.

Vowchurch Ltd has chosen to adopt the cost model in IAS 16 *Property, plant and equipment*.

What is the total net carrying amount of the building at 31 October 20X5?

£456,000	
£475,000	
£570,000	
£665,000	

(d) Knighton Ltd is preparing its first set of financial statements for the three months to 31 December.

The cost of purchases was £120 per unit until 15 November, when the company's supplier increased it to £130 per unit. Purchases and sales took place evenly over the period.

The directors have arrived at three possible alternative ways of valuing inventories at 31 December.

(i) At £120 per unit (cost at the beginning of the period)

(ii) At £130 per unit (cost at the end of the period)

(iii) At £125 per unit (average cost)

Which methods of valuing inventories are allowed, according to IAS 2 *Inventories*?

(i) and (ii)	
(ii) and (iii)	
(i) and (iii)	
All of them	

(e) At 1 November 20X0, Brilley Ltd had an estimated current tax liability of £157,000 and a deferred tax liability of £25,000.

In February 20X1 the company paid corporation tax of £165,000.

At 31 October 20X1, the current tax liability for the year has been estimated at £188,000. The deferred tax liability is £30,000.

What is the total tax expense in profit or loss for the year ended 31 October 20X1?

£185,000	
£193,000	
£196,000	
£201,000	

(f) A liability of uncertain timing or amount is known as:

A contingent liability	
A provision	

Task 1.5

Data

Felley plc acquired 75% of the issued share capital of Haggs Ltd on 1 November 20X0 for £3,400,000. At that date Haggs Ltd had issued share capital of £2,500,000 and retained earnings of £560,000.

Extracts of the statements of financial position for the two companies one year later at 31 October 20X1 are as follows:

	Felley plc	Haggs Ltd
	£'000	£'000
ASSETS		
Investment in Haggs Ltd	3,400	
Non-current assets	5,640	2,920
Current assets	2,880	2,510
Total assets	11,920	5,430
EQUITY AND LIABILITIES		
Equity		
Share capital	4,000	2,500
Retained earnings	3,970	912
Total equity	7,970	3,412
Non-current liabilities	2,000	1,440
Current liabilities	1,950	578
Total liabilities	3,950	2,018
Total equity and liabilities	11,920	5,430

Additional data:

- During the year Felley plc sold goods which had cost £400,000 to Haggs Ltd for £500,000. All these goods remained in the inventory of Haggs Ltd at the end of the year.

- Felley plc has decided non-controlling interest will be valued at their proportionate share of net assets.

(a) **Draft the consolidated statement of financial position for Felley plc and its subsidiary as at 31 October 20X1.**

Felley plc

Consolidated statement of financial position as at 31 October 20X1

	£'000
Assets	
Non-current assets:	
Intangible assets: goodwill	
Property, plant and equipment	
Current assets:	
Total assets	
Equity and liabilities	
Equity attributable to owners of the parent	
Share capital	
Retained earnings	
Non-controlling interest	
Total equity	
Non-current liabilities:	
Current liabilities:	
Total liabilities	
Total equity and liabilities	

Workings

(Complete the left hand column by writing in the correct narrative from the list provided.)

Goodwill	£'000
▼	
▼	
▼	

Picklist for narratives:

Price paid
Retained earnings – attributable to Felley plc
Share capital – attributable to Felley plc

Retained earnings		£'000
	▼	
	▼	

Picklist for narratives:

Felley plc
Haggs Ltd – attributable to Felley plc

Non-controlling interest (NCI)		£'000
	▼	
	▼	

Picklist for narratives:

Current assets – attributable to NCI
Non-current assets – attributable to NCI
Price paid
Retained earnings – attributable to NCI
Share capital – attributable to NCI

Data

Beauvale plc acquired 60% of the issued share capital of Newstead Ltd on 1 November 20X0.

Extracts from their statements of comprehensive income for the year ended 31 October 20X1 are shown below:

	Beauvale plc	Newstead Ltd
	£'000	£'000
Profit from operations	19,700	12,100
Finance costs	(400)	(200)
Profit before tax	19,300	11,900
Tax	(4,900)	(3,600)
Profit for the year	14,400	8,300

Additional data:

- During the year Beauvale plc sold goods which had cost £200,000 to Newstead Ltd for £600,000. Half of these goods remained in the inventory of Newstead Ltd at the end of the year.

- The profit from operations of Beauvale plc includes dividends of £1,800,000 received from Newstead Ltd.

(b) **Draft the consolidated statement of comprehensive income for Beauvale plc and its subsidiary starting from the profit from operations line for the year ended 31 October 20X1.**

Beauvale plc

Consolidated statement of comprehensive income for the year ended 31 October 20X1

	£'000
Profit from operations	
Finance costs	
Profit before tax	
Tax	
Profit for the year	
Attributable to:	
Equity holders of the parent	
Non-controlling interests	

Working

Profit from operations	£'000
Beauvale plc	
Newstead Ltd	
Total inter-company adjustment	

Section 2

Task 2.1

You have been asked to calculate ratios for Hampden Ltd in respect of its financial statements for the year ending 31 October 20X1 to assist your manager in her analysis of the company.

Hampden Ltd's statement of comprehensive income and statement of financial position are set out below.

Hampden Ltd – Statement of comprehensive income for the year ended 31 October 20X1

	£'000
Continuing operations	
Revenue	22,600
Cost of sales	(10,735)
Gross profit	11,865
Distribution costs	(5,424)
Administrative expenses	(4,068)
Profit from operations	2,373
Finance costs	(770)
Profit before tax	1,603
Tax	(294)
Profit for the period from continuing operations	1,309

Hampden Ltd – Statement of financial position as at 31 October 20X1

	£'000
ASSETS	
Non-current assets	
Property, plant and equipment	22,916
Current assets	
Inventories	1,932
Trade receivables	1,808
Cash and cash equivalents	582
	4,322
Total assets	27,238
EQUITY AND LIABILITIES	
Equity	
Share capital (£1 ordinary shares)	8,000
Retained earnings	6,334
Total equity	14,334
Non-current liabilities	
Bank loans	11,000
	11,000
Current liabilities	
Trade payables	1,610
Tax liabilities	294
	1,904
Total liabilities	12,904
Total equity and liabilities	27,238

(a) **State the formulae that are used to calculate each of the following ratios**

(Write in the correct formula from the list provided)

(i) **Operating profit percentage**	▼

Formulae:

Profit from operations/Revenue × 100

Profit from operations/Total assets × 100

Profit from operations/Total equity + Non-current liabilities × 100

Profit from operations/Finance costs × 100

(ii) **Return on capital employed**	▼

Formulae:

Profit after tax/Total equity × 100

Profit from operations/Total equity × 100

Profit after tax/Total equity + Non-current liabilities × 100

Profit from operations/Total equity + Non-current liabilities × 100

(iii) **Current ratio**	▼

Formulae:

Total assets/Total liabilities

Current assets – inventories/Current liabilities

Current assets/Current liabilities

Total assets – inventories/Total liabilities

(iv) **Earnings per share**	▼

Formulae:

Profit after tax/Number of issued shares

Profit before tax/Number of issued ordinary shares

Profit after tax/Number of issued ordinary shares

Profit from operations/Number of issued ordinary shares

(v) **Inventory turnover**	▼

Formulae:

Cost of sales/Inventories

Inventories/Cost of sales

Inventories/Revenue

Revenue/Inventories

(vi) **Trade receivables collection period**	▼

Formulae:

Cost of sales/Trade receivables × 365

Revenue/Trade receivables × 365

Trade receivables/Cost of sales × 365

Trade receivables/Revenue × 365

(vii) **Trade payables payment period**	▼

Formulae:

Trade payables/Revenue × 365

Trade payables/Cost of sales × 365

Revenue/Trade payables × 365

Cost of sales/Trade payables × 365

(viii) **Asset turnover (net assets)**	▼

Formulae:

Revenue/Total assets – current liabilities

Revenue/Total assets – total liabilities

Total assets – current liabilities/Revenue

Total assets – total liabilities/Revenue

(b) **Calculate the ratios to the nearest ONE DECIMAL PLACE.**

(i)	**Operating profit percentage**		%
(ii)	**Return on capital employed**		%
(iii)	**Current ratio**		:1
(iv)	**Earnings per share**		p
(v)	**Inventory turnover**		times
(vi)	**Trade receivables collection period**		days
(vii)	**Trade payables payment period**		days
(viii)	**Asset turnover (net assets)**		times

Task 2.2

Lewis Baingle is interested in buying shares as a means of investment and has heard that some shares are riskier than others. He wishes to assess the merits of two local companies with a view to buying shares in one of them.

Lewis would like to invest in a profitable company but his main concern is that his investment is safe. He has managed to find the most recent financial statements of the companies and you have used these to calculate the following ratios to assist you in your analysis.

	Anica Ltd	Papaca Ltd
Gross profit percentage	45.0%	52.5%
Operating profit percentage	9.0%	11.5%
Gearing	13.3%	71.1%
Interest cover	11.6 times	3.1 times
Quick (acid test) ratio	1.2:1	0.6:1

Prepare a letter for Lewis that includes:

(a) Comments on which company has performed better, based on the ratios calculated and what this tells you about the two companies.

(b) Advice, with reasons based on the ratios you have calculated, to Lewis as to which company to invest in.

....

Task 2.3

(a) State the two conditions that must be met before an asset or a liability can be recognised in the financial statements according to the *Conceptual Framework for Financial Reporting*.

(b) Give ONE example of an asset that is recognised in the financial statements and briefly explain why it meets these conditions.

(c) Give ONE example of an asset that is not recognised in the financial statements and briefly explain why it does not meet these conditions.

BPP practice assessment 5
Phantom Ltd
Answers

Section 1

Task 1.1

(a) **Phantom Ltd**

Reconciliation of profit from operations to net cash from operating activities

	£'000
Profit from operations	1,956
Adjustments for:	
Depreciation	2,898
Dividends received	(200)
Gain on disposal of property, plant and equipment	(756)
Adjustment in respect of inventories (6,552 – 5,544)	(1,008)
Adjustment in respect of trade receivables (6,720 – 5,880)	(840)
Adjustment in respect of trade payables (5,040 – 4,536)	504
Cash generated by operations	2,554
Tax paid	(1,256)
Interest paid	(420)
Net cash from operating activities	878

(b) **Phantom Ltd**

Statement of cash flows for the year ended 31 October 20X1

	£'000	£'000
Net cash from operating activities		878
Investing activities		
Purchases of property, plant and equipment (W)	(12,533)	
Proceeds on disposal of property, plant and equipment (W)	1,498	
Dividends received	200	
Net cash used in investing activities		(10,835)

	£'000	£'000
Financing activities		
Proceeds of share issue (12,000 – 8,000)	4,000	
New bank loans (6,000 – 800)	5,200	
Dividends paid	(166)	
Net cash from financing activities		9,034
Net increase/(decrease) in cash and cash equivalents		(923)
Cash and cash equivalents at the beginning of the year		476
Cash and cash equivalents at the end of the year		(447)

Workings

Proceeds on disposal of property, plant and equipment (PPE)	£'000
Carrying amount of PPE sold	742
Gain on disposal	756
	1,498

Purchases of property, plant and equipment (PPE)	£'000
PPE at start of year	26,890
Depreciation charge	(2,898)
Carrying amount of PPE sold	(742)
PPE at end of year	(35,783)
Total PPE additions	(12,533)

Task 1.2

(a) **Phantom Ltd**

Statement of changes in equity for the year ended 31 October 20X1

	Share Capital £'000	Other Reserves £'000	Retained Earnings £'000	Total Equity £'000
Balance at 1 November 20X0	6,000	2,000	24,198	32,198
Changes in equity for 20X1				
Profit for the year	0	0	831	831
Dividends	0	0	(166)	(166)
Issue of share capital	3,000	1,000	0	4,000
Balance at 31 October 20X1	9,000	3,000	24,863	36,863

Task 1.3

Note: based on the information available at the time this book was written, we anticipate that this task would be human marked in the real assessment.

(a) (i) IAS 40 defines investment property as property (land or a building or both) held to earn rentals or for capital appreciation or for both, rather than for use in the production or supply of goods or services or for administrative purposes; or sale in the ordinary course of business.

(ii) Examples of investment property:

- Land held for long-term capital appreciation rather than for short-term sale in the ordinary course of business

- Land held for a currently undetermined future use

- A building owned by the entity and leased out under an operating lease

- A building that is vacant but held to be leased out under an operating lease

- Property that is being constructed or developed for future use as an investment property

Note: only ONE example is required.

(b) IAS 40 allows two accounting treatments for investment property: the cost model (the property is measured at historic cost less accumulated depreciation and any accumulated impairment losses); and the fair value model.

Under the fair value model, the property is not depreciated. Instead it is remeasured to its fair value (normally its open market value) at the end of each reporting period. Gains and losses on remeasurement (changes in market value) are recognised directly in profit or loss for the period in which they arise.

Task 1.4

(a)

True	
False	✓

Recoverable amount is the higher of fair value less costs to sell and value in use.

(b)

(i) only	
(ii) only	
Both	✓
Neither of them	

(c)

£456,000	✓
£475,000	
£570,000	
£665,000	

	£'
Cost	600,000
Depreciation to 20X4 (600,000 ÷ 20 × 4)	(120,000)
Net carrying amount at 1 November 20X4	480,000
Depreciation for 20X5 (480,000 ÷ 20)	(24,000)
Net carrying amount at 31 October 20X5	456,000

(d)

(i) and (ii)	
(ii) and (iii)	✓
(i) and (iii)	
All of them	

Method 1 is Last-in-First-out (LIFO) and is prohibited by IAS 2. Method 2 is First-in-First-out (FIFO).

(e)

£185,000	
£193,000	
£196,000	
£201,000	✓

	£
Expense for current year	188,000
Adjustment in respect of prior period	8,000
Deferred tax (30,000 – 25,000)	5,000
Tax expense in profit or loss	201,000

(f)

A contingent liability	
A provision	✓

Task 1.5

(a) **Felley plc**

Consolidated statement of financial position as at 31 October 20X1

	£'000
Assets	
Non-current assets:	
Intangible assets: goodwill (W)	1,105
Property, plant and equipment	8,560
Current assets: (2,880 + 2,510 – 100)	5,290
Total assets	14,955
Equity and liabilities	
Equity attributable to owners of the parent	
Share capital	4,000
Retained earnings (W)	4,134
Non-controlling interest (W)	853
Total equity	8,987
Non-current liabilities:	3,440
Current liabilities:	2,528
Total liabilities	5,968
Total equity and liabilities	14,955

Workings

Goodwill	£'000
Price paid	3,400
Share capital – attributable to Felley plc (75% × 2,500)	(1,875)
Retained earnings – attributable to Felley plc (75% × 560)	(420)
	1,105

Retained earnings	£'000
Felley plc (3,970 – 100)	3,870
Haggs Ltd – attributable to Felley plc (75% × 912 – 560)	264
	4,134

Non-controlling interest (NCI)	£'000
Share capital – attributable to NCI (25% × 2,500)	625
Retained earnings – attributable to NCI (25% × 912)	228
	853

(b) **Beauvale plc**

Consolidated statement of comprehensive income for the year ended 31 October 20X1

	£'000
Profit from operations	29,800
Finance costs	(600)
Profit before tax	29,200
Tax	(8,500)
Profit for the year	20,700
Attributable to:	
Equity holders of the parent	17,380
Non-controlling interests (40% × 8,300)	3,320
	20,700

Working

Profit from operations	£'000
Beauvale plc	19,700
Newstead Ltd	12,100
Total inter-company adjustment ((400/2) + 1,800)	(2,000)
	29,800

Section 2

Task 2.1

(a) **Formulae used to calculate the ratios**

(i)	**Operating profit percentage**	$\dfrac{\text{Profit from operations}}{\text{Revenue}} \times 100\%$
(ii)	**Return on capital employed**	$\dfrac{\text{Profit from operations}}{\text{Total equity + non-current liabilities}} \times 100\%$
(iii)	**Current ratio**	$\dfrac{\text{Current assets}}{\text{Current liabilities}}$
(iv)	**Earnings per share**	$\dfrac{\text{Profit after tax}}{\text{Number of issued ordinary shares}}$
(v)	**Inventory turnover**	$\dfrac{\text{Cost of sales}}{\text{Inventories}}$
(vi)	**Trade receivables collection period**	$\dfrac{\text{Trade receivables}}{\text{Revenue}} \times 365$
(vii)	**Trade payables payment period**	$\dfrac{\text{Trade payables}}{\text{Cost of sales}} \times 365$
(viii)	**Asset turnover (net assets)**	$\dfrac{\text{Revenue}}{\text{Total assets} - \text{current liabilities}}$

(b)   Calculation of the ratios

(i)	Operating profit percentage $\dfrac{2,373}{22,600} \times 100$	10.5	%
(ii)	Return on capital employed $\dfrac{2,373}{14,334 + 11,000} \times 100$	9.4	%
(iii)	Current ratio $\dfrac{4,322}{1,904}$	2.3	:1
(iv)	Earnings per share $\dfrac{1,309}{8,000}$	16.4	p
(v)	Inventory turnover $\dfrac{10,735}{1,932}$	5.6	times
(vi)	Trade receivables collection period $\dfrac{1,808}{22,600} \times 365$	29.2	days
(vii)	Trade payables payment period $\dfrac{1,610}{10,735} \times 365$	54.7	days
(viii)	Asset turnover (net assets) $\dfrac{22,600}{27,238 - 1,904}$	0.9	times

Task 2.2

Note: based on the information available at the time this book was written, we anticipate that this task would be human marked in the real assessment.

Sender's address

Lewis Baingle

Address

Date

Dear Lewis,

Performance of Anica Ltd and Papaca Ltd

As you requested, I have compared the profitability of Anica Ltd and Papaca Ltd, based on ratios calculated from their most recent financial statements. I have also compared the two companies in terms of their riskiness for a potential investor.

(a) **Comparison of the two companies**

Gross profit percentage

Both companies have healthy gross profit percentages, but Papaca Ltd is clearly the more profitable of the two. It generates significantly more direct trading profit, relative to its sales, than Anica Ltd.

Operating profit percentage

Again, both companies are reasonably profitable, but Papaca Ltd has the better operating profit percentage of the two. However, the difference between the overall profitability of the two companies is fairly small.

Gearing

Anica Ltd has a much lower gearing ratio than Papaca Ltd. Papaca Ltd appears to have a worryingly high level of debt and would be a very risky investment. In comparison, Anica Ltd has some debt, but this forms only a small proportion of its total financing. On this basis, Anica Ltd would be a much safer investment.

Interest cover

Anica Ltd has a much higher level of interest cover than Papaca Ltd. The ratio suggests that it can comfortably meet its interest payments from its operating profit and that this will continue to be the case even if interest rates rise or profits fall significantly. Papaca Ltd's interest cover is acceptable at the moment, but on this basis again Anica Ltd is clearly a much safer investment than Papaca Ltd.

Quick (acid test) ratio

Anica Ltd has a much better quick ratio than Papaca Ltd. Its liquid assets exceed its current liabilities and this indicates that it should easily be able to meet its payments to suppliers and other short term obligations as they fall due. Papaca Ltd's quick ratio is low enough to suggest that the company has liquidity problems: yet another indication that it would be a very risky investment.

BPP LEARNING MEDIA

(b) **Conclusion**

Because your main concern is the riskiness of your investment I would advise you to invest in Anica Ltd. Anica Ltd is profitable, with no apparent gearing or liquidity problems.

In contrast, although Papaca Ltd is the more profitable of the two companies, it is very highly geared and may have liquidity problems. Taken together, the high level of debt and the low quick ratio are extremely worrying and suggest that the company is in danger of becoming insolvent. Papaca Ltd would clearly be a very risky investment.

I hope you have found this analysis helpful.

Yours sincerely,

Accounting Technician

Task 2.3

Note: based on the information available at the time this book was written, we anticipate that this task would be human marked in the real assessment.

(a) An item that meets the definition of an element (eg, an asset or a liability) should be recognised if:

- It is **probable** that any future economic benefit associated with the item will flow to or from the entity

- The item has a cost or value that can be measured with **reliability**

(b) Plant and machinery is recognised in the financial statements. It meets both conditions:

- It will be used to produce goods that will be sold to generate cash and profits (an inflow of economic benefits)

- It has a cost that is a matter of fact and can be verified (reliable measurement)

Note: other examples of assets that meet the criteria are land and buildings, vehicles, inventories, trade receivables, cash.

(c) Internally generated goodwill cannot be recognised in the financial statements. It meets the first condition, but not the second:

- It contributes to sales and therefore generates an inflow of economic benefits
- It cannot be valued reliably/objectively

Notes